The Vertigo of
Late Modernity

The Vertigo of
Late Modernity

Jock Young

⑤ SAGE Publications

Los Angeles • London • New Delhi • Singapore

SAGE Publications Ltd
1 Oliver's Yard
55 City Road
London EC1Y 1SP

SAGE Publications Inc.
2455 Teller Road
Thousand Oaks, California 91320

SAGE Publications India Pvt Ltd
B 1/I 1 Mohan Cooperative Industrial Area
Mathura Road, New Delhi 110 044
India

SAGE Publications Asia-Pacific Pte Ltd
33 Pekin Street #02-01
Far East Square
Singapore 048763

British Library Cataloguing in Publication data
A catalogue record for this book is available
from the British Library

ISBN 9781 4129 3573 9
ISBN 9781 4129 3574 6

Library of Congress Control Number available

Typeset by C&M Digitals (P) Ltd., Chennai, India
Printed and bound in Great Britain by Athenaeum Press, Gateshead
Printed on paper from sustainable resources

For Jayne

CONTENTS

ACKNOWLEDGEMENTS

This book started out in Stoke Newington and was finished in Parl Slope, Brooklyn. It's backcloth, then, is London and New York, cities of hyperpluralism, hybridism and invention, places of great imagination and potential. It was shaped by debates about the supposed underclass, by increasing punitive responses to social problems, by the rapid rise in the prison population, by racist and nationalist fears of immigration, the failure of the New Labour project, by the riots in France and the North of England, and by 9/11 and the bombings in Madrid and London. Its analysis led me from my previous work on social exclusion to the study of the basis of transgression and vindictiveness and its roots in the rapid changes and insecurities in work, community and the family, to changing perceptions of class, the rise of celebrity and the invisibility of the working poor. It ends with a discussion of the construction of the immigrant as a dangerous other and the social production of evil, whether it is in war or in terrorist attack. It thus crosses subjects and inevitably it crosses disciplines.

In this task I have been helped by a great number of friends and colleagues. Dave Brotherton from John Jay is a constant source of just the right suggestion to read (except the book on ghosts, Dave, I still don't get it). Barry Spunt is a terrific drug researcher and the last romantic, Mike Flynn's energy and insight convinces me that psychology need not necessarily be anodyne and flat. Thanks to Jeff Ferrell, Keith Hayward and Mike Presdee for friendship and boundless enthusiasm for the cultural criminology project. Wayne Morrison, John Braithwaite, Akim Oualhaci, Richard Boon, Pam Brighton, Luis Barrios, Phil Kasinitz, Lynn Chancer, Mark Hamm, Harry Ferguson, Michael Jacobson, Ruth Jamieson, John Pitts – in no particular order, all helped out. Todd Clear and Chris Hale run academic outfits to which it has been a pleasure to belong. Zygmunt Bauman is an inspiration both in terms of the content of his work and the fact that he has given an alternative voice to a sociology which is only too often moribund and prosaic. I have been greatly influenced by three writers who I have never met: Barbara Ehrenreich, Nancy Fraser and Eric Hobsbawm. I worked on earlier versions of some of these ideas with Jayne Mooney, John Lea and Roger Matthews. Thanks to my students at the Graduate Center, CUNY. Many thanks to Caroline Porter who has been a patient and considerate editor and to Catriona Woolner, who has overseen the manuscript from start to finish, adding many insights and flashes of inspiration. Lastly Jesse, Joseph, Fintan and Jake have kept me sane (fairly). This book is dedicated to Jayne.

JOCK YOUNG

1

CROSSING THE BORDERLINE

This book is about cultural borders, it is about borders set up and borders crossed: it is about borders steadfastly erected like some Weberian iron cage and about borders transgressed and broken, it is about borders which intimate difference and borders which facilitate vindictiveness. It is about borders which seem solid and secure, but blur, hybridise, and dissolve. It is about cultural borders which have long lost their fixed spatial moorings, where culture and place no longer have constancy. It is about borders whose normative bases seem at first glance firm, and yet are riven with contradiction and incoherence. It is, in short, about the condition of modernity today which Zygmunt Bauman (2000) calls liquid modernity – where all that is solid melts into air, in contrast to the high modernity of the post-war period where the stolid, weighty, secure work situations of Fordism, undergirded by the stable structures of family, marriage, and community, presented a taken for granted world of stasis and seeming permanency.

What has generated this liquid modernity, this fluidity of norm, institution, and social category so characteristic of our present period? The factors which have brought about this change are well known – mass migration and tourism, the 'flexibility' of labour, the breakdown of community, the instability of family, the rise of virtual realities and reference points within the media as part of the process of cultural globalisation, the impact of mass consumerism, and the idealisation of individualism, choice, and spontaneity. Many of these are far from new, think of mass migration particularly in the United States where it is a key component of its development. Some of the most significant texts in classical sociology have talked about the impact of such forces. For example, Frederich Engels' *Conditions of the Working Class in England* (1969 [1844]) graphically documents the miserable work conditions, family breakdown and social disintegration in mid-nineteenth-century Manchester. Or Durkheim's *Division of Labour* (1951 [1893]), which charts the anomie and rampant individualism consequent on the rapid industrialisation of France at the turn of the nineteenth century.

Indeed some of these developments characterise mid- to late-nineteenth-century capitalism and industrialisation as much as they do our late modern world at the beginning of the twenty-first century. Some, however, although with us throughout modernity, have been ratcheted up in the present period and have become a qualitatively different presence. Take, for example, the role of the mass media where its immense proliferation, its speed and immediacy, its technological advances and its global reach have transformed our existence. Lived experience, once localised and immediate has now become irrevocably interlaced with mediated experience (see Thompson, 1995). Virtual reference points, narratives, fictional and non-fictional, permeate every aspect of our lives. Such a commonality is despatialised, rapid and ever-present. Nor is the impact of the rise of such a mediated society limited to lived experience, it also profoundly affects and undermines our notions of the fixity and concreteness of social concepts. As Jeff Ferrell puts it, 'One of the great social interactionist insights of the last century – that meaning resides not in the thing itself, but in surrounding social and cultural processes – takes on even greater complexity and importance in a world where mass-produced symbols now circulate endlessly amidst the situated experiences of everyday life.' (2006, p. 270). And, as we shall see, such a contested, problematic social reality has resonances not only in the phenomenology of everyday life, but on the tenability and credibility of the social sciences.

Or, if we turn to individualism, we see similarly transformations of its nature and impact. Eric Hobsbawm, in his magisterial *Age of Extremes* (1994) characterises the late-twentieth century as experiencing a cultural revolution of an unparalleled nature. The American Dream of material comfort and the suburbs becomes replaced with a First World Dream extending across the world – harbouring the desires of the privileged and the envy of the rest. Here the point is not brute comfort and material success, but self-discovery and expression, it is not so much arrival as becoming and self-fulfilment, not of hard work rewarded, but of spontaneity and expressivity anew. The comfort-seeking creature of post-war modernity is replaced by the striving subject of late modernity. And if Durkheim's warnings of the *mal d'infiniti* in the late nineteenth century, or Merton's admonition of the incessant nature of material goals in the America of the 1930s (an aspect of his work sadly neglected), conveyed the notion of the human spirit always striving but never fulfilled, heightened individualism in an era of mass consumerism has granted it an even greater resonance today. We are therefore confronted with a combination of factors, some long existing yet unique in their combination, others pre-existent yet transformed in the present period. The impact revolves around three axes, the disembeddedness of everyday life, the awareness of a pluralism of values, and an individualism which presents the achievement of self-realisation as an ideal.

Liquid modernity generates a situation of disembeddedness. This has dual levels: social and individual. Culture and norms become loosened from their moorings in time and place: normative borders blur, shift, overlap, detach. And this precariousness is experienced on a personal level. The individual feels disembedded from the culture and institutions he or she finds themselves in. And to such a situation is presented a pluralism of values: migration, tourism, the mass media and most importantly the variety of indigenous subcultures within society that carry with them the constant nagging awareness that things could be done differently, that we could make different choices. And here it is often small differences, differences of a minor kind which are more disconcerting than norms which are manifestly distinct and somewhat alien. Finally, self-realisation, the notion of constructing one's own destiny and narrative, becomes a dominant ideal. There is, overall, a sense of detachment from the taken for granted social settings and with it an awareness of a situation of choice and freedom. So that which was once experienced as a thing – monumental and independent of human artifice – becomes de-reified and the social construction of reality is glimpsed particularly poignantly in everyday life, especially alarmingly at moments of personal crisis or sudden change.

All of this creates great potentialities for human flexibility and reinvention. Yet it generates at the same time considerable ontological insecurity – precariousness of being. To start with, the bases of identity are less substantial: work, family, community, once steadfast building blocks, have become shaky and uncertain. At no stage in history has there been such a premium on identity, on constructing a narrative of development and discovery, yet where the materials to construct it are so transient and insubstantial. But it is not merely the instability of work, family and community which make the writing of such a narrative difficult, it is the nature of the building blocks themselves. Work in particular is a locus of disappointment – it is the site of meritocratic ideals, of notions of reward and social mobility commensurate with effort, which very frequently it fails to deliver. It is the supposed font of self-realisation yet all too usually a mill of tedium. It is the workhorse of a consumerism which evokes self-realisation and happiness, but which all too frequently conveys a feeling of hollowness, and neverending extravagance, where commodities incessantly beguile and disappoint. Even the real thing seems a fake.

Work does not merely sustain family life, it manifestly intrudes upon it. It is the long commute which cuts into both ends of the day, and where the family becomes the place of tiredness and worn nerves. For the middle class, work is the price to pay for the sparkling family home and the help to clean it and take care of the children while the dual career family is out at work, yet in a strange sense it is often more of an image than a reality. It is real in the glossy magazines of home and garden, it is a caricature in reality. For the working poor, it is the two jobs which make life sustainable, while curtailing family and community, it is time off from seeing one's own children and very often it is the time taken to look after the children of others. None of this should deny for an instant the perennial human joys of companionship of work, marriage and partnership, raising children and the comforts of neighbourliness. It is simply to note that it is precisely these parts of human fulfilment that suffer most … the shoe pinches where it is needed most.

What one finds in late modernity is a situation of contradiction and of paradox. The major institutions have both repressive and liberative potentials. The mass media, for example, carries hegemonic messages justifying the status quo of power – yet constantly in news story and fiction points to the blatant failure and unfairness of the world (see Young, 1981). Cultural globalisation propagates the tinsel values of Hollywood, yet it also carries notions of meritocracy, equality, and female emancipation, while in its global reach and its implosiveness, it serves to stress the interconnections and commonality of the world across economic and social borders (see Thompson, 1995). Even consumerism, as Paul Willis has so ably argued in *Common Culture* (1990) not only sells lifestyle but generates a popular and autonomous demand for individualism and lifestyle of choice which develops, so to speak, on the back of the market place.

Disembeddedness, fluidity, can create the possibilities of seeing through the present institutional set up, of discarding the old traditions, of respect for authority which justify the status quo, of wealth and social division. It thus holds the possibility of a redistributionist approach to social justice and deconstructive approach to identity, yet it can paradoxically offer just the opposite: an acceptance of the world as it is, a mode of 'realism' and an essentialist notion of identity built around one's position of class, gender, ethnicity, place and nation. The outcome is not inevitable or, for that matter, random, but is a product of particular social and political configurations. Of great importance here are perceptual factors, that is the degree to which the basis of economic and social differentials are transparent. In particular I focus upon what I call the chaos of reward and the chaos of identity. As I will argue, the decline of manufacturing industries, the phenomenon of outsourcing, of core and peripheral work personnel, of freelance consultants and advisors, of a proliferating service industry of small restaurants, cafés, childcare and housework – all of these together make the comparison of rewards less obvious. The awareness of class distinction and inequalities was more obvious in the large Fordist bureaucracies of the post-war period, it becomes less tangible in late modernity – all that remains is a generalised feeling of unfairness, a failure of meritocracy which is underscored by widespread redundancies and changes in career. As for identity, the ideal of self-development, of a narrative of self-discovery and personal achievement is difficult in a world where the building blocks seem so insubstantial and contested. All of this makes the creation of a personal narrative difficult. It breeds a feeling of incoherence of half-realised awareness and contradiction. It is not surprising then that at no time in human history has such a recourse been made to fictionalised narratives – the worlds of the soap opera, the thriller, and the romantic novel, a world where there is a beginning, a middle, and an end, a story of substance and fulfilment albeit in a virtual reality.

The genesis of othering

In real life the narrative of life pales beside the narrative of fiction or the ideals of meritocracy, self-fulfilment – the First World Dream. Our narratives seem unfair – they are frequently broken and discontinuous, they have no ending. None of this adds up to a satisfying account, a good story – rather it makes for a feeling of incoherence and bittiness, edged with strong emotions of unfairness both in terms of just reward and social recognition. Note also, it does not make for a neat narrative to be discovered by the diligent researcher: a clear, crisp story to be uncovered and revealed. Yet the longing for existential security, for certainty and solidity often exacerbated by the experience of denigration and stigmatisation remains. So, just as barriers are demolished and rendered permeable, new barriers are erected in the false hope of creating rigidity and secure difference. Such a generation of hiatus of rigid distinctions is seen in many spheres of human activity. Most clearly it is seen in cultural essentialism where, in the process of othering, the self is granted a superior ontology, whether based on class, gender, race, nationality, or religion, and is valorised, given certainty in contrast with the other. Two modes of othering are prevalent: the first is a conservative demonisation which projects negative attributes on the other and thereby grants positive attributes to oneself. The second, very common yet rarely recognised, is a liberal othering where the other is seen to lack our qualities and virtues. Such a *lacking* is not seen, as in the conservative version, as an essential and qualitative difference so much as a deficit which is caused by a deprivation of material or cultural circumstances or capital. They would be *just like us* if these circumstances improved. Thus, whereas for the conservative difference is rendered a perversion, or perhaps an inversion, of normality, for the liberal it is rendered a deviance from a lacking of the normal.

Liberal othering focuses largely on the poor constituted as an underclass, who are seen as being a fairly homogenous group. The poor are seen as disconnected from us, they are not part of our economic circuit: they are an object to be pitied, helped, avoided, studied, but they are not in a social relationship with us. The poor are perceived as a residuum, a superfluity, a

5

dysfunction of a system. Their lives are a product of material or moral determinism, which accentuates the miserable and unsatisfactory nature of their lives. They are not a site of creativity, joy or expressivity – but of a bleak and barren scenario which contrasts with the taken-for-granted satisfactions of the mainstream world.

Let me summarise the key components of liberal othering. 'They' – which is predominantly constituted as 'the poor' – are not so much different from us as suffering from a material or moral deficit, so rather they are a lacking from us. Their crime and deviance is the main focus of the othering, their 'normal' activities, for example their pattern of work and *legal* informal economies, are rendered invisible (e.g. the working poor). Their deviance is seen as a product of this deficit that can be remedied through education and the opportunity of work so as to make up the shortfall of the deficit. Our response to them is therefore not that of demonisation but of actuarial avoidance and judicious help. They are not connected to us either materially or symbolically, rather they are a residuum, separate from us spatially, socially and morally. There are therefore two moments in othering: *diminishing* (they are less than us) and *distancing* (we have no direct social relationship with them).

Both conservative and liberal othering have in common the notion of a gulf between 'them' and 'us', a distancing, and both gain strength for the centre by diminishing the moral nature of the margins. The difference is that conservative othering involves the notion of suggesting that the deviant is alien – an inversion of 'our' values while liberal othering stresses a lacking, a deficit of value. Correspondingly, whereas conservatives focus on policies which are punitive or exclusionary, liberals focus on inclusionary measures which are educational and rehabilitative. However, importantly, in both modes the deviant does not threaten order, rather the deviant – whether internal or external to our society – helps to shore up order. Othering, then, is a key process which maintains order. I wish to argue that this late modern binary, in either of these modes, permeates public thinking and official discourse about deviants in our midst and extends to images of other cultures, countries, nationalities and religions and, with it, notions of immigration and population movement. Further, that such a binary is pivotal in much social scientific thinking, not only in the conceptualisation of the other and the deviant, but in the production of knowledge itself.

Ontological insecurity then gives rise to the search for clear lines of demarcation, crisp boundaries in terms of social groups (both in terms of the othering of deviants and conventional notions of multiculturalism and ethnic distinctions). On the level of the social sciences, this is reproduced in the search for clear definitions and in the assertion of an objectivity which suggests a gulf between the investigator and the investigated, together with the denial that any social relationship occurs across this hiatus with the implication of the rationality and integrity of the culture of the investigator and the relative irrationality and unsubstantiveness of the investigated.

The attractions of hiatus

Thus such a binary notion of human nature and social order extends throughout notions of ontology and sociology, into areas of social scientific epistemology and method. It was while working on *The Exclusive Society* (1999) that I encountered this problem of hiatus and dualism so characteristic of the social condition of late modernity. It is inherent in the particular notion of social exclusion as isolation – of a segment of the population being physically and morally excluded from the mainstream, detached from the body of 'normal' or 'middle' class people and above by impermeable physical and social barriers. It is encountered in the accompanying notion of cultural difference, whether expressed in the form of cultures alien to our own or more commonly cultures which lack our rationality and solidity. It is implied by the ontological or essential differences between people: it occurs in notions of cultural globalisation, where the dominant cultures of the First World are seen as being initially hermetically separate from the cultures of the Third World, and that these pristine worlds of difference are simply obliterated by global forces, as if there was a time quite recently when they were 'uncontaminated' and a time soon when they will disappear. It is the rhetoric behind the clash of civilisations where orientalist notions of the world conjure up an apocalyptic battle as if those 'civilisations' could possibly have been miraculously separate. It is the central weakness of much methodology in the social sciences which seeks to set up definitions of social entities as if they were akin to animal species having some Linnaean separateness or essence, a unique DNA, which we can simply grasp by an act of systematic description. Thus we ask 'what is terrorism?' as if it were a fact out there and not a function of our phenomenological view, our perceptual position and does not blur irredeemably with conventional warfare. And the same, of course, is true of attempted definitions of all social categories; think of violence, pornography, prostitution, rape, the gang, or indeed suicide. A belief that there is some hiatus between the conventional and the deviant – clearly criticised by Durkheim in his elegant discussion of the blurring of the concept of suicide and underscored by his evocation of the society of saints, where lines of delineation are subject to change over time, yet are reaffirmed with the same intensity as to their naturalness and distinctiveness. And although such a concept of blurring and change, of 'overlap' and 'shift' (see Matza, 1969) is characteristic of all societies, I will argue that it is all the more so today, in the era of late modernity, where norms are daily contested and blurred, and where the movement in levels of social

7

tolerance, the process of defining deviancy up, has become a part of every-day life. Moral borders, in short, blur and move with a speed that is easy to perceive and palpable in their impact.

For the critical anthropologists Akhil Gupta and James Ferguson, a major part of the mispresentation of culture and politics is a presumed isomor-phism, the assumption that place, space and culture inhabit a coincident territory. Globally this is seen in maps which present 'the world as a collec-tion of "countries" ... an inherently fragmented space, divided by different colors into diverse national societies, each "rooted" in its proper place' and each with 'its own distinctive culture and society' (1997, p. 34). On a cul-tural level they point to various processes which, particularly in late moder-nity, drastically undermine such an isomorphism: immigration – the movement of people across borders, the mixture of cultures in the nether-worlds of the borderlands which belie discrete demarcations, multicultural-ism within societies and the whole phenomenon of hybridity where cultures transform by selective addition and recombination. And to this one should add a paramount factor: the existence of cultural reference points within the media which electronically criss-cross the world and show no respect for borders.

In a world where culture is less fixed to place, cultures are more capable of such hybridity and recombinance. But note the immigrant group enter-ing a 'host' culture is already changed, there is no distinct before and after in a world of globalised media. Immigrants arrive from abroad not with a pristine alien culture but with one which is already hybridised. The immi-gration myth of a hitherto pure culture facing assimilation and looking back home with nostalgia is far from the truth. Further, that of course hybridisa-tion occurs both ways, both 'immigrant' and 'host' is transformed.

Yet less one should enter a freeform world of post-modern choice, a gym-nastic of cultural dexterity and change, we should note the obvious. That is, not only do cultures blend and overlap, but such recombination occurs not in a situation of freedom, but in a world of power and domination. 'We all inhabit', as Renato Rosaldo puts it, 'an interdependent late-twentieth-century world marked by borrowing and lending across porous national and cultural boundaries that are saturated with inequality, power, and domina-tion' (1993, p. 217). Further, as Gupta and Ferguson trenchantly argue, 'the presumption that spaces are autonomous has enabled the power of topog-raphy successfully to conceal the topography of power' (1997, p. 35). The notion of the separateness, spatial, cultural and social, occludes power.

Looking within societies, then, we could learn much from anthropologists with their more global perspectives. It would allow us, for example, to avoid what Paul Gilroy (1993) calls ethnic absolutism which would believe that 'white' and 'black' cultures are hermetically separate and distinct. Yet we must be aware of the power of dominant cultures. If we take New York City for example, where a remarkable 37% of the population are officially born outside the United States – well over 40% if we allow for the many people who have reason to avoid the census (and London and Toronto are not far behind in the size of their immigrant populations) we perhaps can no longer, as my students constantly remind me, talk of minority populations. Rather we have cities of minorities where people reinvent themselves, their traditions and their futures. Yet there can be little doubt about the strength of middle-class America, its culture of individualism, meritocracy and constitutionalism – its belief in itself and the American Dream. Hybridity then is not a relationship between equals – the biological analogy is to this extent a misnomer. The understanding of difference within the late modern cities must take cognizance of this just as it must be sensitive to resistance, separateness, recalcitrance and dogged difference. At the very least, methodology whether in survey work or in ethnography must take note of shadow opinions, ambivalence and contradiction as well as appraising the tendency of those lower in the social structure to give the 'correct' answer – the response of the hegemony, to those they surmise as being 'above' them in the social hierarchy.

The notion, then, of a disjointed world of hiatus and chasm obfuscates reality and disguises power; but as Gupta and Ferguson put it, 'the irony of these times is that as actual places and localities become even more blurred and indeterminate, *ideas* of culturally and ethnically distinct places become even more salient. It is here that it becomes more visible how imagined communities come to be attached to imagined places. As displaced peoples cluster around remembered or imagined homelands, places or communities in a world that seems increasingly to deny such firm territorialized anchors in their actuality' (ibid., p. 39). And such an irony, of course, spreads to powerful groups who fondly imagine and recreate past worlds of homogeneity and tranquillity, and extends to the social scientist who seeks just such a fixed anchor to establish claims of objectivity and dispassionateness. For positivistic social science, not unlike the insecure citizen of late modernity, desperately needs a secure narrative, an unquestioned structure, a reified world, with distinct borders and clear demarcations. It needs a steady platform from which to observe, and clear-cut entities to scrutinise and to measure. And just as the ontologically uncertain citizen attempts to assuage feelings of social vertigo and insecurity by the magic of othering, so positivist sociology and criminology attempts to achieve the scientific goal of objectivity by distancing from its subject, by creating a hiatus where social relationship is denied, by an act of scientific othering (see Young, forthcoming).

Finally, let me add that corresponding to a sociology, ontology and methodology of hiatus there is a politics. That is, for the right, the lower part of the social structure is seen as detached and useless, it is at best a burden,

9

CROSSING THE BORDERLINE

at worst a danger, a population of incorrigibles, largely composed of immigrants, who must be controlled, surveyed and excluded. They are a negative point around which politics must be mobilised; their very exclusion an othering which gives identity to the politics of the 'normal majority'. For liberals they are an other who must be helped, manipulated, made to conform through the regimens of education and work. Here we have a politics of inclusion but it is inclusion into a system of work tedium and little reward, an existing structure of inequality which is scarcely questioned.

The poor are either our problem (the right) or their problem (the liberal left) not that their problems are *our* shared problems, that the problems of instability of work, the family, community, the uncertainty of income and the vertigo of identity are spread right across the levels of the vast majority of citizens. Such exclusionary processes resonate through the social structure. What is necessary is not a politics of hiatus but of unity. Militating against this are two currents running through our social structure which enunciate fundamental differences and evoke schism.

The insecure citizen, beset by the forces of globalisation and change, seeks to escape the vertigo of the late modern world by reaching out for strong lines of identity and grasps out at difference. Let me give an example: Thomas Frank, in his fascinating book *What's the Matter with Kansas? How Conservatives Won the Heart of America* (2004), starts with the puzzle of how the poorest counties in the United States are often those most solidly Republican. How poor people, whose communities are decimated and lives are manipulated by big business, can vote for a party which represents the very rich and corporate America. A rural America, let us remind ourselves, where there are now more prisoners than farmers and where prisons and gambling have become major industries. His argument is that the Republicans have managed, in an ingenious manner, to claim to speak for the common man, and that this party of billionaires and CEOs have cast the liberal élite as the real enemy. It constructs an upright agenda of traditional conservative values, pro-life, anti-abortion, Christian virtues, and couples this with neo-liberal economic policies. This conservatism of the common man delivers them to the Republican ballot box which, with a dreadful irony, results in massive tax cuts for those earning over $300,000 a year and economic policies which close down manufacturing industry and militate against the small farmer.

But there is more to this than sheer populism or, to put it another way, one always has to explain the popularity of populism. The vertigo of late modernity, I would argue, leads large sections of people in the lower to middle part of the class structure to experience what Nietzsche called *ressentiment*, a feeling of anger, bitterness, powerlessness, which searches out culprits and mobilises difference. Such an attitude scorns what it sees as an alliance between the do-gooders and the ne'er-do-wells, between the liberal élite, the latté liberals, propriety with their adherence to what Pope Benedict calls the 'dictatorship of relativism' and the urban poor of wastrels and losers. It draws firm lines of virtue like a cape around itself in terms of sexual propriety, military prowess, patriotism, Christian values and the conservative agenda. Such a moral revanchism receives a strong narrative from war, a narrative which the liberals incessantly try to undermine, it constructs a politics of hiatus, it is, as Nietzsche put it, 'through these opposed values that gulfs are cleft in the social plane which a veritable Achilles of free thought would shudder to cross' (2005, p. 2).

I am concerned, then, with this politics of hiatus: with the sociological basis of this process of othering and exclusion. Yet this is not the end of the story. In the meantime, below this populist discontent, lower in the atmosphere of unease, a parallel revanchism of virtue begins to unfold. For among a small but significant minority of immigrants to the First World, and most potently their children, an experience of embracing the Western values of liberty, equality and fraternity, yet witnessing exactly the opposite on the streets, in the slum estates, in the run-down schools produces a revulsion which poses an alternative vision of propriety, dignity and piety, a movement which would exclude the excluders, an attempt to create a counter orthodoxy of othering. This book will start by detailing the foundation of an underclass and end by examining the roots of terrorism; it will trace how the mechanisms of social exclusion attempt to deal with the vertigo of late modernity: with the fear of falling and the stigma of being cast out.

Core to this is a critique of the phenomenology of hiatus: that is of a gulf between subject and object, of the notion of an underclass detached from the class structure, of aetiologies which attempt to explain deviant behaviour whether it be crime, terrorism, or riots in terms of motivations and desires separate and distinct from those of the 'normal'. In engaging with this I will critique the process of othering, whether of a liberal or conservative variety, and of methodologies, whether based on survey research, the interview, or ethnography, which propose a radical detachment between researcher and researched. To deny the sociology of hiatus necessitates opposition to any politics, whether of the right or the left, which reaffirms division either in the toleration of gross economic inequality or in the invocation of essential differences between individuals or groups within society. Our task, then, is to build a transformative politics which tackles problems of economic injustice and builds and cherishes a society of genuine diversity.

The vertigo of late modernity

Imagine a society of saints, a perfect cloister of exemplary individuals. Crimes, properly so called, will there be unknown; but faults which appear venial to the layman will create there the same scandal that the ordinary offense does in ordinary consciousnesses. If, then, this society has the power to judge and punish, it will define these acts as criminal and will treat them as such. For the same reason, the perfect and upright man judges his smallest failings with a severity that the majority reserve for acts more truly in the nature of an offense. Formerly, acts of violence against persons were more frequent than they are today, because respect for individual dignity was less strong. As this has increased, these crimes have become more rare; and also many acts violating this sentiment have been introduced into the penal law which were not included there in primitive times. (Calumny, insults, slander, fraud, etc.)

(Émile Durkheim *The Rules of Sociological Method*, 1964 [1895], pp. 68–9)

I have talked of how insecurities in economic position and status, coupled with feelings of deprivation in both these spheres, engender widespread feelings of ressentiment both in those looking up the class structure and those peering down. Such insecurities can be experienced as a sense of vertigo and, outside of the charmed sphere of the contented minority, such uncertainties are tinged with anger and dislike. Further, that such processes have a wide resonance throughout society, underscoring many of the anxieties and obsessions of contemporary life.

Vertigo is the malaise of late modernity: a sense of insecurity of insubstantiality, and of uncertainty, a whiff of chaos and a fear of falling. The signs of giddiness, of unsteadiness, are everywhere, some serious, many minor; yet once acknowledged, a series of separate seemingly disparate facts begin to fall into place. The obsession with rules, an insistence on clear uncompromising lines of demarcation between correct and incorrect behaviour, a narrowing of borders, the decreased tolerance of deviance, a disproportionate response to rule-breaking, an easy resort to punitiveness and a point at which simple punishment begins to verge on the vindictive. Some of these things are quite blatant, they are the major signposts of our times, the rise in the United States of a vast Gulag of 2.2 million people in prison and 1 in 34 of the population in prison, on probation, or parole at any one time, the draconian drug laws, the use of terrorist legislation to control everything from juvenile gangs to freedom of speech. Some are quite banal, the obsession with the politically correct, the attempt to fit the population into rigid but ever-changing ethnic categories, the policies of zero-tolerance in the United States: the move from policing felonies to the policing of misdemeanours, the shenanigans of New Labour over the control of undesirable behaviour, ASBO enters the English language (even becoming a verb: 'to be ASBO'd'), Anti-Social Behaviour Coordinators are advertised in the job columns of The *Guardian* (an anarchist's dream I would have imagined) while a British Home Secretary stands up at the 2005 Labour Party Conference and announces his intention 'to eliminate anti-social behaviour' by 2010 (a statement of Canute-like munificence – goodness knows what he would make of Durkheim's society of saints). Moral panics abound, as I write, in Britain the media are obsessed with binge drinking, as if public drunkenness were some new phenomenon to these islands (see Hayward, 2006), while the concept of 'binge' shrinks palpably, now consuming four drinks in a row becomes considered a pariah act of wanton debauchery. The model Kate Moss is publicly pilloried for snorting a line of cocaine, an activity which a very large part of the upper middle class of London (including, of course, journalists and very many MPs) have got up to at some time or another. Journalists lurk in toilets with cocaine testing kits in order to hound those celebrities who have got beyond themselves. The great fashion houses and perfume makers withdraw their contracts and sponsorship, although as the fashion editor of The *Guardian*, Jessica Cartner-Morley (2005) has pointed out – make a great play on their edginess: of being risqué, of peddling the forbidden (witness the perfumes Opium, Poison, Obsession, the aesthetics of anorexia, juvenile sexuality, belts, buckles, bondage, etc.). Moss goes into rehab, like a penitent to a nunnery in the Middle Ages, although not for half a lifetime but for two weeks. And, spurred on by her newsworthiness, the sponsorship of the model near the end of her career is quickly renewed. Redemption is so much quicker in late modernity.

The sources of late modern vertigo are twofold: insecurities of status and of economic position. Although such a feeling of unsteadiness permeates the structure of society, it is particularly marked in the middle classes in the American sense of everyone from the middle level manager to the skilled worker, it is less so among upper middle class professionals, whose skills and professional organisations protect them from threat, or from the working poor and below who have precious little distance to fall. This involves, as all commentators concur, a wide swathe of workers, but particularly those whose status is closely welded to economic position. That is those whose lifestyle (holidays abroad, car, house, private education for children, domestic help, etc.) is so dependent on standard of living. Those for whom the realms of class and status are rightly fused. Here fear of falling is fear of total loss of everything – it threatens their loss of narrative, of a sense of modernity where life involves personal progress in career, in marriage, and in the community they choose to live in.

Pluralism, the shock of the different; the encounter with diversity face to face in the cities, on tourist visits abroad and through the global implosion of media imagery and actual realities, produces at the most a sense of disorientation. It points to the possibility that things could be different and that rational discourse need not lead to the same conclusions as in one's own culture; it de-reifies and de-familiarises – making the familiar no longer obvious and taken for granted. But disorientation alone does not precipitate feelings of anger and ressentiment. Indeed, among the secure and contented middle class, pluralism brings out the sense of the international flâneur; for the sophisticated well versed in the cultures of Europe and the frisson and energies of the United States, the awareness and enjoyment of diversity is an integral part of one's lifestyle. And, of course, so too is the sampling of the myriad cultures and cuisines of the city. This is a key factor behind gentrification, the move back into the city – just as those more threatened moved out in the evacuation of the inner cities subsequently known as 'white flight'. Thus, for the secure middle class, such encounters with diversity corroborates rather than threatens their ontology, their way of life, their sense of themselves. But this is not so for a wide swathe of the middle class whose jobs are threatened and who feel resentment towards those that they perceive as an underclass detached from decent society yet living on their taxes and making none of the daily sacrifices that they have to make. Let us look at how this pans out in terms of seemingly unrelated events across the social structure.

Turbo-charged capitalism

Edward Luttwak, in an article written in 1995 entitled 'Turbo-Charged Capitalism and its Consequences', and subsequently expanded into a book (1999), presents us with three sets of figures. The US aeroplane company Boeing on 10th August 1995 had its shares quoted at $65, representing 77 times the earnings of the shares in the previous four quarters, while in the same week the International Association of Machinist and Aerospace Workers (who are a major union at Boeing) publicised the findings of a survey which showed that 50% of their members, who overwhelmingly see themselves as middle class, felt their jobs to be insecure and only 20% felt themselves to have security of employment. Lastly, concomitant to this was the extraordinary size and nature of the American Gulag – by the end of 1994, 2.8 million Americans were either on probation, parole and in prison at any point of time – one American in every 189 being actually incarcerated: a total of 1.5 million in all Federal, State and local jails. Of course, as we have seen, the figures look bleaker every year: today there are 2.2 million incarcerated at any one time. Luttwak asks us to look at these three seemingly disparate sets of figures abandoning the 'one-thing-at-a-time pragmatism' of Anglo-Saxon thinking and commit the 'teutonic vice' of looking for systemic connections in human life.

On our behalf, Luttwak ties together these three statistics. He starts with the process of globalisation: the deregulation of markets which opens up Boeing's aeroplane sales to the world while at the same time outsourcing the production of airframe parts anywhere in the globe where labour is cheap. Couple this with the computerising of much repetitive labour and one has a downsizing of the work force which results in remarkable acceleration of profits. Staff are laid off not only in bad times, as in the past, but also, most significantly, in times of prosperity in order to achieve a more lean and effective core of workers. Thus we arrive at the second set of figures. Boeing employees are correct to feel insecure in their jobs and their anxiety is compounded by the fact that decent jobs in the primary labour market are harder and harder to find while marginal and low paid service sector jobs expand and both formal and informal support for the unemployed is in decline. As he puts it, sardonically:

> what 'flexibility' amounts to as far as employed labour is concerned is that every year millions of Americans bereft of supporting families (forget the generous cousins that unemployed Andalusians and Greeks can still count on, or the functioning nuclear families of France or Italy – in contemporary America not even brothers and sisters help one another), and facing a six-month limit on unemployment compensation (as opposed to 12 or even 24 months in Western Europe) must and do accept even drastically reduced earnings to work at all, so that jobs in retailing and small service businesses of the dog-washing variety can expand *ad infinitum* (it will soon be unnecessary to brush one's own teeth). (1995, p. 6)

Thus a middle class sector of the population once part of Galbraith's vaunted 'constituency of contentment' has due cause for anxiety. For the shift is from a good job with fringe benefits to drastic drops in income, possible loss of highly mortgaged homes, and inability to sustain children in college. Such stress induces illness without the health insurance to support it. 'Health-cost trauma should become a recognised medical syndrome', Luttwak notes ironically, 'it is certainly more genuine than its Gulf War counterpart' (ibid., p. 7).

He then turns to the final set of statistics: the awesome size of the American Gulag and its attendant system of 'corrections'. 'Turbo-charged capitalism' not only consigns a large section of the middle class into a state of insecurity and anxiety (entire industries rise and fall much more swiftly than before – downsizing proceeds apace) – it also generates an underclass who are *perceived* as economically useless and, in turn, high crime rates which have created no-go areas in each and every great American city.

'No society', he warns, 'can fail to pay a heavy price for widespread middle-class insecurity.' (ibid., p. 7). One symptom of this insecurity is the draconian reflex of punishment which forms the core of the American prison explosion ('one strike and you are out', mandatory prison sentences, etc.) but more widely is the broader urge to punish and prohibit which characterises contemporary US society. He refers not only to the war against drugs which is the second reason for the prison expansion, but the vast range of new prohibitions: smoking, fatty foods, sexual harassment, pornography, use of derogatory language, etc. From the quasi-criminal to the politically incorrect, all manner of behaviour, attitude and gesture is subject to

15

taboo and control. The always criminal becomes more criminalised, the quasi-criminal becomes criminal, and, around these, large penumbra of informal prohibitions arise. Of course some of these activities are doubtful and unsavoury. Yet as Luttwak notes, 'Because each prohibition has its own plausible defence, only their sheer number and great diversity reveal their common origin. They are all expressions of the same deep resentment' (ibid.). And he adds a historical dimension: 'It is no coincidence that prohibitions multiply when the middle class is especially insecure. It has all happened before, and there is no need of a Gestapo when so many Americans volunteer to do the job themselves by pursing their lips, narrowing eyes (just ask any smoker or fatty eater in public), and by voting for the least tolerant candidate available in one election after another' (ibid.)

Take note of what Luttwak has achieved in a brief essay. He has grounded the changes both in crime and in penality in the economy and the economic changes in the forces of globalisation. He has dealt with *both* crime and penality and he has located the American prison expansion in the general culture of intolerance. Now there is much that could be criticised in these sweeping generalisations. There is a general lack of mechanisms: how and where is exclusion translated into crime? (it is automatic and obvious in Luttwak's formulation), how does the culture of intolerance give rise to more people in prison? (what about the role of law and order politicians, the prison industry, the judiciary?), how does insecurity and anxiety give rise to intolerance and scapegoating? (rather than sympathy and identification with the underdog). All of these things and more – some of which I will touch upon and develop in the next chapter, Edward Luttwak in his remarkably un-'Anglo-Saxon' way has suggested fundamental connections between the economy and the twin elements of crime and punishment.

Finally, Luttwak views 'turbo-charged capitalism' as the way of the future. It is most emphasised in the United States but, as his recent book points out, its source is the powerful current of globalisation, a process occurring in all advanced industrial countries. It involves a transition from the market place being used to support society to one where all of society is mobilised to support the market place.

Luttwak adroitly places globalisation, downsizing, the rising rate of imprisonment, crime in the inner cities, and the increasing intolerance of deviant behaviour (defining deviancy up in Daniel Moynihan's terms) as phenomena which exist in the same social system. He suggestively connects economic insecurity to punitiveness and intolerance but what he does not do is explain the mechanisms which bring these seemingly disparate facts together. Through concepts such as moral indignation, ressentiment, bulimia and essentialism, I will attempt, in this book, to point to the social processes and psychodynamics which give rise to both widespread vindictiveness and transgressive anger.

2

BLURRING THE BINARY VISION

In *The Exclusive Society* (1999) I contrasted the inclusive world of the post-war period of the 1950s and 1960s with the more exclusionary social order of late modernity in the last third of the twentieth century and beyond. Eric Hobsbawm's (1994) 'Golden Age' of high employment, job security and stable marriage and community is contrasted with a more insecure and divided society that followed it. For, whereas the Golden Age granted social embeddedness, strong certainty of personal and social narrative, a desire to assimilate the deviant, the immigrant, and the stranger, late modernity generated both economic and ontological insecurity, a discontinuity of personal and social narrative and an exclusionary tendency towards the deviant.

In my research I started from the most immediate and apparent manifestations of social exclusion in late modern societies. I sub-divided these exclusions into three layers: the labour market, civil society and the State. Within the labour market I noted the decline of the primary labour market, the expansion of a secondary labour market characterised by insecurity, short-term contracts and multiple career trajectories and a penumbra of those on the margins, an underclass of those who are structurally unemployed and spend a lifetime idle or working for poverty wages.

Corresponding to this exclusion from the labour market was the exclusion from civil society: an underclass left stranded by the needs of capital on housing estates either in the inner city or on its periphery. Those who, because of illiteracy, family pathology or general disorganisation, were excluded from citizenship, whose spatial vistas were those of constant disorder and threat and who were the recipients of stigma from the wider world of respectable citizens. The welfare 'scroungers', the immigrants, the junkies and crack heads: the demons of modern society. And lastly, such a second class citizenship was demonstrated and exacerbated by the focus of the criminal justice system, by their existence in J.A. Lee's (1981) graphic phrase as 'police property' and by the extraordinarily disproportionate presence of the immigrant and the poor within the penal system.

Such a dualism is captured by John Galbraith's (1992) contrast between the 'contented majority' and an underclass of despair, with respectability on the one hand and stigma on the other, a world of civility and tranquillity over and against that of crime and mayhem. It underscores much of the contemporary usage of the phrase 'social exclusion'. However, I became increasingly sceptical of the various accounts of this process where social exclusion is presented as a sort of hydraulic process, where the tides of inclusion have risen leaving behind the destitute and the feckless, without any reference to the dynamics of social antagonism and conflict (e.g. Wilson, 1987; Social Exclusion Unit, 1999a). Moreover, such a separation was invariably constructed as a binary of inclusion/exclusion where the excluded exist in an area which is spatially segregated and socially and morally distinctive. From this perspective, crime is a product of a disorganisation characterised by joblessness, weak family, inadequate schools and disintegrated communities, and where the causal mechanism is quite simply lack of control in each of these closely inter-linked arenas.

It soon became clear to me that such a dualism was fundamentally misconceived. It echoed the conventional wisdoms of the subject, to be sure, but it did not adequately grasp the social and spatial terrain of the late modern city nor the dynamics of the actors who traverse it. It rightly suggests barriers and divisions but wrongly exaggerates their efficacy and solidity: it mistakes rhetoric for reality, it attempts to impose hard lines on a late modern city of blurred demarcation and crossovers. It posits a hermetic localism in an age of globalisation. Furthermore, it neither captures the intensity of the exclusion – the vindictiveness – nor the passionate resentment of the excluded, while painting a far too calm and rational picture of the fortunate citizens – the included.

Let us first examine the components of the social exclusion thesis:

1 THE BINARY that society can be divided into an inclusive and largely satisfied majority and an excluded and despondent minority.
2 MORAL EXCLUSION that there exists a vast majority with good habits of work, virtuous conduct between citizens, stable family structures and a minority who are disorganised, welfare dependent, criminal and criminogenic, who live in unstable and dysfunctional families.
3 SPATIAL EXCLUSION that the excluded are isolated from the included, that stronger and stronger barriers occur between them and that these borderlines are rarely crossed. Furthermore, that the fortunate classes create guilded ghettos which systematically exclude the poor.
4 THE DYSFUNCTIONAL UNDERCLASS that the underclass is a residuum which is dysfunctional to itself and to society at large, both in its cost in taxes and in its criminogenic nature. It is the 'dangerous classes' of the Victorians underwritten by the taxes of the Welfare State.'
5 WORK AND REDEMPTION that the provision of work will transform the underclass: changing their attitudes of mind, habits of dependency, cultures of hedonism, criminal tendencies and dysfunctional families, and transport them into the ranks of the contented and the law abiding.

This thesis is held by writers of various theoretical and political dispositions: whether it is the 'social isolation' of William Julius Wilson (1987), the 'hyperghettoization' of Loic Wacquant (2001), the warnings of 'Indian style reservations' by Richard Herrnstein and Charles Murray (1994), 'the New Bantustans' of Mike Davis (1990), the language and rhetoric of New Labour's Social Exclusion Unit (1999a), 'the dual city' of Manuel Castells (1994), 'the geographies of exclusion' of David Sibley (1995) or the New York of nightmares and dreams portrayed in Tom Wolfe's *Bonfire of the Vanities* (1988). And parallel to the segregation of the poor is the 'guilded ghettos', self-imposed isolation of the middle classes whether it is in 'the gated communities' of Los Angeles, so well publicised by Mike Davis (1990), or 'the fortress city' of Susan Christopherson (1994), or 'the hyper-anaesthetized play zones' which are the 'flip side narrative of the "jobless ghetto"' (2000, p. 91) of Christian Parenti.

I have also become increasingly suspicious of explanations of crime which are constituted around notions of opportunities, on one side, and lack of controls, on the other. Such a rational choice theory of crime is prevalent across a wide spectrum of theorists (e.g. D. Garland, 2001; Felson, 2002), while instrumental rationality is implicit in many of the classic texts (e.g. Merton, 1938, 1957). In this the motivation for crime is usually mundane, the illegal relief of deficit or the simple taking of opportunities when there is a deficit of control. I have no doubt that much crime is mundane, instru-mental and opportunistic in motivation and that there are people whose response to crime is cool, calculated and rationalistic. But an awful lot of crime, from joyriding to murder, from telephone kiosk vandalism to rape, involves much more than an instrumental motivation. Work in cultural criminology, influenced by Jack Katz's seminal *Seductions of Crime* (1988) with roots in the early work of the sociology of deviance of the National Deviancy Conference in Britain and the Birmingham School of Cultural Studies, was greatly developed in the work of writers such as Jeff Ferrell (1997), and Stephen Lyng (1990) and more recently in Mike Presdee's *Cultural Criminology and the Carnival of Crime* (2000), and Keith Hayward's (2004) *City Limits: Crime, Consumerism and the Urban Experience* whose work all points to the wide swathe of crime that is expres-sive rather than narrowly instrumental.

Cultural criminology reveals almost exactly the opposite of Felson's world of mundane crime stressing the sensual nature of crime, the adrena-line rushes of edgework – voluntary illicit risk-taking and the dialectic of fear and pleasure. The existential motivational structure they explore inverts the very basis of routine activities, opportunities and control theory. Here the motivation to commit crime is not mundane but the revolt against the mundane – rules are transgressed because they are there, risk is a chal-lenge not a deterrent (see Morrison, 1995) and the steady increase in control, 'the creeping criminalisation of everyday life' as Mike Presdee puts it (2000, p. 159), provokes transgression rather than conformity.

What is of great importance about this investigation into the existential foreground of crime is that it reveals the *intensity* of motivation and links this to a background of a world where pleasure has to be seized despite the intense commodification of consumer culture, where control must be struggled for in a situation of ever increasing rationalisation and regulation and where identity is threatened by the instability of social narratives. As Keith Hayward points out, 'put simply, many forms of crime frequently perpetrated within urban areas should be seen for exactly what they are, an attempt to achieve a semblance of control within ontologically insecure worlds' (2002, p. 225). And to this intense drive for ontological certainty, for defining moments of pleasure and release, I would add the anger fuelled by economic insecurity and deprivation. Thus the intense emotions associated with much urban crime relates to significant and dramatic problems in the wider society. What is important here is a criminology which insists that, in a world of broken narratives, where economic and ontological insecurity abounds, that the nature of crime and the response to it is far from mundane; that the actors are far from pallid creatures calculating the best manoeuvres through the social world in order to minimise risk and maximise contentment and that much of the dynamic behind crime is resentment and much of the response to it vituperative. Crime has its excitement, its drama, its seductions and punishment, similarly, its vindictiveness, its hostility, its thinly concealed satisfactions. In contrast the criminology espoused by rational choice theory, with its images of opportunism and control, is quite simply the criminology of neo-liberalism and its truth claims are as limited as those that depict society as held together simply by contractual relations of a marketplace. Furthermore, not only is the discourse of cultural criminology in strong contrast theoretically to neo-liberalism, the very appeal of the transgressive, the anxiety-provoking, the transcendent, is in itself a reaction to a world dominated by institutions and discourses dominated by neo-liberalism (O'Malley and Mugford, 1994).

Such a position does not deny the rational component of action, but suggests that rationality is a great deal more complex than rational choice suggests and that both ends and means are shaped and energised by human culture and passion (see Sahlin, 1976). In the area of criminology it certainly does not make for a neat division between crimes of gain and crimes of passion. It should be further noted that cultural criminology encompasses not only the passions of crime but the often heated emotions involved in public and responses to crime by police and other members of the criminal justice system. Nor should it be thought that such an approach is restricted to crime and its control. Social action in general is ill-served by rational choice theory (e.g. Coleman, 1990). Thus, although cultural criminology has formed a cutting edge for this approach, conformist behaviour, often law-abiding, often with no relationship whatsoever to law, must be understood in its intensity. Often that which looks like it is without energy, a habit without motive and thinking – the day-to-day commitment to workaday routines, the day-to-day route to work, the picture postcard 'happy' marriage – involve an intensity which only becomes obvious when it unravels and unfolds. What I am suggesting then is that both the sociology of transgression and rule breaking and the sociology of 'realism' where the actor accepts the world in all its injustices and limitations, retreating under the carapace of habit into the secure world of the daily grind, with everything in its place, falls under the same theoretical rubric. That is, passion both in the spectacular and the commonplace. We can widen this analysis out then not only from the sociology of crime and deviance to the sociology of 'normality' and conformity. And, more obviously, we can also widen our analysis to include the sociology of war, terrorism and genocide.

Not only is there a close symmetry between the aetiology and phenomenology of crime and punishment, particularly of violent crime and state violence, but there are also close parallels with crimes occurring in war (by both sides), in terrorism and the response to it, and in the development and enactment of genocide. Further, much has been made of the striking similarities between the violence of conventional crime and the violence of war (not least being the young, male, working-class actors themselves) and the parallels between the war against crime and war itself. Indeed the emerging criminology of war seems to bring together the narratives of crime and of war and remedying the surprising ignoring of war (see Jamieson, 1998), and of genocide see (Morrison, 2003) by conventional criminology.

I wish now to examine the structure of social inclusion/exclusion, focusing on three areas: firstly the blurring of boundaries in terms of the binary conception of social exclusion; secondly the cultural implosiveness of late modernity and the phenomenon which I term 'bulimia'; and thirdly a critique of the dual city depiction of spatial segregation.

Blurring the boundaries

Let us turn to the notion of the binary of inclusion and exclusion with the associated notions of spatial, social and moral separation. I wish to argue that it is the blurring of these boundaries which is the key to the dynamic of antagonisms within society both of the poor towards the well off and of the better off to those below them. Note that I wish to contest this thesis, not from a perspective that there are no widescale disparities in late modern society, nor that areas of the city are not particularly blighted by crime and that their inhabitants experience social exclusion and stigmatisation.

21

Surely all of this is true and should be a target and priority of any progressive policy. But the construction of the problem in a binary mode obfuscates the issue, while the notion of social exclusion ironically exaggerates the degree of exclusion while underestimating the gravity of the problem. The danger of the concept of social exclusion is that it carries with it a series of false binaries: it conveys the notion of actors being either included or excluded – being on one side of the line or the other; it ignores the fact that problems occur on both sides of the line, however much one has clusters in one area rather than another and, more subtly, it conceals the fact that the 'normality' of the majority is itself deeply problematic.

The binaries of social exclusion

Society at large	The underclass
The unproblematic	The problem
Community	Disorganisation
Employment	The workless
Independence	Welfare dependency
Stable family	Single mothers
The natives	The immigrants
Drug free	Illicit drug use
Victims	Criminals

The concept of social exclusion implies that there is some homogenous underclass, the repository of much of the current portfolio of vices or deficits which contrasts with a relatively stable, virtuous majority of the included. In fact they are, as Herbert Gans (1995) has pointed out, an extremely heterogeneous group. Furthermore, as John Hills and his associates (2002) have indicated, the individuals concerned are often mobile throughout their lives and exist in extraordinarily varied levels along any scale of inclusion and exclusion. The image that I used in *The Exclusive Society* was that of a beach and the creatures upon it:

The mode of exclusion is, therefore, different from the past and corresponds to the realities of the present. It does not present itself as an on/off switch of inclusion or exclusion: either you're inside society or you're not. Rather it is a sifting process which occurs throughout society, for exclusion is a gradient running from the credit rating of the well off right down to the degree of dangerousness of the incarcerated. Its currency is risk, its stance is *actuarial* – calculative and appraising. The image of society is not that of a core of insiders and a periphery of outsiders but more that of a beach where people that are assigned to a gradient of positions in a littoral fashion. And, to stay with this metaphor, at the top of the beach there is the privileged sipping their cocktails, their place in the sun secured whilst at the bottom there are creatures trapped in the sea who can only get out with great effort and even if so are unlikely to survive. The beach has its gradient in between but this does not preclude at its extremes sharply segregated worlds whether it is of the super-rich or the underclass. (1999, p. 65)

There is a tidal movement, centripetal and centrifugal, there is little that is static or secure (see also Byrne, 1999). In contrast, the conventional image of the excluded as similar and static betrays, by its very homogeneity and fixity, its true nature, an ideological category, the bringing together of folk devils in the process of othering. Further in respect of the patterning of problems: unemployment, poverty and economic insecurity are scarcely unknown outside the designated areas – indeed quantitatively they are overall more prevalent in the supposedly secure majoritarian heartlands of society than they are in the selected minority of 'excluded' areas. And the same, of course, is true of illicit drug use, community disorganisation, unstable family structures, etc. In the case of the notion of 'the normal majority' it assumes that, in this world, class differentials are somehow insignificant, that paid work is an unambiguous benefit, that 'stable', family life is unproblematic, licit psychoactive drug use is less a problem than illegal drug 'abuse', etc. Furthermore, it assumes that the transition from the social excluded to the majority via the vehicle of work will miraculously solve all these problems.

But we can go further than this for there is widespread evidence that the culture of contentment – which John Galbraith (1992) talks of: a 'contented majority' who are all right thank you, doing fine and sharing little in common or concern for the excluded minority – are a myth. The demands for a more and more flexible labour force coupled with the leap forwards in automation and the sophistications of computer software has caused great reverberations of insecurity throughout the employment structure. Redundancy, short-term contracts, multiple career structures have become the order of the day. Furthermore, as the Joseph Rowntree Foundation Report, *Job Insecurity and Work Intensification* (Burchell, 1999), discovered, redundancy not only causes chronic job insecurity but the workers who remain have to work longer hours and expand their skills to cover the areas of those dismissed (op. cit., p. 60). For those in work, the length of the working day increases: it is, of course, easier for the employer to ask for more and more time when security of employment is uncertain. *The market does not compete in hard places, it goes for the soft tissue of time and vulnerability*. Moreover, while in the past the income of one wage earner was sufficient to maintain a family, the dual career family has now become a commonplace where both partners are immersed in the labour market. And if, in the economic sphere, precariousness and uncertainty are widespread so too in the domestic sphere: divorce, separation, single parenthood are endemic, with the pressures of work merely adding to the instability of the late modern family.

Bulimia: not exclusion but inclusion/exclusion

There is a strange consensus in recent writings about the underclass. Both writers of the right and the left concur that what one has is not a separate culture of poverty as earlier conservative and radical writers presumed (e.g. Edward Banfield, 1968 on the right, or Michael Harrington, 1963, on the left), but rather that what has occurred is a breakdown of culture (see Murray, 1984; Wilson, 1987). Thus William Julius Wilson (1987), in his influential 'social isolation', thesis, points to the way in which whole areas of the inner city, having been formed around the previous needs of manufacturing industry, are left stranded as capital wings its way to find more profitable dividends elsewhere in the country or abroad. While the middle and respectable working classes escape to the suburbs, the less skilled remain behind bereft of work and, indeed, role models who display work discipline and the values of punctuality and reliability. The loss of work, in turn, leads to a lack of 'marriageable men' who can earn a family wage and engenders the rise of single mothers in the ghetto – and the role model of the family, parallel to that of work, is likewise diminished.

Charles Murray (1984), writing from the opposite political perspective, comes to surprisingly similar conclusions. His causal sequences are, of course, very different: it is not lack of work that causes the problem but lack of willingness to work, engendered by an 'over generous' Welfare State which creates 'dependency' among the poor. Such a dependency manifests itself in a lack of motivation to work and single mothers living on welfare. Thus the effects on attitudes to work and the family are similar and the perceived consequences, a high rate of crime and incivilities, identical. Murray is, of course, often criticised as a 'culturalist' in the underclass debate although he explicitly denies that this is his position. Thus in his rejoinder to critics he rejects the culture of poverty thesis noting 'How can people read my extensive descriptions of causation, all of which focus on the way in which members are responding sensibly (at least in the short term) to policies that have been put in place around them [i.e. the Welfare State and thus dependency] and then cite surveys regarding a 'culture of poverty' to refute me? The burden of my argument is that members of the underclass are *not* sunk in a cultural bog ...' (1996, p. 83).

All of these assessments of the morals of the poor are those of *deficit*: in the recent writers they lack our values, in the earlier writers they have different values which are seen as deficient. That is, there is present-day emphasis in the literature on what I have described as liberal othering (an othering in terms of lack of our values rather than the more conservative othering which suggests values alien to our own). And, as it is, all of them describe a fairly similar value system or lack of it, namely short term hedonistic, lacking in restraint, unwillingness to forgo present pleasures, aggressiveness and willingness to use violence to achieve desired goals. In short, a spoilt, petulant, immature culture at the bottom of the social structure.

In *The Exclusive Society* I set out to examine this picture of mores at the bottom of the social structure. I decided to look at the American black underclass as a test case for surely, if this thesis were true, it would be among these supposed outcasts of the American Dream that this distinct, localised and anomic deficit culture would be found. In particular I looked at Carl Nightingale's (1993) brilliant ethnography of the black ghetto of Philadelphia, *On the Edge*. What Nightingale discovered confounded such an image. For instead the ghetto was the apotheosis of America. Here is full immersion in the American Dream: a culture hooked on Gucci, BMW, Nikes, watching television 11 hours per day, sharing the mainstream culture's obsession with violence, backing Bush's involvement in the Gulf War, lining up outside the cinemas, worshipping success, money, wealth and status – even sharing in a perverse way the racism of the wider society. The problem of the ghetto was not so much the process of it being simply excluded but rather one which was all too strongly included in the culture but, then, systematically excluded from its realisation. All of this is reminiscent of Merton but where, in a late modern context, the implosion of the wider culture on the local is dramatically increased. We have a process which I likened to bulimia of the social system: a society which choruses the liberal mantra of liberty, equality and fraternity yet systematically in the job market, on the streets, in the day-to-day contacts with the outside world, practices exclusion. It brands as 'losers' those who had learnt to believe that the world consisted of 'winners' and 'losers'.

Crossing the borderline: against the dual city thesis

If you stand where the kites fly on the summit of Parliament Hill in Hampstead, on a clear day you will see, about half-way between the spires of St Michael's church in Highgate and the steel-and-glass skyscrapers of the City of London, the six immense tower blocks of Nightingale Estate. They stand, in two ranks of three, almost in the centre of Hackney. It is less than four miles from Hampstead and Highgate in space, but if social distances were measured in miles it would be half-way round the globe. The gulf between the inner city and the desirable neighbourhood is a measure of the wide gap between wealth and poverty in Britain.

The inner city is the social antipodes of middle-class Britain, a universe apart, an alien world devoid of almost every feature of an ideal environment. It is the place where all our social ills come together, the place where all our sins are paid for.

(Paul Harrison, *Inside the Inner City*, 1983, p. 21)

There are imaginary geographies which place imperfect minorities in marginalized locations: in a social *elsewhere*. These locations consist of protected zones which ensure the reproduction of those who inhabit them, who are separated from the majorities living outside. These geographies of exclusion associate *elsewhere* with that which is contaminated, filthy, offensive to morality and olfaction.

(Vincenzo Ruggiero, *Crime and Markets*, 2000, p. 1)

Thus the underclass is constructed as an Other, as a group with defective norms who contrast with the normal majority. And here in this region lies all sorts of crime and incivilities. From this perspective of essentialising the other, the demand is to locate the problem areas: where exactly *are* the demons, so to speak? The powerful seek, in Tod Gitlin's poignant phrase, 'to purge impurities, to wall off the stranger' (1995, p. 233). Thus the underclass is said to be located within the clear cut ghettos of the inner city sink estates or the long lost satellite slums at the cities' edge. But, in fact, there is no such precision here: the poor are not as firmly corralled as some might make out. Thus, as Gerry Mooney and Mike Danson write, in their critique of the 'dual city' concept, based on their research in Glasgow – a city, some would say, of extreme cultural and economic contrasts:

The conclusion which is drawn from the analysis of poverty and deprivation in contemporary Glasgow presented here is not one which lends support to the dual city model. ... This is not to deny, however, that there is an uneven distribution of poverty in the city or that poverty is concentrated in certain areas. What is being contested is the usefulness of the dual city argument for our understanding of such distributions and the processes which contribute to it. ...

The language of the two city/dual city argument is one which is seriously flawed by definitional and conceptual difficulties. Despite the continuing use of concepts such as polarisation, underclass, exclusion and marginalisation, we are little clearer about the underlying factors which are viewed as contributing to such processes. In this respect the dual city perspective and its implicit arguments about growing socio-spatial polarisation are plagued by ambiguity and vagueness.

In discussions of the emerging 'tale of two cities' in Glasgow, the attention which the peripheral estates received does not relate directly to the levels and proportions of poverty to be found there. In part this is a consequence of reluctance to define adequately the areas or social groups concerned. Further *within* peripheral estates there is a marked differentiation between the various component parts in terms of unemployment, poverty and deprivation. This is almost completely neglected in the dominant picture of these estates which has emerged in recent years which stereotypes the estates as homogeneous enclaves of 'despair' or 'hopelessness'. (1997, pp. 84–5)

Similarly, John Hagedorn points to the variegated neighbourhoods in Milwaukee which he studied 'a checkerboard of struggling working class and poor families, coexisting even in the same block, with drug houses, gangs and routine violence.' (1991, p. 534). Maybe urban geographers of all political persuasions would like more of a clear cut cartography than is healthy but, in reality, the contours of late modernity always blur, fudge and cross over.

Yet the influential social commentator, Manuel Castells advocates the concept of dual city as the fundamental urban dualism of our time:

It opposes the cosmopolitanism of the elite, living on a daily connection to the whole world ... to the tribalism of local communities, retrenched in their spaces that they try to control as their last stand against the macro-forces that shape their lives out of their reach. The fundamental dividing line in our cities is the inclusion of the cosmopolitans in the making of the new history while excluding the locals from the control of the global city to which ultimately their neighbourhoods belong. (1994, p. 30).

While elsewhere Castells suggests that the tribes, far from experiencing hybridism and a coming together, are sharply divided, they are 'a variety of social universes, whose fundamental characteristics are their fragmentation, the sharp definition of their boundaries and the low level of communication with other such universes' (1991, p. 226). In this conception the rich live in late modernity whereas the poor are trapped in locality, tribalism and the past. Such a notion, tied to that of a class divide based on information, fails to grasp the cultural penetration of globalisation. For, as John Tomlinson points out:

those marginalized groups for whom 'locality is destiny' experience a *transformed* locality into which the wider world intrudes more and more. They may in all sorts of ways be the 'losers' in globalisation, but this does not mean that they are excluded from its effects, that they are consigned to cultural backwaters out of the mainstream of global modernity. Quite to the contrary, it seems to me that the poor and marginalized – for example those living in inner-city areas – often find themselves daily closest to some of the most turbulent transformations, while it is the affluent who can afford to retire to the rural backwaters which have at least the appearance of a preserved and stable 'locality'. (1999, pp.133–4)

Thus, in terms of mass communication, they encounter messages and commodities from all over the world, while the inner city area in which they live becomes multi-ethnic and diverse due to labour immigration. They are exposed to what Dick Hebdige (1990) calls a 'mundane cosmopolitanism' just as real or perhaps more significant than the rich tourist who travels the world in a fairly sanitised fashion from chain hotel to chain hotel, from airport lounge to airport lounge. And cultures of distant places, either through the media or on the streets, become incorporated in the local cultures particularly of the youth (see Back, 1996). Further, the notion that the cosmopolitan élite is the true site of hybridity whilst the masses of people exist in separatist tribes is far off the mark. Thus Dave Morley, in his *Home Territories: Media, Mobility and Identity* (2000), is incorrect when he argues that rather than hybridity there has been an increased 'ethnification' of public space where borders remain sharp and all too real. He cites approvingly the criticism of Dick Hebdige (1992) and Celeste Olalquiaga's (1992) analysis of the lower East Side of Manhattan – with their aesthetic and cultural valorisation of identity as applying only to the cosmopolitan (and bohemian) élite and not to the migrants who live there.

My feeling is that this critique mistakes the nature of hybridisation: crossover, the picking up of cultural elements from the 'host' society and from wider virtual sources occurs relentlessly in situations of cultural globalisation as do attempts to 'ethnify', to create/recreate traditional values from back home. Both hybridisation and ethnification are products of globalisation – the first sometimes consciously, but more frequently unconsciously – the latter more purposively and in reaction against what is perceived as cultural encroachment. Hybridity sneaks in the door and can even coincide with the nostalgic and the traditional.

Thus the spatial, cultural, and informational separation is scarcely as strict as is frequently suggested because of powerful underlying economic and cultural reasons. Thus, for this reason, one would be critical of Zygmunt Bauman when he writes of Washington DC:

> One difference between those 'high up' and those 'low down' is that the first may leave the second behind - but not vice versa. Contemporary cities are sites of an 'apartheid a'rebours': those who can afford it, abandon the filth and squalor of the regions that those who cannot afford the move are stuck to. In Washington, DC ... there is an invisible border stretching along 16th Street in the west and the Potomac river in the northwest, which those left behind are wise never to cross. Most of the adolescents left behind the invisible yet all-too-tangible border never saw downtown Washington with all its splendours, ostentatious elegance and refined pleasures. In their life, that downtown does not exist. There is no talking over the border. The life experiences are so sharply different that it is not clear what the residents of the two sides could talk to each other about were they to meet and stop to converse. As Ludwig Wittgenstein remarked, 'If lions could talk, we would not understand them'. (1998a, p. 86).

This eloquent expression of the dual city thesis is wrong, not in its sense of division, but in its sense of borders. For the borders are regularly crossed and the language spoken on each side is remarkably similar. The most obvious flaw in the argument is that of gender: maids, nurses, clerical staff move across into work everyday. Women, as William Julius Wilson argues in *When Work Disappears*, are more acceptable to the world outside of the ghetto than their male counterparts. It is after all 'home boys' who stay at home. But bellhops, taxi drivers, doormen and maintenance men regularly ply their way across the invisible borders of Washington DC. It is not, therefore, just through television that the sense of relative deprivation of the poor is heightened, it is in the direct and often intimate knowledge of the lives of the affluent.

The functional underclass

What is not accepted, and indeed is little mentioned, is that the underclass is integrally a part of the larger economic process and, more importantly, that it serves to maintain the living standard and the comfort of the more favored community ... The economically for-tunate, not excluding those who speak with greatest regret of the existence of this class, are heavily dependent on its presence.

The underclass is deeply functional; all industrial countries have one in greater or lesser measure and in one form or another. As some of its members escape from deprivation and its associated compulsions, a resupply becomes essential. But on few matters, it must be added, is even the most sophisticated economic and social comment more ret-icent. The picture of an economic and political system in which social exclusion, how-ever unforgiving, is somehow a remediable affliction is all but required. Here, in a compelling fashion, the social convenience of the contented replaces the clearly visible reality.

(John Galbraith, 1992, pp. 31–2)

Yet it is common to portray the underclass as not wanted, as a social residuum. They are the people who were left behind in the urban hinter-lands as capital winged its way to places where labour was cheaper, they are those whose labour is no longer required and who, furthermore, are 'flawed consumers' as Zygmunt Bauman (1998b) would have it, whose income is insufficient to render them of any interest to those selling the glittering commodities of late modern society. They are the casualties of globalisation and the new technology: they are the useless class, a segment of society which has become detached and irrelevant. As Ralf Dahrendorf put it: 'They are, if the cruelty of the statement is pardonable, not needed. The rest of us could and would quite like to live without them' (1985, p. 20). They are not simply of little use because their presence has dysfunc-tions for the rest of society: they have no uses but great costs. These dys-functions are said to take two forms. Firstly, the underclass is a source of crime and incivilities, it is viewed as a dangerous class; secondly, the residuum are costly, an ever-increasing burden on the hard pressed taxpayer.

David Rieff in *Los Angeles: Capital of the Third World* (1993) writes of the close physical proximity of the professionals and the underclass in Los Angeles, their interdependence yet the chasm that separates their lives. Frank Webster captures this well when he comments:

Illustrations of this are easy to find. On the one hand, maids are an essential element of the professionals' lifestyles, to cook, to clean, to look after children, to prepare for the dinner parties held in the gaps found in the frenetic work schedules of those deep into careers in law, corporate affairs, trading and brokerage. The maids, generally Hispanics, ride the infamously inadequate public transit buses to points in the city where their employers may pick them up in their cars to bring them home to clean up breakfast and take the children off to school. On the other hand, visitors are often struck by how verdant are the gardens of those living in the select areas of LA. Often they make the assumption that 'anything grows here in this wonderful sunshine'. But they are wrong: Los Angeles is a desert and gardens need most intensive care to bloom. They get it from an army of mainly Chicano labourers which arrives on the back of trucks very early in the mornings to weed, water and hoe – for a few dollars in wages, cash in hand.

In spite of this dependence, which obviously involves a good deal of personal inter-action, the lives of the two groups are very far apart. Of course this is largely because they occupy markedly different territories, with members of the poor venturing out only to service the affluent on their terms as waiters, valets, shop assistants and the like; the underclass also inhabit areas which the well-to-do have no reason (or desire) to visit. (1995, pp. 205–6)

The dual city where the poor are morally segregated from the majority and are held physically apart by barriers is a myth. The borderlines are regularly crossed, the underclass exists on both sides anyway, but those who are clustered in the poorer parts of town regularly work across the tracks to keep the well-off families functioning. *The work poor keep the work rich going: indeed, it is only the availability of such cheap 'help' that enables the dual career families to continue.* The situation of the dual income family and their need for support is well documented in Nicky Gregson and Michelle Lowe's *Servicing the Middle Class* (1994). The class relations of this emergent form was well summarised by the Hunts when they wrote:

Hired help on a single-family basis involves a category of workers that must be paid out of the take-home earnings of the nuclear unit. Consequently, the dual-career family is premised upon the increased use of a class of workers locked into a standard of living considerably lower than their employers ... it would provide the liberation of one class of women by the continued subjugation of another. (Hunt and Hunt, 1977, p. 413)

Neither are the poor excluded morally, they are far from socially isolated, the virtues of work and the stable nuclear family are daily presented to them. For not only do they actually directly physically experience it in their roles of nannies, kitchen help, as waiters in restaurants and cleaners and bell boys in hotels – they receive from the mass media a daily ration of these virtues, indeed one that is in excess of that consumed by those who work in the primary labour market.

The boundaries of bulimia

Physical, social and moral boundaries are constantly crossed in late modernity. As we have seen, they are transgressed because of individual movement, social mobility, the coincidence of values and problems both sides of any line and the tremendous incursion of the mass media which presents city-wide and indeed global images to all and sundry while creating virtual communities and common identities across considerable barriers of space. Boundaries are crossed, boundaries shift, boundaries blur and are transfixed.

The ghettos of the poor and the rich are not islands of isolation: they are porous vessels in which osmosis of a very calibrated kind occurs. As depicted by the isolation theorists, the gilded ghetto keeps the poor out and the ghetto of the poor is an institution which keeps the underclass in. This is simply not their constitution: the ghettos of the rich are dependent on the work of the poor – they could not exist without it. The production of food, household goods, the utilities of electricity, gas and water are, of course, all provided at a distance. But the myriad tasks needed to maintain the living standards of the well-off are all provided by the stream of servants and of service agents who move daily from their homes in the poorer parts of town. The paradox, then, is that the gated community needs to be permeable in its barriers, but that the osmosis is one-sided. For the rich do not know or care to enter the ghettos of the poor. East New York, in Brooklyn, is, for example, *terra incognito* to the middle-class inhabitants of Park Slope in Brooklyn, but a procession of maids, nannies, car drivers, porters, washers up and shelf fillers traipse out of East New York to the brownstones, hospitals and restaurants of Park Slope.

The socially excluded do not, therefore, exist in some 'elsewhere' cut off spatially, socially and morally from the wider society. To suggest this is not to say that physical barriers do not occur. Traffic is often scheduled so as to cut off parts of town, transport systems leave whole tracts of the city dislocated from the rest, and gated communities occur both in the fortunate and unfortunate parts of the city. It is not to deny that a characteristic of late modern society is the setting up of barriers, of exclusion. Nor is it to ignore the cultural divisions that are set up within society propelled by misconception and prejudice. Indeed the discourse about social exclusion with its binary structure is itself part of such an attempt to construct moral barriers and distinctions. Rather, it is to say that such physical parameters are exaggerated, that the virtual communities set up by the mass media easily transcend physical demarcations, and that values are shared to a much greater extent than social isolation theorists would suggest. Of course subcultural variations exist within society but that's what it is, *subcultural*: a variation in accentuation of core values rather than a deficit or difference in value.

The binary language of social exclusion fundamentally misunderstands the nature of late modernity. Here is a world where borders blur, where cultures cross over, hybridise and merge, where cultural globalisation breaks down, where virtual communities lose their strict moorings to space and locality. The late modern city is one of blurred boundaries, it was the Fordist city of modernity which had a segregated structure, a division of labour of specialised areas, a Chicago of concentric rings. Now the lines blur: gentrification occurs in the inner city – deviance occurs in the suburbs. It is a world of globalisation not separation, of blurring not strict lines of demarcation, it is culturally a world of hybrids not of pedigrees, of minor not major differences – the very decline in the physical community and rise of its virtual counterpart means that it is impossible for an underclass to exist separately.

Once again none of this is to suggest that considerable forces of exclusion do not occur but the process is not that of a society of simple exclusion which I originally posited. Rather it is one where both inclusion and exclusion occur concurrently – *a bulimic society* where massive cultural inclusion is accompanied by systematic structural exclusion. It is a society which has both strong centrifugal and centripetal currents: it absorbs and it rejects. Let us note first of all the array of institutions which impact the process of inclusion: the mass media, mass education, the consumer market, the labour market, the welfare state, the political system, the criminal justice system. Each of these carries with it a notion of universal values, of democratic notions of equality and reward and treatment according to circumstance and merit. Each of them has expanded throughout the century and has been accompanied by a steady rise in the notion of citizenship encompassing greater and greater parts of the population in terms of age, class, gender and race. And within the period of late modernity the mass media, mass education and the consumer and labour markets have, in particular, increased exponentially. Each of these institutions is not only a strong advocate of inclusive citizenship, it is also paradoxically the site of exclusion. The consumer markets propagate a citizenship of joyful consumption yet the ability to spend (and sometimes even to enter) within the mall is severely limited, the labour market incorporates more and more of the population (the entry of women into paid work being the prime example) yet, as André Gorz (1999) has so astutely stressed, precisely at the time when work is seen as a prime virtue of citizenship, well paid, secure and meaningful work is restricted to a tiny minority. The criminal justice system is on paper a paragon of equal rights. The British *Police and Criminal Evidence Act* 1984, for example, governs among other things the powers of stop and search. It is a veritable cameo of neo-classicist notions of equality of citizens in the face of the law and the need for 'democratic' suspicion, yet on the streets, in practice, policing is indisputably biased in terms of race and class (see Mooney and Young, 2000). Politics is an hourly interjection of radio and television, the mass media speak on our part for 'the common good', and 'the average' man and woman – they even parade and interview joe public with regularity yet the vast majority of people feel manifestly excluded from political decision-making. Indeed even the tiny minority of active party members often feel impotent and uninfluential. Mass education is the major transmission belt of meritocratic ideas, it is the nursing ground of equal opportunity yet, as subcultural theorists from Albert Cohen to Paul Willis have pointed out, its structures serve to reproduce class divisions, and to exacerbate resentment. Lastly the mass media has a pivotal role; it has grown immensely and occupies a considerable part of waking life. In 1999, for example, the average person in England and Wales watched 26 hours of television, listened to 19 hours of radio every week, and read, on top of that, mass circulation newspapers and magazines. That is 40% of one's waking life spent watching TV or listening to the radio, rising to 60% of your free time if you are lucky enough to be in work. The lower down the class structure the citizen – the more socially excluded if you want – the more mass media is consumed. Thus, paradoxically, cultural inclusion is the inverse of structural inclusion. The media carry strong notions of the universal citizen and they, of course, depict the other institutions: the world of consumption, work, education, politics and criminal justice. Yet despite this overall commitment to social order, the very stuff of news is the opposite: disorder, breakdown, mayhem, injustice (see Young, 1981). To take the criminal justice system as an example: crime and police stories are a staple of both factual and fictional mass media and the miscarriage of justice is a major theme. From the murder of Stephen Lawrence to the Cincinnati riots, from the Guildford Four to Rodney Hill, police prejudice, corruption and incompetence is paraded daily. The mass media is a spectacular noticeboard of exclusion – it has all the characteristics of a bulimic narrative: it stresses order, justice and inclusion (the backcloth of the news) yet it highlights disorder, injustice and exclusion (the foreground). The contrast between a bulimic society and an exclusive society can be seen if one compares Western liberal democracies (and perhaps the new South Africa) with an explicitly exclusive society, the South Africa of Hendrik Verwoerd and P. W. Botha. Here one had explicit spatial and social exclusion, a multiculturalist apartheid based on racist distinctions, a controlled mass media which refused (on the whole) to report police brutality and which extolled divisions. It was both exclusivist culturally and exclusivist structurally (see Dixon, 2001).

The phenomenon of cultural globalisation fundamentally ratchets up this process of bulimia. Television dramas, news and advertisements, contain not only plot, story and product but a background of expectancies and assumptions. First World culture permeates the globe and carries with it notions of equality, meritocratic values, civil liberties – it proselytises not only expectancies of standard of living but notions of freedom and citizenship.

I want to suggest that it is the bulimic nature of late modern societies which helps to explain the nature and tenor of the discontent at the bottom of the social structure. It is rooted quite simply in the contradiction between ideas which legitimate the system and the reality of the structure which constitutes it. But the tensions between ideals and reality exist only because of the general and manifest awareness of them. Both the punitive anger of the righteous and the burning resentment of the excluded occur because the demarcation lines are blurred, because values are shared and space is transfixed, because the same contradictions of reward and ontology exist throughout society, because the souls of those inside and those outside the 'contented minority' are far from dissimilar, sharing the same desires and passions, and suffering the same frustrations, because there is no security of place nor certainty of being and because differences are not essences but mere intonations of the minor scales of diversity.

The very intensity of the forces of exclusion is a result of borders which are regularly crossed rather than boundaries which are hermetically sealed. No caste-like social order would be as transfixed with crime nor so ready to demonise and pillory the other. For it is an altogether unsatisfactory exclusion: borders and boundaries are ineffective; they create resentment but do not achieve exclusivity. For the 'excluded' regularly pass across the boundaries whether physically or virtually: they sense injustice, they *know* about inequality, whereas those 'lucky' enough to be 'included' are not part of the 'culture of contentment' which John Galbraith famously alludes to, rather they are unsure about their good fortune, unclear about their identity, uncertain about their position on the included side of the line.

But to understand the nature of the forces of exclusion, the barriers set up to man the social structure, we must go further and look at the predicament of the 'included'.

The precariousness of inclusion

We have discussed in the process of bulimia how the excluded are included in the norms, and social world of the wider society. But we can blur the binaries further for we must now understand how the social predicament and experience of the insiders parallel those of the outsiders and how this process is the key to understanding some of the most fundamental antagonisms within late modern society.

In order to understand this we must first of all distinguish the two basic facets of social order within advanced industrial societies. Firstly the principle that rewards are allocated according to merit, that is, a meritocratic notion of distributive justice. Secondly, that people's sense of identity and social worth is respected by others, that is, justice of recognition. When the first is infringed we speak of relative deprivation and when the second is violated we talk of misrecognition and ontological insecurity (see Fraser, 1997). If we examine the terrain of late modernity in these key areas of distributive justice and justice of recognition we find a high degree of uncertainty. My assessment is that in both these areas late modernity brings with it a sense of randomness: a chaos of reward and a chaos of identity. To take distributive justice first of all, the unravelling of the labour markets and the lottery of who finds themselves in each sector, the rise of a service industry consisting of diverse and disparate units, the seemingly random discontinuities of career, the profligate and largely unmerited rewards in the property market and in finance, all give a sense of reward which is allocated by caprice rather than by the rules of merit. My suggestion is that a generation which has been extensively instructed in the values of meritocracy are confronted with chaos in the market of rewards and this engenders a feeling of relative deprivation which does not have the easy comparative points of position in industry within standardised careers characteristic of Fordism, mass manufacturing industry and the Golden Age but is instead more individualistic in its envy, more internecine in its rivalry.

Secondly, in the area of recognition, of sense of worth and place, of ontology, there has been a parallel chaos. This is fuelled largely by the widespread discontinuities of personal biography both in the world of work and within the family, coupled with the undermining of a sense of locality – of physical place of belonging. This disembeddedness (see Giddens, 1991) creates an ontological insecurity – an identity crisis: the most ready response to this being the evocation of an essentialism which asserts the core, unchanging nature of oneself and others. This consists of three stages, firstly an insistence of some essential and valued qualities (whether cultural or biological) which are associated with the individuals in question (whether of masculinity, 'race', class, religion or ethnicity), and secondly the denigration of others as essentially lacking these virtues. Furthermore, that such a process of mobilising negative essences with regards to others creates prejudices, exclusions and stereotypes within society which further fuel the feelings of ontological insecurity of others. That is there is, in other words, a third stage where those who are thus 'othered' and essentialised, create a hardening of themselves (the most typical example being the hardening of machismo) in order to combat their humiliation and exclusion from society. The process of othering has, therefore, a self-reinforcing circularity.

It is important to note how such a process of othering, of mutual dehumanisation, promotes and facilitates violence. This mobilisation of aggression involves the two components of a feeling of economic injustice (relative deprivation of some sort) and feelings of ontological insecurity. Thus, in order to create a 'good enemy', we must be able to convince ourselves that: (1) they are the cause of a large part of our problems; (2) they are essentially different from us – inherently evil, intrinsically wicked, etc. This process of resentment and dehumanisation allows us to separate them off from the rest of humanity (us) but it also permits us to harden ourselves to deal with the special instance of a threat. We can act *temporarily* outside of our human instincts because we are dealing with those who are acting inhumanely. This technique of neutralisation permits the transgression of our general prohibitions against violence. It goes without saying that such a process of essentialisation occurs not only domestically, for example, justifications of violence against gays and the vituperative feelings of the general public towards 'vicious thugs', but also in terms of the dramatisation of evil between, say, the First World and its terrorists.

Both crime and punishment are areas greatly affected by these uncertainties. Relative deprivation especially when coupled with misrecognition and disparagement can readily lead to crime. The classic domestic instance is economic marginalisation of a group accompanied by police harassment. Similarly cultural globalisation projects images of the 'good life', economic success, the pleasures of consumption and of lifestyle indeed, the relative longevity of life itself around the globe, while economic globalisation opens up the whole world as a market place generating, in many instances, economic insecurity and subordination. Such a scenario is tailor-made for global relative deprivation across the borderlines between the First and Third Worlds, just as cultural dominance engenders the need for counter-images constructed out of tradition and essentialisation. Out of such an existential terrain, fraught with economic envy, ontological insecurity and righteous indignation, fundamentalism flourishes and terrorism readily takes roots.

The focus on the underclass

Relative deprivation can also occur where someone higher in the class structure looking down can see undeserved rewards unmatched with the disciplines of work and restraint. Further, just as the relative deprivation and ontological uncertainties of the poor can lead to crime, so perhaps more paradoxically, the deprivation and insecurity of the more wealthy can lead to feelings of punitiveness. As we have seen, the hard working citizen of the majority perceives a world where rewards seem allocated in a chaotic fashion. These rewards have become so diffuse that it is difficult to see rhyme or reason in society at large; hostility at this chaos of rewards tends to focus on the very rich or those at the bottom of the structure. That is, those who are very obviously paid too much for the amount of work they do and those who are paid for doing no work. In other words it fastens on the more obvious violators of meritocratic principle, namely the super rich and the underclass. The antagonism towards the idle rich and, for example, members of the Royal Family or company directors who allocate themselves incommensurate rewards, I have documented elsewhere (Young, 1999).

The underclass, although in reality a group heterogeneous in composition and ill defined in their nature, is a ready target for resentment (see Gans, 1995; Bauman, 1998b). Re-constituted, rendered clear cut and homogenous by the mass media, they became a prime focus of public attention in the form of stereotypes: 'the undeserving poor', 'the single mother', 'the welfare scrounger' etc., and an easy focus of hostility. Such stereotypes derive their constitution from the process of essentialising, so widespread because of the prevalent crisis of identity, that is, of negative images, the very opposite of the 'virtues' of the included, thus casting the social world into the binary mould which I have discussed previously. Thus, if the chaos of reward creates ready hostility towards the underclass, the chaos of identity grasps upon them as a phantasmagoric Other with all the opposite characteristics of the world of honest hardworking citizens and, therefore, a ready prop to their ontological security.

But note the paradox, here, an underclass which is, in fact, very similar to the rest of society, generates antagonism and distancing. The poor become more like the more wealthy, at the same time as they are 'othered' by them; the degree to which the poor become more like the rest, the more they resent their exclusion. Indeed, as we shall see, it is the narrowing of cultural differences which allows resentment to travel both ways along this two-way street. Thus, Zygmunt Bauman insightfully notes how it is the very similarity of aspiration which the underclass has which exacerbates the dislike of them just as it is this self-same aspiration, when thwarted, which creates discontent among the excluded. Thus in his critique of Lawrence Mead he writes:

> The underclasses offend all the cherished values of the majority while clinging to them and desiring the same joys of consumer life as other people boast to have *earned*. In other words, what Americans hold against the underclass in their midst is that its dreams and the model of life it desires are so uncannily similar to their own.' Further, and the other side of the coin, 'it is logic of consumer society to mould its poor as unfilled consumers' [yet] ... 'it is precisely that inaccessibility of consumer lifestyles that the consumer society trains its members to experience as the most powerful of deprivations. (1998b, p. 73)

Crime and the narrowing of differences

Feelings of discontent, of unfairness both in terms of material reward and recognition, are experienced either when cultural differences diminish or when those that were once similar began to be regarded differently. That is because discontent relates to relative, not absolute deprivation (see Runciman, 1966). Thus discontent rises: when migrants are assimilated or when lower classes are granted citizenship or when ethnic groups, once separate, become part of the mainstream, coupled with blockages of social mobility, limited access to privileged labour markets and public prejudice and denigration – in short, an incomplete meritocracy. The importance, then, of the ethnographies of Carl Nightingale (1993) on the black under-class of Philadelphia and Philippe Bourgois (1995) on the Puerto Ricans of the East Harlem barrio of New York City, is that they root discontent in the *narrowing* of cultural differences. In the first case Nightingale traces how much of African–American culture of the South is lost in the assimilated generation growing up in the Northern cities and, in the second, how it is the second generation Puerto Rican immigrants becoming more 'American' who experience the greatest discontent.

Thus the breakdown of spatial and social isolation in late modernity, which I have documented – a consequence of globalisation, the mass media, the con-sumer market and mass education – leads to a diminishing of cultural differ-ences and a rise in discontent both within nations and between nations.

Globalisation and the generation of domestic and global discontent

The twin forces of economic and cultural globalisation thus impact together with considerable effect both domestically and globally. Although the extent and level of economic globalisation is debatable (Hirst and Thompson, 1999) the impact is worldwide. The poor are not left behind stranded in the inner cities deserted by capital, they live in intense and self-involved market places and their eyes are on the outside world. The Third World peasant may not contribute much to the world economy and to the triad of the United States, Europe and Japan (see Thompson, 2000) but this does not mean they are outside the forces of economic globalisation: their coffee is sold on the world markets, they buy coca-cola at their local stall. Furthermore, the cultural globalisation which encompasses the global market raises people's aspira-tions, threatens their identities, and fuels their discontent.

I wish to argue that the discontent, arising out of the material and onto-logical uncertainties which globalisation engenders, has compelling parallels both on a domestic and a global level. Moreover, that these discontents col-lide with and exacerbate each other. For brevity's sake I will outline this process schematically:

1. *Widening of income differentials*   On a domestic level there has been a widening of income differentials in the First World (for the US see Mishel et al., 2001) whereas on the global level there has been a growing gap between the rich and poor nations (see UN, 1999).

2. *Cultural globalisation and relative deprivation*   Widening income differ-entials, however severe, do not in themselves generate discontent. What does is the relative deprivation generated by cultural globalisation. Internally

in the First World the poor are regaled with images of consumption and meritocracy while encountering structural inequality and unfairness. Furthermore while worldwide cultural globalisation parades standards of consumption, health care, and material well-being which are presented as human universals yet are palpably unfairly and grossly distributed. The saturation of media exposure both in the poorest parts of the First World and the far reaches of the globe in the context of gross inequalities has a bulimic quality.

3. *Globalisation and the crisis of identity*   The impact of neo-liberal policies in the First World exhorting a flexibility of labour and underwritten by economic globalisation and advances in automation generates instabilities of employment, career and community while putting great stress on family life (see Currie, 1997). Parallel to this, the individualism of a market society generates marital and family upheaval. All in all biographies become constituted by broken narratives, a situation of social disembeddedness occurs and there is widespread crises of identity. The impact of cultural globalisation in the Third World is to threaten tradition, undermine taken-for-granted realities and destabilise identity. Although such a crisis of identity envelops major swathes of the population, this is particularly acute among the poor who suffer both economic and political marginalisation. That is, domestically they feel not only economically discarded, but also misrecognised and disrespected, whereas globally minority groups and whole nations and cultures feel both economically dependent and politically sidelined.

4. *Relative deprivation and ontological insecurity*   The combination of material deprivation and ontological insecurity engenders attempts to secure identity by essentialising one's own culture and endeavouring to harden this identity by blaming and negatively essentialising others. Such a process of dehumanising the other in order to secure oneself, provides a major technique of neutralisation with regards to the use of violence. That is, if unfairness provides a rationalisation for violence, dehumanisation permits it.

5. *The narcissism of minor differences*   Such a crisis of identity evokes the need for hardened and distinct identities whether they be centred around machismo, community, nationality or religion. This has both a difficulty and an urgency given that, in an era of cultural globalisation, cultures once distinct have become, both within a nation and internationally, more similar. Thus, as Carl Nightingale (1993) shows in his study of the black underclass of Philadelphia, or as Michael Ignatieff has vividly shown in *The Warrior's Honor* (1999) with his examination of the Croatian–Serbian conflict, differences have to be actively constructed. Thus, in Freud's terms, 'the narcissism of minor differences' engenders passionate and intense conflicts (1929, see also Blok, 1998). Traditions are invented and differences improvised

whether it is the generation of masculine cultures of an almost burlesque nature (at precisely the time where male–female gender differences are narrower) or the evocation of myth and legend in Northern Ireland and the Balkans.

6. *Identity wars*   Nancy Fraser, in *Justice Interruptus* (1997), argues that the present period has been characterised by the politics of identity rather than that of class. Class, of course, has scarcely disappeared, but perhaps more accurately class politics are often enveloped in a discourse of identity. Crime in this present period similarly manifests itself in a concern with identity, the instrumental crime of the past seems to be superseded by crimes of passion, rage against humiliation, and concerns with expressivity and lifestyle. Similarly, Kaldor and Vashee (1997) talk of the new wars – the 'wars of identity' – with ethnic group pitted against ethnic group or, on a more global scale, 'crusades' of the West against 'terror' where a fundamentalist president, using the language of fundamentalism, sets himself up against the forces of fundamentalist Islam.

3

THE SOCIOLOGY OF VINDICTIVENESS AND THE CRIMINOLOGY OF TRANSGRESSION

Oh tell me brave Captain why are the wicked so strong?

How do the angels get to sleep when the devil leaves his porch light on?

(Tom Waits, 'Mr Siegal', *Heartattack and Vine*, Asylum, 1980)

I have discussed the crossing and blurring of boundaries in late modernity. I wish to argue that, not only is such a breakdown of demarcations characteristic of the times of economic and cultural globalisation we live in, but that such a spatial, social and moral overlap is the key to the changing characteristics of crime and punishment today. Namely that the criminology of transgression and the sociology of vindictiveness must be understood in the context of the social dynamics generated by the implosive nature of the cultural systems and the contradictory nature of the spatial and social structures which both permit and restrict mobility. Furthermore, that not only are there strong parallels between the dynamics of crime and the desire to punish, but that there are close similarities between violence associated with 'common' criminality and the violence of war and terrorism.

Relative deprivation downwards, a feeling that those who work little or not at all are getting an easy ride on your back and your taxes, is a widespread sentiment. Thus, whereas the 'contented' middle classes may well feel sympathy towards the underclass, indeed their 'relative satisfaction' with their position may translate into feelings of charity, those of the much larger constituency of discontent are more likely to demand welfare to work programmes, stamp down on dole 'cheats', etc. Such a response, whatever its rationality, is not in itself punitive: it is at most authoritarian but it is not necessarily vindictive. But tied to such a quasi-rational response to a violation of meritocratic principles is frequently a much more compelling subtext which seeks not only to redress a perceived reluctance to work but to go beyond this, to punish, demean and humiliate (see Hallsworth, 2000; Pratt, 2000).

The key features of such resentment are disproportionality, scapegoating and stereotyping. That is, the group selected is seen to contribute to the problems of society quite disproportionally to their actual impact (e.g. teenage mothers, beggars, immigrants, drug users) and they are scapegoated and depicted as key players in the creation of social problems. Their portrayal is presented in an extraordinarily stereotypical fashion which bears little relationship to reality. Thus in *The Exclusive Society* I note how there seems to be a common narrative on the depiction of such late modern folk devils which extends from 'single mothers' to 'drug addiction'.

Svend Ranulf, in his pathbreaking book *Moral Indignation and Middle Class Psychology* (1964 [1938]) was intrigued by the desire to punish those who do not directly harm you. Such 'moral indignation', he writes, is 'the emotion behind the disinterested tendency to inflict punishment [and] is a kind of disguised envy' (1964, p. 1). He explores this emotion using the concept of 'ressentiment' which was first used by Nietzsche in his condemnation of the moral basis of Christian ethics and developed by Max Scheler in his *Das Ressentiment im Aufbau der Moralen* (1923). Ressentiment has within it the impulse, as Merton put it, to 'condemn what one secretly craves' (1957, p. 156). Ranulf's innovation was to locate ressentiment sociologically and to tie the source of envy to restraint and self-discipline. Thus he writes:

the disinterested tendency to inflict punishment is a distinctive characteristic of the lower middle class, that is, of a social class living under conditions which force its members to an extraordinarily high degree of restraint and subject them to much frustration of natural desires. (1964, p.198)

It cannot be an accident that the stereotype of the underclass: with its idleness, dependency, hedonism and institutionalised irresponsibility, with its drug use, teenage pregnancies and fecklessness, represents all the traits which the respectable citizen has to suppress in order to maintain his or her lifestyle. Or as Albert Cohen famously put it, 'The dedicated pursuit of culturally approved goals, the eschewing of interdicted but tantalising goals, the adherence to normatively sanctioned means – these imply a certain self-restraint, effort, discipline, inhibition. What effect does the propinquity of the wicked have on the peace of mind of the virtuous?' (1965, p. 7). Such a social reaction is moral indignation rather than moral concern. The demons are not the fallen and the pitiful which fixate the philanthropist, rather they, at once, attract and repel: they are the demons within us which must daily be renounced. Thus the stereotype of minorities is not a wholly negative identity, for as Homi Bhabha reminds us, in a telling phrase, it is a 'complex, ambivalent, contradictory mode of representation as anxious as it is assertive' (1993, p. 70).

The rigours of late modernity extend such restraints and insecurities far beyond a narrow class band. A large part of the population are subject to relative deprivation and ontological uncertainties and on top of this the pressures and restraints necessary to function exacerbate this even further. To survive in the late modern world demands a great deal of effort, self-control, restraint. Not only is the job insecure and poorly paid, the hours worked are long – extra hours are expected as a sign of commitment and responsibility – children are often not seen for long after the long commute home – *people talk of 'quality time' as a euphemism for 'little'* – the weekends seem short and enjoyment has to be snatched often with the liberal aid of alcohol. The dual career family more and more becomes a norm with the planning both of adults' and children's schedules that this entails.

Let us summarise the restraints:

- increased working hours (see Schor, 1993; Gorz, 1999)
- increased intensity of work (see Burchell, 1999)
- increased commuting (see Knox, 1995)
- dual career family (see Garland, 2001; Taylor, 1999; Gregson and Lowe, 1994).

It is the experience of restraint and sacrifice which turns simple displeasure (a sense of unfairness) into vindictiveness. Furthermore, the climate of work pressure and job uncertainty pervades a wide swathe of the class structure, it is not restricted to the lower middle classes, which Ranulf pinpointed, in line with much of the thinking at the time with its concerns about the rise and social basis of fascism (see also the discussion of Luttwak, in Chapter 1). Moreover this climate of restraint exists on the top of the problems of job security and fairness of rewards and the crises of identity – we thus have a three layered process, each layer contributing to the process of the demonisation of the underclass:

1 *Sense of economic injustice*   The feeling that the underclass unfairly live on our taxes and commit predatory crime against us fuels the dislike and fear of the underclass.

2 *Crisis of identity*   The underclass readily become a site for establishing identity by asserting the binary them and us, where 'us' is normal, hardworking and decent, and 'them' is a lacking of these essential qualities. It is such essentialism which demonises the underclass – constituting them as a homogenous, clear cut, dysfunctional entity.

3 *The situation of restraint*   It is the projection of all the problems of restraint that supplies the *content* of the demonisation: the various supposed facets of underclass life; teenage pregnancy, single mothers, substance abuse, criminogenic cultures, highly racialised (e.g., the focus on immigrants and asylum seekers).

Such a process is, of course, not that of simple envy. The lawyer does not want to be a junkie, the professional woman certainly did not want to be a teenage mother, the bank manager could not countenance being a street beggar, the life of the new wave traveller does not instantly draw the careful couple from

THE SOCIOLOGY OF VINDICTIVENESS

Croydon (an English suburb). Certainly not: for both real and imagined reasons, the lives of such disgraced 'Others' are impoverished and immiserised. No one would want to swap places with them. But their very existence, their moral intransigence, somehow hits all the weak spots of our character armour. Let us think for one moment of the hypothetical day of the hypothetical 'included' citizen on the advantaged side of the binary: the traffic jam on the way to work, the hours which have been slowly added to the working day, the crippling cost of housing and the mortgage which will never end, the need for both incomes to make up a family wage, the delay in having children so that the woman's career can get established, the fear of biological timeclocks and infertility, the daily chore of getting the children to school across the crowded city, the breakdown of locality and community, the planning of the day of two careers and two children (thank God for the mobile 'phone!), the lack of time with the children, the fear of missing out: 'they've grown up before you knew it', the temptations and fears of the abuse of alcohol as a means of enjoyment, in the time slots between the rigours of work.

It is surely not difficult to see how an underclass who, at least in stereotype, are perceived as having their children irresponsibly early, hanging around all day with their large families, having public housing provided almost free, living on the dole, staying up late drinking and taking exotic, forbidden substances and, on top of all that, committing incivilities and predatory crimes against the honest citizen, are an easy enemy. They set off every trigger point of fear and desire.

Fear of falling

Underlying all of this is the ever present possibility of downward mobility, of a descent into the underclass, a loss of control, of dignity, a process all the more possible as automation and outsourcing threatens wider and wider swathes of the population. Nowhere is this better described than by George Pelecanos, the crime writer, who captures well this fear as well as the tale of two cities which touch yet are divided by a hiatus of illusion and indifference:

You hear about race in Washington, but to be honest the whole thing's more about class than it is about race, and that's what I try to write about. Anyone who's so-called middle class here is just one step above poverty. They've got the car, and the house, but it's *all* on credit; they're one pay cheque away from the poor and the junkies and the dispossessed, and that's why they hate them, that's what breeds the fear ...

What did we grow up in? This great dichotomy of Washington. This federal city existing in the middle of this working-class city, and the two of them never touch. You've got this famous Capital dome looming over the streets where you see nothing but despair and poverty and drugs and crime. It's right there, man, and the government is right there, it's right in front of them, and they don't do a god damn thing about it. Not a god damn thing.'

Interview with George Pelecanos, The *Guardian*, 16 July 2000, p. 13

Resentment is more than just unfairness when someone receives a reward disproportionate to their merit. Resentment is when someone short circuits the whole marketplace of effort and reward, when they are perceived as getting exactly what they want without any effort at all – or more precisely exactly what *you* want and can only achieve with great effort. But there is an extra twist to this: an additional ratchet up of the situation. Because the equation of merit and reward has shifted in late modernity from an emphasis on merit to a focus on reward. Effort, delayed gratification, meriticious progress towards a goal has given way to immediacy, gratification now, short term hedonism. Work may well be valued, as André Gorz suggests, but hard graft is not. The whole tenor of a society, based on a lavish underwriting of credit, an economy based on the exhortation to possess *now*, is that of a consumer society based on instant gratification. The old values of hard work leading to a deserved reward – the Keynesian formula of working hard and playing hard, characteristic of the Golden Age of modernity (see Young, 1971) gives way to a society where the consumer is the paragon and spontaneity the king. Restraint, planning and control of behaviour may be the necessary undergirding of the included citizen but there is no one out there to admire or congratulate such sacrifices. Furthermore, there is a strange irony here because, whatever the political perspective on the underclass, whether they are seen to have alternative values or a lacking of them, their behaviour is seen to epitomise spontaneity, short-term hedonism, lack of planning, immediacy. All the classic statements with regards to lower class culture highlight this combination, whether it is Walter Miller writing in the 1950s or Charles Murray writing today. And if those on the right see this as a collation of individual failures, those on the left see it as a fairly rational plan of action given the unpredictability and insecurity of any long-term future. For if everything is uncertain you might as well enjoy yourself while you can.

The circle becomes complete: just as the excluded absorb the values of the wider society which both incorporates them and rejects them, the values of the wider society and the margins begin to converge. The central ethos of late modern capitalism becomes like the ethos of the ghetto. Conservative commentators, of some acuity, have noted this convergence. William Kelso, for example, argues against Wilson's isolation thesis that 'the problem with the black underclass is not that it is isolated from mainstream values but that it has adopted an exaggerated version of society's emancipated and often chronic culture' (1994, p. 173). And Myron Magnet, the author of *The Dream and the Nightmare* (1993) and reputedly a great influence on President George Bush II, locates the problem of the underclass not in their individual failings but in the influence of the new middle-class values which have devalued all the things which would get you out of poverty (such as hard work and marital stability) and valued all of the things which keep the poor in poverty (taking drugs, personal liberation, valuing leisure rather than work). What these writers fail to do is relate these values to the changes in late modern capitalism and to the exigencies of life today. Not only do such market values of immediacy permeate all corners of society, the situation and predicament of people become more similar and favour short-term solutions and immediate pleasures. Thus Gabriel and Lang, in their insightful study of the late modern consumer society note how:

The weakening of the Fordist Deal suggests to us that Western consumerism has entered a twilight phase. During the high noon of consumerism, the face of the consumer was clear ... The pursuit of happiness through consumption seemed a plausible, if morally questionable, social and personal project. Today, this is far more problematic. The economic conditions have become fraught ... insecurity is experienced across social classes ... Proponents of consumerism live in the hope that tomorrow will see another bright day. We think this vision is the product of wishful thinking ...

A far more realistic picture is that casualization of work will be accompanied by casualization of consumption. Consumers will lead precarious and uneven existences, one day enjoying unexpected booms and the next sinking to bare subsistence. Precariousness, unevenness and fragmentation are likely to become more pronounced for ever-increasing sections of Western populations. Marginality will paradoxically become central. (1995, pp. 189–90)

Towards a criminology of transgression

But what of the underclass? Precisely the same forces that shape the resentment of those higher in the structure to those below, serve to constitute the feelings of exclusion in the lowest point of the structure. Thus relative deprivation and a crisis of identity affect both parts of society although the direction of the hostility so conjured up and the poignancy of its impact are very different indeed.

In the case of the underclass the acute relative deprivation forged out of exclusion from the mainstream is compounded with a daily threat to identity: a disrespect, a sense of being a loser, of being *nothing*, of humiliation. The source of this systematic disrespect lies, of course, in the dynamics of deprivation, identity crisis and restraint among those in the secondary labour market – the precariously included which I have outlined above. It is crystallised in particular in the institutions of policing, where the poor become the overwhelming focus of police attention, a 'police property' (Lee, 1981), which serves to help constitute collections of youths, street gangs as a group and where the police become central characters in the narrative of the streets. It is important to underline how the humiliation of poverty and the humiliation of lack of respect interact – both on a day-to-day level and on an ideological level, that is, problems of gross economic and status inequality. To take the latter, first as Bauman has pointed out (1998b), income inequality and status inequality (and in turn the politics of redistribution and recognition) are not separate arenas but misrecognition and disrespect *justifies* income inequality. Thus the poor are seen to be inadequate, dependent, have the wrong personal skills and attitudes as if in a social vacuum and in more extreme cases poverty is simply rationalised as a product of biology or culture.

It is the double stigma of poverty and lack of respect which shapes the life and cultural resistance of the underclass. And all of this, of course, not in a situation of alienation from the mainstream society but the very reverse. For social bulimia involves the incorporation of mainstream social values of success, wholehearted acceptance of the American (or First World) Dream, and a worship of consumer success and celebrity. It is this cultural incorporation which puts the sting into the humiliation of exclusion – it is much easier to ignore a system one despises than a system one believes in.

How is such a double stigmatisation reacted to? Let us first note that the situation of poverty in late modernity would seem to be qualitatively different than that in the past. Bauman (Bauman and Tester, 2001), for example, contrasts the dignity, solidarity and self-respect of many working class people in the Great Depression of the 1930s. And, as for crime, accounts of that time stress its utilitarian nature (to tackle directly material needs) and the external targets of crime rather than crime within the group (see Hood and Jones, 1999).

Today the poor often seem to exist in self-blame and mutual hatred (see, for example, Seabrook, 1984, Sennet and Cobb, 1993), Loic Wacquant talks of the Hobbesian nature of the ghetto poor ('You just gotta be alert Louie in this neighbourhood here. *You gotta be alert* – know what it is? It's the *law of the jungle*. Louie: *bite or be bitten*. And I made my choice long time ago: *I'm not* gonna be bitten, *by no one*. Which one do you choose?' (former gang leader of the Black Gangsters Disciples, in Wacquant, 1998, p. 133), a theme which is reiterated in Philippe Bourgois' harrowing 'Just Another Night in a Shooting Gallery' (1998).

And crime, of course, becomes internecine rather than directed at the wealthy. There is no shortage of punitive violence among the poor. For example, The homicide rate for blacks in the United States is 8.6 times that of whites and one must remember that the vast majority of black homicides (94%) are intraracial – black upon black (see Mann, 1993; DeKeseredy and Schwartz, 1996). In Donald Schwartz's study of inner-city Philadelphia over a four year period (1987–1990) a staggering 40% of black men in their twenties had been to a hospital emergency room at least once for some serious injury resulting from violent assault (Schwartz et al., 1994; Currie, 1998). It would be more precise to use statistics by class, but these are few and far between, and while undoubtedly blacks are much poorer than whites, the existence of a not inconsiderable black middle class in the United States, with a considerably lower homicide rate, serves to significantly soften these figures – dramatic as they are. The poor predate the poor quite apart from their markedly unfavourable predicament as victims of corporate, white collar and State crimes. Yet we must not overstate the case. There is a truth in this but it is, of course, only a partial truth. The lens of the criminologist tends to focus on a particular aspect of working class culture and obfuscate all else. Thus it overemphasises despair, misery, internecine conflict and determinism. All of these things occur, but this narrative of pathology is only one story of the slum or the ghetto. Two other vital and important narratives also transfix this world. One of these is the narrative of resilience and resistance. Bring this lens to the ghetto and you will find everything from determination to get on in the world as it is (see Newman, 1999) to symbolic resistance to rebellion (see Brotherton and Barrios, 2004). Not all humiliation ends in pathology. Lastly, there is a narrative of fun and excitement. It has taken the recent advent of cultural criminology with its accent on subcultural creativity, the adrenaline rush of transgression, and the revolt against boredom to overturn this (see Chapter 2). Of course those in the sociology of youth culture have regularly used such a lens (see Brake, 1980; Frith, 1983). For the ghetto is a place of joy as well as one of fear, the wellspring of popular music, a theatre of the streets, a posture which the youth of the suburbs emulate, a place of creativity as well as determinism.

Yet none of this can allow us to ignore the false consciousness of self-blame. For it is not only that the included, the more comfortably off, are punitive and blaming of the underclass, the poor are self-blaming and punitive to each other. How does this come about? I would point to two factors: the chaos of reward, which I have mentioned previously, and the tendency for a shift from a politics of class to a politics of identity and with it the rise of celebrity.

In any other society the chaos of reward might be experienced merely as the arbitrary nature of destiny and fate: the random allocations of lady luck. But in a society where meritocracy is pronounced in every television programme, media and schoolyard, such a chaos is felt as an unfairness. In the Fordist structures of high modernity such unfairness involved comparisons between the serried ranks of roughly equivalent jobs in industry, in the public bureaucracies. The rise of the service industries, of part-time contracts, of outsourcing to a myriad small firms, the short time nature of any job and the decline of the lifelong narrative of work, each stage with a predictable increase in income, make such large scale comparisons less possible. Relative deprivation changes, in Runciman's (1996) terms, from 'fraternal' (comparisons between individuals on equivalent level or disputes between levels of reward) to 'egoistic' (comparisons between atomistic individuals).

The effect of the chaos of reward is, of course, exerted throughout the social structure. For the included, however, there is one frontier that seems clear and distinct, that between those that work and those who are 'work shy' – the chaos of reward, therefore, underwrites the targeting of the underclass. But for those at the bottom of the structure, lack of work often looks like self-failure and the allocation of the meagre state handouts and provisions on the basis of need rather than 'merit' generates divisions between individuals and frequently between ethnic groups.

The rise of celebrity

While poverty is deplored, success is celebrated. The rise of celebrity, the extent to which it replaces notions of class and traditional conceptions of authority, is a key transformation in late modernity. Laurence Friedman, in his brilliant book *The Horizontal Society* (1999) points to the distinguishing features of the celebrity. They are famous, of course, but also they are ordinary and familiar. People feel they know them, that they can speak directly to them. Above all it is:

> a celebrity society of mobility. The boy from the ghetto can earn millions as a basketball player. The kid next door can become a rap star or a talk-show host. The girl down the block can become another Madonna or a Hollywood star. Celebrities can communicate easily with ordinary people. They do not speak an arcane, élitist language. This is because they *are* ordinary persons. (1999, pp. 34–5)

And Friedman stresses the sense of accident or fate seemingly behind celebrity. Anyone might become a celebrity: 'Fixity has vanished. Lightning can always strike. Anything can happen. Anything does' (ibid., p. 35). The celebrity is like us, is talented but lucky, is chosen by us not imposed upon us – but most important of all the celebrity *deserves* their money and their prestige. The success of celebrity echoes the chaos of reward. As Bauman puts it:

> No longer the moral tales of a shoeshine boy turning into a millionaire through hard work, parsimony and self-denial. An altogether different fairy tale instead, of chasing moments of ecstasy, spending lavishly and stumbling from one stroke of luck to another, with both luck and misadventure being accidental and inexplicable and but tenuously related to what the lucky and unlucky did, and seeking luck, as one seeks a winning lottery ticket, in order to chase more fun and have more moments of ecstasy and spending more lavishly than before. (Bauman and Tester, 2001, p. 118)

And, of course, the luck of celebrity is enacted in the instant fame of *Big Brother* or the speedily fabricated success of *Pop Idol*.

There seems little doubt that the poor celebrate the celebrity. The conspicuous consumption of the ghetto, the immersion in the mass media, the values of luck and excitement, and even the fact that a *few* of their number escape to become stars of music, sport and entertainment – all make for a close attraction. The celebrity becomes, so to speak, a *delegate* for a particular social group. He or she is their representative in the limelight. It is for this reason that so many black people supported O.J. Simpson, however shaky the evidence. For it was not him on trial as much as the representative of their group.

As for the wider society I have more reservations: the need for daily restraint, the valuing of meritocratic achievement, the emphasis on hard work *despite* the general debt based accentuation on consumption, now all make for a certain ambiguity rather than undiluted enthusiasm. Despite this the pre-eminence of the politics of status and identity and the emergence of celebrity as the apex point of stratification over the older politics of class and arguments over redistribution is a general phenomenon (see Fraser, 1997; Bauman, 2001). It is detrimental in several ways: it conceals the massive divisions in society between the super-rich, on one hand, and on the other, those that sell their labour or are unable to do so, and the possible alliance between them. Indeed, by collating wealth and celebrity it presents as *natural* that only a few people are the focus of overwhelming financial and status privilege.

Let us conclude this section by the astringent comments of Laurence Friedman on celebrity:

Very little seems to be left of the old class-based rage – rage at the cruel, unfair way the world distributes its goods; it has been extinguished, except for a few dying embers. Not many people, it seems, connect their own sufferings and privations, their own hunger and longings, with the wealth they see all around them. To the contrary, the money of the rich smells sweet to them. For Marxists, capitalist wealth was blood money, money squeezed from the sweat and muscles of starving workers, money poisoned by poverty, disease, and death; money was greed, exploitation; it was man's oppression of man. Contemporary money is radically different; magically, it has been washed clean of these bad associations. The public mind connects it with fun: with the world of sports and entertainment. The new (and glamorous) rich are movie stars, rock-and-roll musicians, baseball and soccer players, heroes of TV sitcoms. These are indeed the most visible rich. They breed no resentment. Indeed, the masses seem all too eager to contribute their share of the rents and the tributes. ...

All this has a profound effect on politics as well as on policies. It explains why, in the 1990s, a politics of low taxes, flat taxes, or even no taxes has become so popular; the progressive income tax has been radically flattened out; death taxes are cut or (in California) eliminated; yet masses of people, who themselves barely scrape by, who have no job security, let alone an estate to worry about, go to the polls and reelect the rich and the representatives of the rich. They refuse to throw the rascals out or to storm the Bastille. Indeed, these masses direct their hatred and disgust, in the main, not against the blatant rich but against those who are worse off than they are: the poor, racial minorities, immigrants, and everyone who is the total inverse of a celebrity. The lifestyle of the rich and famous is the opium of the masses 1999, pp. 46–7)

Humiliation and rebellion

I'll chill like Pacino, deal like De Niro, Black Gambino, die like a hero.

(Rakim 'Juice (Know the Ledge)', Nightingale, 1993, p. 184)

Carl Nightingale's ethnography of the black Philadelphian underclass makes the brave, almost audacious leap of understanding that the culture of the ghetto is not one of isolation and alienation but involves a whole-hearted yet desperate embracing of mainstream American values. And indeed all the portfolio of values are available out there: the stress on consumption and immediacy, on machismo, on the use of violence as a preferred means of settling problems both in movies and in military adventures (and more recently in movies about military adventures) and in racist stereotypes and divisions. Nightingale sees such a process as an over-accentuation of the mainstream (rather like Matza and Sykes' (1961) celebrated depiction of juvenile delinquency and subterranean values) and that this is *compensatory*; it eases the pains and humiliations of poverty and racism. Although I think this description of ghetto values is perceptive and accurate, I worry about the rather psychologistic causality here, with, for example, the invocation of 'psychic relief' and the notion that further psychological pain comes from religitimating the very values which 'created their hurtful memories' (see, for example, 1993, p. 218, 55n). In this it is remarkably similar to the 'reaction formation' invoked 40 years earlier by Albert Cohen in his classic *Delinquent Boys: The Culture of the Gang* (1955). Rather, it might be useful if we return to the two stigmas which the poor confront, that of relative deprivation (poverty and exclusion from the major labour markets) and misrecognition (lower status and lack of respect). Both of these are forms of humiliation, with poverty among abundance the most humiliating stigma of all (Bauman and Tester, 2001, p. 154). Such a crisis of identity, a need to combat a feeling of being a 'nobody', a 'loser', a worthless person, produces precisely the same process of essentialisation which I have described earlier, experienced by those who are part of the socially included – however

THE SOCIOLOGY OF VINDICTIVENESS

precariously and tenuously. But it is done with a much greater intensity and with a different context and outcome. That is, the generation of a notion of hardness, a fixity, a difference of self based on gender (e.g. hypermasculinity), ethnicity, 'turf' (locality), and age (e.g. the gang). This is seen most in hypermasculinity where, as Nightingale points out, by the fifth or sixth grade 'the bright eyes of the boy students start to glaze over in preparation for assuming a tough look' (1993, p. 47). The children metamorphose before one's eyes. And such a process of essentialising oneself is greatly facilitated by essentialising others. But it is not the rich and the celebrated who are othered, it is not vertical but horizontal divisions: by men against women, by ethnic group against ethnic group, by gang against gang, by locality against locality. Even the essentialising projections of the better off, the othering of the poor becomes utilised by the poor to essentialise themselves. Witness the widespread self referral as 'nigga', the cult of 'badness', the ethical inversion of 'motherfucker', 'pimp' or 'b-boy'.

The humiliation of poverty finds its 'magical' solution in the cult of consumerism, in children who learn the trademarks BMW, Nike, Gucci from an early age, who value designer labels, watches, and blatant jewellery. For, unlike the labour market, the consumer society allows easy and universal entry – the sneakers and gold chains are within reach. The American poor eat their way to obesity in pursuit of the American Dream. Yet they are flawed consumers, the market welcomes micro-consumerism just as it flaunts wealth while excluding the poor. The response of consumerism merely exacerbates relative deprivation rather than alleviating it. And as for the hardened response of hypermasculinity, such cultures of toughness, as Paul Willis pointed out in his classic *Learning to Labour* (1977), merely traps them in the lowest part of the structure. Thus in *In Search of Respect* (1995) Philippe Bourgois details, with grim fascination, how the street-identity cultivated by the men from El Barrio which incorporates limited social skills, assumed gendered arrogance and involves an intimidating physical presence, rendered them well nigh unemployable in the burgeoning FIRE service sector of Manhattan, and appeared clumsy and illiterate to their often female supervisors:

They cannot walk down the hallway to the water fountain without unconsciously swaying their shoulders aggressively as if patrolling their home turf. Gender barriers are an even more culturally charged realm. They are repeatedly reprimanded for offending co-workers with sexually aggressive behavior. (Bourgois, 1995, p. 143, see also the discussion in Jay Macleod's *Ain't No Makin' It*, 1995)

The major point of all of these ethnographers who work within the rubric of social reproduction theory – influenced by the seminal work of Paul Willis – is that it is not simply that structures oppress the agents, but that the social agents themselves contribute in a pyrrhic fashion to their exclusion and oppression: 'In the process, on a daily level [of searching for respect] they become the actual agents administering their own destruction and their community's suffering' (Bourgois, 1995, p. 143).

The satisfactions of transgression

He looked at the briefcase filled with money, the grocery bag filled with cocaine, the briefcase and the bag side by side in the corner of the room. Funny how neither one meant a damn thing to him. The money couldn't buy him anything better than he had right now, than he had felt that afternoon: the risk of just taking something you decided was yours, the head-up feeling in your stride afterward when you were walking away. *The ride* ... It was all about the ride.

... Cooper was going to take this ride as far as it would go 'cause it *felt* good. Course, he knew the way it was going to end, the same way it always ended for guys like him who never had no chance, and didn't give a good fuck if one came along. The point of it all was to walk like a motherfuckin' man; if you had to, go down like one, too.

(George P. Pelecanos (1998) *King Suckerman*)

As a criminal I have been a lamentable failure. Whatever money I have gained by crime, I could have earned as a labourer in half the time I have spent in prison. My character, which is uncompromising and addicted to taking risks, was a guarantee that I could not be a success as a thief or a bandit. But money has always been a secondary goal; crime has always been directed to more powerful objectives. I took to crime as a course which was dictated by life itself; success or failure in the actual commission of criminal acts was never a matter of much concern to me, nor did they stand in the way of what I was really seeking, which was a particular kind of life style.

Also I am not a really materialistic person. Money has never been, or ever will be, my primary object. Inside or outside, I was always liked by my own kind. My life was always exciting and dramatic; wherever I was, I was part of the action. Psychologically, I had the satisfaction of personifying the counter-culture with which I identified myself, and I found this was confirmed by my notoriety and prestige. I embodied the supreme virtue of the criminal underworld, and I revelled in the greatest compliment it can bestow – gameness.

(John McVicar (1979) *McVicar: By Himself*, pp. 197–8)

I have noted how the response of the included to the poor is more than simply a meritocratic desire to ensure that benefits are drawn fairly and work is not actively avoided. There is a vituperative quality posited on the back of the rationale of control. Similarly with regards to crime, the punitive turn has a vindictiveness which goes beyond the principles of neo-classicism and deserved punishment. Just so with crime: the criminality of the underclass is not simply a utilitarian affair involving the stealing of money or property for food or drink or drugs for that matter – although all of these elements are indeed part of the motivation. Violence is not just a simple instrument for persuading people to part with their cash nor a management technique in the corporate world of organised crime. Drug use is not a prosaic matter of the pleasures of the poor – an alternative psychoactive experience to gin and tonic or a light and bitter, after a hard day at the office. Rather it involves, all of these things, but above all it has a transgressive edge. For the transgressors are driven by the energies of humiliation – the utilitarian core is often there, but around it is constructed a frequent delight in excess, a glee in breaking the rules, a reassertion of manhood and identity. It is this insight, as we have seen, that the cultural criminologists – Ferrell (1997), Presdee (2000) and Hayward (2004) – have highlighted in their critique of neo-liberal criminology (e.g. Felson, 2002, Garland, 2001) with its depiction of crime as an outcome of rational choice which occurs in a situation of easy opportunity within a rubric of institutions of weak control.

In this revision of the conventional liberal wisdoms of the causes of crime we need to re-examine the classic texts. For Robert Merton (1938) crime was an alternative route to the American Dream. In his famous typology it was an 'adaptation' or an 'adjustment' where the 'strain' of not having access to legitimate opportunities led to recourse to illegitimate avenues. The goals of success were unaltered, the cash to achieve them merely was achieved by illegal means. Jack Katz in his *Seductions of Crime* (1988) (a major influence on the new cultural criminology) points out that the Mertonian vision of crime simply does not fit the phenomenology of crime: the versatility, the zest, the sensuousness of the criminal act. He points to the attractions of evil, the ways of the 'badass', the transforma-tive magic of violence. All of this is very much to the point, but in his cor-rect emphasis on the neglected foreground of infraction, the heightened mental state of the offender, he rejects the structural background. Any such determinism he sees as a gross materialism, a liberal apologia which attempts to link too easily structural poverty to crime – bad background to bad behaviour. I think Katz throws the baby out with the bath water, to simply invert the conventional wisdom by highlighting agency and rejecting structure. Our job is to emphasise both structure and agency and trace how each constitutes the other (see Willis, 1977; Bourgois, 1995; Macleod, 1995, and social reproduction theory, also Giddens, 1984, dis-cussion of structuration). The structural predicament of the ghetto poor is not simply a deficit of goods – as Merton would have had it – it is a state of humiliation. And crime, because it is driven by humiliation not by some simple desire to redistribute property, is transgressive. The theory of bulimia which I have proposed, involves incorporation and rejection, cul-tural inclusion and structural exclusion, as with Merton, but it goes further than this, emphasising that this combination of the acceptance followed by rejection generates a dynamic of resentment of great intensity. *It is Merton with energy, it is Katz with structure.*

For Merton (1938) crime was an alternative route to the American Dream and this prognosis was developed by Richard Cloward and Lloyd Ohlin, so that for the citizen cut off from legitimate opportunities and where illegitimate chances were readily available, criminal behaviour was as normal as going out to work. The rich subcultural tradition that followed Merton represented today by theorists such as William Julius Wilson (1987, 1996), carry forward this analysis presenting forcefully the notion of crime occurring where there is 'social isolation' from the world of work.

Loic Wacquant's hustlers, for example,

> do not ... experience ... rejection from the labour market as a major trauma. This is because holding a stable and well paid portion, a 'legit job' liable to guarantee a modicum of security, has never been part of his horizon of expectations: where marginalization becomes part of *the order of things*, it deprives one even of the consciousness of exclusion. (1998, p. 13)

Anyway, legitimate jobs simply do not compete with the criminal.

> What good would it be to take the 'legit route' when the resulting rewards are so meager and almost as uncertain as those more immediate and palpable even if they come at high risks, offered by the street economy? (ibid., p. 14)

Contrary to this, I have argued throughout that marginalisation does have an impact. Philippe Bourgois' crack dealers in East Harlem, for example, were far from unaware of the world of legitimate work. They were ridden with self-doubt about their exclusion, had fantasies about being a 'normal working nigga', had been in work, and had been humiliated by the world of work – simultaneously wanting to be legitimate and despising it, but far from being oblivious of it (see 1995, Ch. 4). It is this humiliation that leads to the transgressive nature of much crime, however utilitarian its core. It is this transgression which means that although crime may be a substitute for work, it is rarely *like* work as many theorists would like us to believe. For example, it is not just the psychotropic qualities of cocaine that make cocaine dealing an erratic, violent and irascible affair, nor do the international aspects of its trade make them cartels like the corporations that deal in margarine or aluminium.

The 'crime as work' metaphor is one that is hopelessly overburdened. In its higher echelons organised crime has always involved the brash, the brazen and the extravagant. Dick Hobbs, in his excellent obituary of John Gotti, the New York Mafia boss, cites him as saying to his underlings 'You got to go in there with your suits and your jewellery ... Put it in their face. When people go to the circus, they don't want to see clowns. They want to see lions and tigers, and that's what we are' (2002, p. 18). And lower down the pile anyone who believes that cocaine dealers are lower managers of a distribution company and that their guns are just there to enforce contracts because of the lack of legal protection, are suffering from an acute dose of neo-liberalism. Just go to the right club in Dalston, East London, or Brixton in the South, look at the gold, the jewellery, watch how the action mixes with the ragga and the jungle, look at the swagger, listen to the patois: the guns are not just instruments they are sexy, his is not a job, it's excitement, this is not an alternative to work, it is a sensual riposte to labour. Jack Katz in an exemplary passage cites Robby Wideman,

Straight people don't understand. I mean, they think dudes is after the things straight people got. It ain't that at all. People in the life ain't looking for no home and grass in the yard and shit like that. We the show people. The glamour people. Come on the set with the finest car, the finest woman, the finest vines. Hear people talking about you. Hear the bar get quiet when you walk in the door. Throw down a yard and tell everybody drink up. ... You make something out of nothing. (1988, p. 131)

Wideman must have had Merton in mind, Katz notes ironically, and adds:

The aspiration is not what is advertised on television. Robby Wideman was not incapable of identifying what drove him; it was to be a star — something literally, distinctively transcendent. (ibid., p. 315)

Edgework, ontological certainty and utopia

Roger Matthews, in his study of armed robbers (2002), makes the important point that much of the mundane descriptions of crime emanating from offenders, particularly prison studies, are learnt responses which play down the attractiveness of robbery, pretend remorse, and explain their behaviour in terms of a need for money or unfortunate circumstances. These, he feels, are part of the repertoire of excuses strategically developed in prison with an eye on parole and early release. He notes, amusingly, how his interviews suddenly liven up and become more animated and excited when describing the *actual* robberies. Matthews proceeds to incisively demolish rational choice theory. The actual motivation of many, he argues, is the feeling of control and the adrenaline buzz of excitement rather than the rational pursuit of money. These two quotes from armed robbers illustrate his point well:

It's just like when you do coke, you get a rush out of it, but when you've got a gun in your hands, people are listening to you. They're doing as they are told. You're in full control. It's just brilliant. You're just there. You're the man. You're like God.

Always high, always on a high like, get off on doing the buzz, the buzz of actually doing the whatever like, job, 'cos we do burglaries as well, like, get off on that get off on whatever. To actually do a job and walk out of a sort of like bank, post office, when you got sort of like twenty or thirty grand, you can't get a better buzz than that. (2002, p. 36)

To explain this he turns to cultural criminology and particularly Stephen Lyng's concept of 'edgework' (1990). Here, as I noted earlier, in a world where pleasure is increasingly commodified and control of one's life extremely limited: going to the edge and grasping control out of chaos can be both reassuring and immensely pleasurable. Ontological certainty is seized from a situation of uncertainty and threat to being. Armed robbery fits this bill, as does hard drug use and even the more minor crimes of shoplifting and casual violence can have their satisfactions. Mike Collinson captured this well when he wrote:

Edgework represents a sometimes spontaneous search for dramatic self within a world of alienation and over-socialisation. Being on the edge, or over it – beyond reason and in passion – is momentarily to grasp a spiritual and a romantic utopia. (1996, p. 435; see O'Malley and Mugford, 1994, Matthews, 2002, p. 145)

From turf war to real war

We have seen in Carl Nightingale's study of the black ghetto of Philadelphia the extent of the immersion of the urban poor in the consumer culture of the United States. This is paralleled by an embracing of the notion of violence as an immediate and ready means of solving problems, whether it is in the advocacy of 'forceful parenting', the enthusiasm for Hollywood 'action' movies, or support for Bush I in the first Gulf War. And, of course, it is precisely the young men of such a culture who provide a high proportion of the front line soldiers. For, as John Galbraith has pointed out, the poor contribute greatly to the soldiers who risk death, whereas the children of the middle-class 'community of contentment' provide very few combat troops. Thus, at the time of the first Gulf War, he notes 'writing this during the days when the conflict was under way and much applauded, I asked the Harvard dean responsible for student matters how many of his charges had rallied to the war or been commanded thereto, he replied 'very few'. I pressed for a precise figure. He replied 'zero' (1992, p. 141).

Paul Willis depicts the development of the culture of lower working-class boys as a 'Pyrrhic victory'. First they see through their predicament and then create a culture of hardness and machismo to protect them against humiliation. Yet it is this heavy culture of resistance which traps them in this predicament. 'The cultural celebration', he notes wryly, 'has lasted it might seem just long enough to deliver him through the closed factory doors' (1977, p. 107). In these days of unemployment and 'new wars' the contemporary culture of machismo delivers, not so much to the factory floor, as to the front line.

Hip hop across the borders

I have argued against the use of binaries, against the current discourse on social exclusion which contrasts an included citizen who is contented, secure and ontologically certain over against the excluded member of the underclass who lacks all of these positives. I have criticised the notion of the dual city where lines are not crossed and where each part of the binary inhabit different moral universes. None of this dismisses the very real physical and social exclusions which rack late modern societies and the system driven stigmatisation and othering which characterise these relations. But such an intensity of exclusion – and the corresponding resentment of the excluded – is propelled by the similarities of values and the transgression of borders. The world of late modernity abhors separateness just as it avidly sets up barriers. Globalisation means nothing if it does not imply transgression: of a world brought closer together and the diminishing of cultural differences. How often does one have to say there are no strict lines of demarcation in late modernity? Even in the most ethnically segregated cities of the West – Washington D.C., Philadelphia and Los Angeles – the barriers are daily breached by the mobility of labour and the all pervasive penetration of the mass media. The values of the majority constitute the normative life of the minority and generate the bulimia which fuels their discontent. The very similarity of the underclass, indeed its over-identification with the values of consumerism and hedonism, sets itself up almost like an unwitting target for the resentment of the included. Each facet of their behaviour mocks the daily restraints of the included. Yet there is fascination here as well as disliking and fear. The culture of the underclass with its compensatory masculinity, resorts to violence and rampant individualism – all over-accentuations of the wider culture, which in turn influences film, fashion and popular music. The street scripts the screen and the screen scripts the street. The culture of the excluded becomes the culture of the included, or at least the young and those precariously included, who grow to be a larger and larger part of the population. Hypermasculinity resonates far out of the ghetto: the swagger and misogyny of rap stirs the resentment of the white poor and extends further to the swathes of young men in the respectable and lower middle classes who no longer can feel continuity and certainty in their lives. The borders are transgressed, the boundaries are criss-crossed, the centre begins to resemble the margins just as the margins resemble the centre.

4

CHAOS AND THE
COORDINATES OF ORDER

I have argued so far that the phenomenology of everyday life, the experience of late modernity, presents itself to people in the form of a chaos of reward and of identity. That is, in the form of an incoherent sense of unfairness on one hand, while on the other hand a pervasive ontological insecurity: an inability to meet the heightened metanarratives of meritocracy and self-fulfilment. In this chapter I want to explore these coordinates of order in the key areas of distributive justice and identity. In doing so I want to examine the rise of identity politics and the supposed decline in the politics of class.

The last third of the twentieth century witnessed a remarkable transformation in the lives of citizens living in advanced industrial societies. The Golden Age of the post-war settlement with high employment, stable family structures, and consensual values underpinned by the safety net of the welfare state has been replaced by a world of structural unemployment, economic precariousness, a systematic cutting of welfare provisions and the growing instability of family life and interpersonal relations. And where there once was a consensus of value, there is now burgeoning pluralism and individualism. A world of material and ontological security from cradle to grave is replaced by precariousness and uncertainty and, where social commentators of the 1950s and 1960s berated the complacency of a comfortable 'never had it so good' generation, those of today talk of a risk society where social change becomes the central dynamo of existence and where anything might happen. As Anthony Giddens put it: 'to live in the world produced by high modernity has the feeling of riding a juggernaut' (1991, p. 28; see also Berman, 1983; Beck, 1992).

Such a change has been brought about by market forces which have systematically transformed both the sphere of production and consumption. This shift from Fordism to Post-Fordism involves the unravelling of the world of work where the primary labour market of secure employment and 'safe' careers shrinks, the secondary labour market of short-term contracts, flexibility and insecurity increases, as does the growth of an underclass. It results, in Will Hutton's catchphrase, in a '40:30:30' society (1995) where 40% of the population are in tenured secure employment, 30% in insecure employment, and 30% marginalised, without paid work or working for poverty wages. We may quarrel with the figures – and they are to my mind overly optimistic – but the unravelling is a key feature of late modernity.

Secondly, the world of leisure is transformed from one of mass consumption to one where choice and preference is elevated to a major ideal and where the constant stress on immediacy, hedonism and self-actualisation has had a profound effect on late modern sensibilities (see Featherstone, 1985; Campbell, 1987). These changes both in work and leisure, characteristic of the late modern period, generate a situation of widespread relative deprivation and heightened individualism. Market forces generate a more unequal and less meritocratic society, market values encourage an ethos of every person for themselves. Such a process is combined with a decline in the traditional forces of informal social control, as communities are weakened by high levels of geographical mobility and frequently left to decay as capital finds more profitable areas to invest and develop. At the same time, families are stressed and fragmented by the decline in communities and their support systems, together with the reduction of state backup in terms of childcare and funding, coupled with the more intense pressures of work (see Schor, 1993; Wilson, 1996; Currie, 1997).

The journey into late modernity involves both a change in perceptions of the fairness of distributive justice and in the security of identity.

Class and identity in the twenty-first century

Nancy Fraser in her influential *Justice Interruptus: Critical Reflections on the Post-Socialist Condition* (1997) outlines two types of politics: those centring around distributive justice and those centring around the justice of recognition – that is, class politics and identity politics. She points to the rise in prominence of the latter – a phenomenon which I will attempt to explain later in this chapter. But what concerns me here is to develop and explain this distinction as a basis for an analysis of social order and political legitimacy. In *The Exclusive Society* (1999) I point to the two fundamental problems in a liberal democracy: the need to distribute rewards fairly so as to encourage commitment to work within the division of labour, and the need to encourage respect between individuals and groups so that the self-seeking individualism characteristic of a competitive society does not lead to a situation of war of all against all. Individuals must experience their rewards as fair and just and they must feel valued and respected.

Let us develop this distinction between the sphere of distribution and that of recognition. Central to distributive justice is the notion of fairness of reward and in modern capitalist societies this entails a meritocracy, that is, where merit is matched to reward. Recognition involves the notion of respect and status allocated to all, but if we stretch the concept a little further, it also involves the notion of the level of esteem or social status being allocated justly. Indeed both the discourses of distributive justice and recognition have the notion of a basic equality (all must receive a base level of reward and respect as part of being citizens) but on top of this, rather than a general equality of outcome, is a hierarchy of reward and recognition dependent on the individual's achievements.

It is important to note how such processes of reward and recognition are not merely passive activities. It involves the active creation of the individual as well as the response of society. You work and develop talents which are allocated rewards, you create meaning and identity, which is responded to by those around you and society in general. The individual, thus, creates a narrative of life which tracks the development of a moral career, which prospers or declines whilst building a sense of self and identity which is more or less reflected in the accord of others.

What terms are we to use when distributive justice or recognition is wanting? When material reward is unjustly allocated we commonly use the term relative deprivation, when recognition is denied someone we call this ontological insecurity. But let us finesse these further: we can talk of two aspects of unfairness, insecurity and deprivation, and the two dimensions, economic and ontological (Figure 4.1).

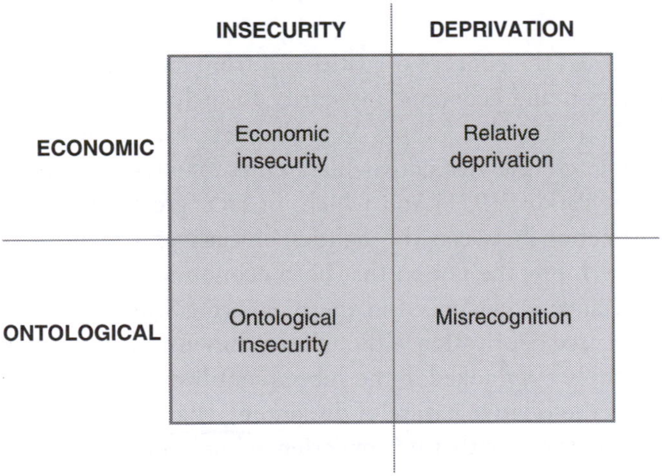

	INSECURITY	DEPRIVATION
ECONOMIC	Economic insecurity	Relative deprivation
ONTOLOGICAL	Ontological insecurity	Misrecognition

Figure 4.1   The four dimensions of disaffection

These categories can occur quite independently of each other: it is possible to have a high income yet feel insecure in one's job (e.g. a bond trader on the Stock Exchange) or to suffer relative deprivation in terms of income (e.g. a small shopkeeper) yet be secure enough in one's job. Similarly, it is possible to be insecure about one's identity yet experience no feelings of disrespect towards oneself (e.g. the person whose marriage has failed and whose community is disintegrating). While, across the categories economic and ontological, it is only too possible to be a successful second generation immigrant in a professional job but be disrespected by the police and representatives of the 'official' world. However, as I will argue, certain combinations of injustice can produce great discontent and stress. For example, two well researched combinations are in the areas of crime and punishment. A major cause of crime lies in deprivation that is, very frequently, the combination of feeling relatively deprived economically (which causes discontent) and misrecognised socially and politically (which causes disaffection). The classic combination is to be marginalised economically and treated as a second rate citizen on the street by the police. Secondly, as I have argued earlier, it is the combination of widespread economic and ontological insecurity among the 'middle classes' which engenders a punitive response to crime and deviancy.

However, my argument is that all of these forms of injustice are prevalent in late modernity. For, as we shall see, in the process of the transition from modernity to late modernity, powerful currents shake the social structure transforming the nature of relative deprivation, causing new modes of misrecognition and exclusion, while, at the same time, being accompanied by widespread economic and ontological insecurity. The purchase of each of these currents impacts differentially throughout the social structure by each of the prime social axes of class, age, ethnicity and gender.

I have widened the concept of justice out from its usual concern with relative deprivation and economic insecurity to include problems of identity and status. In a way, this follows Max Weber's discussion of stratification which pinpointed the distinctive hierarchies of class and of status (see Weber, 1958; Parkin, 1971) and which, in fact, greatly influenced Nancy Fraser's distinction between the politics of class and identity (see Fraser, 2000). Furthermore, the notion that both economic and status deprivation are of importance is evidenced in the pioneering work of W. J. Runciman (1966) on relative deprivation, although the dimension of status deprivation is almost entirely overlooked in the subsequent literature. It is important to keep in mind the relative nature of discontent, that is the subjective aspect of injustice and the way that it is experienced only in the context of expectations and comparisons. That is, injustice is only perceived as unfair if there is a social expectation of equality of reward and status.

But let us now turn to unravel the profound changes in the social world which have generated widespread experiences of injustice and uncertainty in both the spheres of distributive justice and identity. Let us first look at the various factors which have changed in the structuring of reward in late modern societies, noting that such a chaos of reward is engendered by several closely interrelated processes:

- *Decline in comparability*   The huge Fordist organisations of the post-war period allowed for easy comparisons of the reward due for each level of skill and performance. Such a parity of reward was extended across industries and reinforced by the widespread collective regulations of trade unions, many of which evolved a multi-occupational base. The decline in manufacturing industry and the rise of service industries undermined the size of such monolithic entities and the use of outsourcing, freelance work and consultancy greatly reduced the basic core of the manufacturing base. The category service industry is something of a bogus or chaotic category (see Sayer, 1992) containing as it does the knowledge industries (such as universities and hospitals) which are, in fact, one of the major remnants of a mass employment with comparability by rank and skill and the small shops, restaurants, and individuals who provide the services of groceries, numerous cuisines, dry-cleaning, day care, nannies, home cleaning, etc. Both of these types of service industry expand, the first a remaining bastion of comparability, the second with little systematic basis. Underscoring all of this is the precipitate decline in trade union membership and nationally agreed employment standards.
- *Loss of narrative*   Gone are the jobs which lasted from graduation to retirement, from diploma to gold watch. These provided not only a sense of embedded identity (of which more later) but also, so to speak, a narrative of gradual incremental reward – a pay structure which was certain, just, and seemingly natural. In its place multiple careers occur, sometimes chosen, sometimes abruptly the result of end of contract or downsizing. Short-term contracts reinforce this predicament with many institutions having a predominance of short-term contracts over stable, tenured jobs (American universities would be a prime example of this).
- *Arbitrary reward*   The successful firm today increases its productivity and reduces its staff. Downsizing occurs across industry from manufacturing to high tech – from the steel towns to Silicone Valley. The indescribable sense of arbitrariness when people with high skills who are good workers in successful industries lose their jobs is described in such books as Susan Faludi's *Stiffed* (1999), or in the songs of Bruce Springsteen, where local economies decline, communities disintegrate and people oscillate between self-blame and vindictiveness. Such a sense of the precariousness of work encompasses vast swathes of the population. It creates what one of Tony Blair's speech writers noted, in an inspired moment: 'an upper class, an underclass and in between an increasingly nervous class'. But this hard luck industry is coupled with the rise of the equally arbitrary good luck industry. The gambling industry creates millionaires every day, while rises in house prices generates an enormous equity among home owners. A person on a reasonable income in Britain, say £30,000 a year after tax, would need to work 33 years without spending a penny to accumulate the £1,000,000 in equity which very many owners find themselves with. Indeed, their regular reward in terms of the increase of value of the property they live in is often greater than their income from work.

The undermining of the meritocracy

If you don't play the game,

You can't live the dream.

(Advert for the New York Lottery, bus stop, NYC, 2003)

All of these three factors: lack of comparability, broken narratives and arbitrariness, are profoundly unmeritocratic for they bring into doubt what is merit and, most profoundly, whatever it is, if it is rewarded. None of this would matter two figs if we lived in a society whose highest values were luck, fortune, and destiny. But we do not, for a whole host of our key institutions carry the central legitimation of capitalist society – meritocracy. Of course, the betting shop, the lottery, the psychic on the high street, and the evangelical churches of the poor which promise merit rewarded in the next life, all provide ample proof of public scepticism, but the belief in the dream, persists. It is this combination of anxiety, unfairness, and randomness which contradicts the core beliefs of justice and generates a groundswell of a sense of unfairness and often a confused and undirected undercurrent of anger. But it is a sentiment which finds it difficult to get a clear fix on the divisions of class and privilege as did previous generations.

All of this engenders an experience of the flattening of the class structure (see Friedman, 1999). It is not that class has disappeared, indeed class is most apparent, and is a constant concern and discussion point for everyone. Indeed, the behaviour and values of the upper class and lower class are a central part of the focal interests of our times. But the terms of reference of 'upper class' and 'lower class' have been fundamentally re-written, recast from the ends of a continuum to points of orientation of moral approval and approbation, while in between what was once a register of fine differentials, the serried ranks of unskilled and skilled manual, lower middle class, professional, have now become to be perceived as flattened – not disappeared as in a post-modern dream (e.g. Pakulski and Waters, 1996), but rather the terrain is occluded, it is no longer obvious. The rice terraces of the post-war class structure have been replaced by the uneven turf of a field ploughed hither and thither in confusing directions. Instead of working class and upper class, we now have underclass and celebrity and in between a middling class, contemptuous and fearful of those below them, appreciative and covetous of those above them. This new stratification is epitomised in the common usage of 'middle class' in America to mean anyone with a steady job (and perhaps health insurance) and by the extraordinary media focus on the celebrity – the glittering other at one side of the spectrum and the underclass at the other.

The middling class is riven by differences, but these divisions are experienced more of identity than of economic class: gender, age, ethnicity, sexual orientation and physical ability become more concrete to people, and out of this a politics of identity begins to superimpose itself upon those of class.

Changes in the perceived class structure

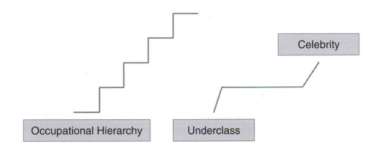

The shift from a society concerned with distributive justice, from one concerned with recognition, from the politics of class to those of identity, is a common one in the literature of late modernity (see Friedman, 1999; Fraser 1997; Pakulski and Waters, 1996). But not only are these claims sometimes overdrawn, the reasons why such a change occurs remains largely unexplained. My contention is, as I have argued, that the process rests on fundamental changes in the structures of production and consumption.

We have seen how the great shift in consciousness that accompanied late modernity was from aspirations and desires which were in terms of material comfort, well-being and sufficiency to those which stressed meaning, identity, self-enjoyment and expression. The American Dream, just as it became the *realisable* dream of all the First World (and the hopes and envy of all the rest) has become transformed: the patent obviousness of success – the house in the suburbs together with car, large kitchen, and well mown garden – no longer fully satisfy. In truth, all the trimmings of material comfort are still desired – perhaps all the more so – but nowadays it is simply not enough. Meaning has become important, finding yourself rather than merely arriving: work, friendship, marriage, community, all these institutions are now scrutinised for their contribution to a narrative of self-fulfilment. And such a personal narrative – so difficult to firmly construct in late modernity – becomes elided with a sense of the need for personal enjoyment, a life where the 'good' things were appreciated – a life which is rich rather than drab, exciting rather than boring.

Accompanying this transition is a whole series of connected shifts in what is valued: the 'gentrification' of the inner city, the movement back into

CHAOS AND THE COORDINATES OF ORDER

Table 4.1   First World Dreams

	Post-war Dream	Dream of late modernity
Life goals	Ends taken-for-granted Material contentment Arriving	Ends questioned Identity Expressivity Finding yourself
Ideals of work	Instrumentality	Meaning
Value orientation	Deferred gratification	Immediacy Lack of boredom
Leisure	Taking it easy	Frisson
Desired space	Suburb	The city
The admired	The rich	The celebrity
Politics	Politics of class	Politics of identity

town, the elevation of status over class – of celebrity over 'mere' wealth, the politics of class being succeeded by the politics of identity (see Table 4.1). Once again, it is not that redistributive politics have disappeared – far from it – nor that a sense of unfairness and injustice is not a fundamental moving force in society and in politics. On the contrary: the striking contrast between meritocratic ideals and structural possibilities occurs with greater severity, but it is experienced on a far more individual level and the patterns and shape of class differences becomes occluded. In particular, the lines between welfare recipients and workers becomes perceived much more clearly than they actually are, while the stratifications between middle and working class become less certain, and at the top a 'deserving' celebrity élite provide fixed points of admiration and of reference. Furthermore, particularly in North America, the patterns of collective inequalities become seen through the lens of identity politics. That is, the success in reward of black against white, ethnic group compared to ethnic group, whether it is housing, education, or income.

But my concern is not only the mystification of class but the search for identity. The intensity of desire for expressivity, fulfilment and identity in late modernity emerge from a series of circumstances which both foster and frustrate its accomplishment. For just as the aspiration for identity arises preckely at the time that the building blocks of identity become more insubstantial and nebulous, just as the desire for expressivity rises the world seems less able to provide meaning and fulfilment, just as enjoyment becomes a premium, the forces of rationalisation and commodification place social boredom on the agenda.

Let us look first of all at the forces which give rise to the search for identity and expression. A key text here, because it captures the contradictory nature of this process, is Paul Willis' book *Common Culture* (1990). Paul Willis is a master of irony. His most famous text, *Learning to Labour* (1977) has the subtitle 'How do working class boys get working class jobs?'. Thus he sets the question: how does a class society reproduce itself? His answer is that the 'lads' see through the irrelevance and humiliation of their education in the light of the labouring jobs to which most of them are heading. They set up an anti-school culture of resistance which is anti-intellectual, sexist and often racist. Yet in this process of resistance they have a pyrrhic victory because it is precisely such traits which deliver them to the lowest part of the market place. Willis' irony in his later book shifts from the area of work to the area of consumption and has a more optimistic message pointing to inadvertent gains rather than inevitable losses.

Willis points to the rise of consumerism in the post-1970s period as one which has unleashed the most extraordinary levels of individualism and demand for the spontaneous and the immediate. He derides those many commentators who see consumerism as an enslaving mechanism: the pessimistic thesis which sees the exploitation of work being reproduced in leisure – the supposed realm of freedom. The fault in this, he argues, is that the analysts see the human actors in too passive a light – as mere ciphers who are condemned to act out the input of advertising, the imperatives of the consumer market. He thus challenged the notion of a hegemony of desire which constantly directs and subverts the aspirations of the mass of people. He shares tradition with Marxists such as Marshall Berman who, in *All That's Solid Melts into Air* (1983), points to the way in which capitalism throws up constantly its own contradictions. The two subversive principles which consumerism engenders are choice and spontaneity. Thus Willis writes:

> Modern capitalism is now not only parasitic upon the puritan ethic, but also upon its instability and even its subversion … The market is the source of a permanent and contradictory revolution in everyday culture which sweeps away old limits and dependencies. The market's restless search to find and make new appetites raises, wholesale, the popular currency of symbolic aspiration. The currency may be debased and inflationary, but aspirations now circulate, just as do commodities. That circulation irrevocably makes or finds its own new worlds. (1990, pp.19, 20–7)

And, he adds, with flourish:

> Commerce and consumerism have helped to release a propane explosion of everyday symbolic life and activity. The genie of common culture is out of the bottle – let out by commercial carelessness. Not stuffing it back in, but seeing what wishes may be granted, should be the stuff of our imagination. (ibid., p. 27)

What we have then is a shift to expressive identity: an elision of meaning and excitement. But this stress on finding oneself/enjoying oneself is confronted with a series of obstacles and weak building blocks. For parallel to the chaos of reward is the chaos of identity. Earlier we examined the series of changes which have disrupted and unsettled the narratives of meaning which the late modern person creates for him/herself. Disembeddedness of family, work, and community disrupted the narrative whilst the presentation of pluralism of value makes for the constant awareness of choice, reflexivity and, inevitably, uncertainty. Identity is always precarious in late modernity – thus precisely at the time that there is greater stress on finding a fulfilling identity, there is less means to generate such a stable narrative.

The shift to identity politics

The struggle for recognition is fast becoming the paradigmic form of political conflict in the late twentieth century.

(Fraser, 2000, p. 11)

Let us examine more closely Nancy Fraser's claim and her carefully nuanced analysis. In a lively debate between Axel Honneth and Nancy Fraser (2003), Honneth points to the fact that many of the major social struggles in history have involved claims for redistribution *and* claims for respect and recognition. Indeed Edward Thompson made his major target of criticism those on the left who wrote histories as if they were only a reflex of economic interests and did not involve resistance and protest, locally based and identity bound (see his magnificent *The Making of the English Working Class*, 1968). Honneth (2003) perceives Fraser's notion of a shift from the politics of class to that of identity as in part a reflection of an overgeneralisation of the American experience, but he then goes further than this in saying that the struggle for recognition is the key component of all such social conflicts.

Let us put this in context. As we have seen, Fraser's argument has two aspects, one that problems of social justice involves two interwoven yet analytically distinct elements – that of distribution and that of recognition – which, rather inelegantly, she terms 'perspectival dualism' and which, as we have seen, owes much to Weber's classic distinction between class and status. Secondly, that problems of identity, of recognition, have become central to politics, to some extent replacing the politics of class. The major thrust of such a dualism is against economic reductionism – witness Thompson – and it is, therefore, ironic that Honneth in his debate with Fraser is positing just the opposite type of 'monism', namely a reduction of everything to culture. As we have seen, there is undoubtedly no empirical coincidence between class and status: sometimes it coincides, sometimes it does not. Fraser acknowledges the cultural turn, but she maintains a separateness between the cultural and the economic, particularly so in that it is in present-day neo-liberal societies that the market is manifestly and purposively *more* rather than less autonomous. Furthermore, culture or status is also transformed in late modernity.

In her reply to Honneth, 'Social Justice on the Edge of Identity Politics' (2003), Fraser examines the concept of status as it was originally used in terms of traditional societies. She creates an ideal typical pre-capitalist society stratified by status. She notes that it would have five major characteristics: it would be sharply bounded, inter-cultural contacts would be restricted to the margins and hybridism minimised; it would be institutionally undifferentiated – the same cultural template would regulate all forms of social interaction; it would be all-pervasive, no subcultures with different values would occur; it would be uncontested; and lastly it would be legitimate, there would be no principled basis for challenging it. Grant that this characterisation, like any ideal type, is heavily overdrawn, but Fraser then, in an interesting thought experiment, contrasts this with modern society. Here none of these conditions hold and she details many of the changes in late modernity which we have already discussed. There are no sharp boundaries, external cultural influences penetrate deep into society: hybridisation is endemic. There is a widescale differentiation of norms between institutions, a strict hierarchy of status is seen as inegalitarian and illegitimate, and above all there is a pluralism where 'virtually none of the [dominant] narratives, discourses and interpretative schema go unchallenged; all are contested, rather than, as social actors struggle to institutionalize their own horizons of value are authoritative ... there is a dynamic regime of ongoing struggles for recognition' (Fraser, pp. 56–7). Such an analysis parallels that of the critical anthropologists such as Gupta and Ferguson whom we discussed in Chapter 1 and, like them, she is only too ready to stress that such a pluralism is not a struggle of equal weight. Dominant values favouring, for example, whites, heterosexuals, men and Christians exist and these have strong correlates in the hierarchy of social class. Yet status, contest and the politics of identity are intense and ever-present.

In a sense, Fraser's analysis is descriptive rather than explanatory, and it exists on a level of macro-politics rather than the sociology of actors. I have attempted so far to put the transition to late modernity in a more sociological context. The struggle for identity occurs in the context of an economic order which stresses the building of lifestyle and identity but in which the building blocks are less and less substantial. It is in the context of the chaos of rewards and the chaos of identity that we begin to understand the way in which the politics of identity becomes central in late modernity.

In a world in which the individual is presented with a pluralism of values, the basis of developing definition of status at odds with the more widespread, dominant culture is ever-present. This pluralism, combined with the ideals of expressivity, of finding, discovering, creating one's identity, makes such a construction of contrary values ever possible. Fixed ideas of status work best where the culture is homogenous, relatively sealed off from the outside world and where the ideals are simple material contentment rather than identity.

The effect of the chaos of reward is to make comparisons of class more difficult yet the stress on meritocracy scarcely diminishes feelings of unfairness. This occlusion of class makes the *displacement* of class concerns around the focus of identity all the more likely; this is not to deny the authenticity of contests for status and recognition, but to point to reasons why overtly class politics should be markedly less to the fore in late modernity. But there are also inherent differences between class and status which help explain the shift.

In the present period the gaps between the entwined threads of wealth and recognition are manifest: status interweaves with class, income interweaves with recognition as Fraser points out, and indeed Max Weber before her. But it is not identical, it is not reducible. The down at his heels rock star may be broke, doesn't know where the money's gone (blames the agent), yet can walk in a room and all heads will turn – he is a star, a celebrity, admired and talked about. The chief executive officer of a multi-million dollar firm may have annual bonuses which would put a sizeable municipality in the shade, but has less status than a good and well-loved doctor within an established general practice. Sometimes the strands of class and status seem far apart, sometimes they seem remarkably close. The war against the poor, the denigration of the underclass is precisely that – an attempt to fuse together poverty with individual failure, lapses in morality – the loser deserves to lose and has to lose attitude if they are going to enter the ranks of the winning class.

The distinction between injustices of distribution and identity is useful because their bases are distinct and because status is much more amenable to subversion than wealth and poverty. Status is determined by social approval, by accolade from significant publics. Yet these politics can be diverse and the granting of status is in the behest of each of them. Money is by its very nature universally recognised, status is not. A singer may have a cult following, be swooned upon by some and totally ignored by others. More profoundly, youth cultures can create counter-status hierarchies. And they can do this as an act of resistance; style, fashion, taste can be mobilised as counter balances to the established straight world as it is. Teenagers excel in this: the history of youth culture is a tale of subterfuge. Middle-class kids will create a culture of grunge out of Oxfam shops and charity stores – they will purposely try to reverse their class position while working-class kids can appropriate items of style from their betters, take signifiers from the wider world and put them into a tailspin, change their velocity, their impact, their meaning. Here again the concept of hybridisation is too tame, too organic – a better metaphor is that of bricollaging, of choosing, cherry-picking key cultural items and reinterpreting them: gay culture, for example, has a wonderful history of this in its playful appropriation of the masculine and the macho into its queer opposite.

Status then is much more manipulable than class as its basis is in relevant publics rather than the class conditions of the market place. This is not to say, of course, that market positions are a function simply of the economic, the market itself is socially embedded and constituted and the access to markets, whether legal or illegal, formal or informal, is subject to social construction but none of this is as manipulable and contestable as is status, particularly in the context of the pluralism of late modernity.

Antecedents of the cultural shift

We are now in a position to unpack the elements which underscore the cultural shift. First of all we have noted the social and economic underpinning: the loss of embeddedness in work, family and community necessitating the constant reinvention of personal narratives; the development of individualism, and concern with lifestyle on the back of the consumer society; the rise of a First World Dream concerned with the quality of life and self-development as well as simple material comfort; the rise of a mediated reality where cultural reference points circulate the globe in the process of cultural globalisation. All of these changes provide some sociological underpinning to Nancy Fraser's observations.

Such a cultural shift, however, does not, as postmodernist commentators maintain, lead to 'a death of class' (Pakulski and Waters, 1996). Fraser's perspectival dualism with the two interweaving threads, class and status, the politics of distributive justice and identity, which interweave yet have relative autonomy, is of great analytical use here. But the tight concurrence of class and status unravels in late modernity – both because of a more autonomous market place and the rise of an intense cultural world. Status loosens its moorings from the class structure. The increasingly pluralist basis of esteem permits the rise of resistance, of subcultures which consciously or unconsciously, explicitly or implicitly, set themselves up against the hegemony. The increasing occlusion of class makes the displacement of class politics by identity politics more likely. But it would be wrong – as is common in much radical subcultural theory – to view such cultural conflicts, such revolt through style or resistance through ritual as merely displacement phenomena where culture is a somewhat confused shadow of the real conflicts of class. Some cultural forms are like that and this is true

CHAOS AND THE COORDINATES OF ORDER

of conflicts of the powerful as much as the dispossessed – but others go beyond this. Resistance to routine, the creation of cultures of pleasures, of new scenarios of desire, of self-development and exploration revolve round not so much the traditional conflicts over the distribution of rewards, as the contested foundations of the good life. The late modern era was heralded by the rise of hippie culture, by the new bohemia, a pot pourri of post-scarcity lifestyles and blueprints (see Hall, 1969; Young, 1973). There has been a constant tendency of much radical criticism to belittle subsequent youth cultures as merely adaptations to failure, or at least signs of resistance, rather then experiments in living. Resistance to tedium, establishment of solidarity and community, explorations of pleasure and desire from Woodstock to Ibiza, from rave culture to 'the gang' – all tend to be overlooked in their creativity and innovativeness. Further, the day-to-day rebellion against the taken for granted, from the little resistances and subversions in the workplace and domestic life, to the moments of transcendence in popular music, actions counter to the neo-liberal hegemony of work and consumption, are part and parcel of the grain of everyday life. It should not surprise us that, in a world which is both drastically unequal and overlaid with tedium, discipline and regimentation – what Alain Touraine calls the programmed society (1971) – that resistance occurs everywhere, sometimes in surprising places, and sometimes, of course, not to our pleasing.

This being said, one of the most central elements in the exploitation of the lower class involves the active concealment of relationships of class under the rubric of culture. Othering is, of course, one of the most central aspects of denigration. The phenomenon of othering the poor, which I have described earlier, is essentially a process of obfuscating *relationships* of class by justifications of culture – or the lack of it. Witness the denial of class connection – the presentation of the poor as outside of the economic circuit, the creation of *distance* and hiatus and the process of *diminishing* – the portrayal of inferior positions as a result of inferior cultures or inferior socialisation. Thus relationships of class and gross redistributive inequalities are reduced to problems of culture and most particularly the deficit of culture. That is, the poor become visible only in their presumed lacking of middle-class culture. Let me give an example of such dismissal – just an aside from a magazine article: 'One thing is certain – Lewinsky is not trailer-park trash as has often been portrayed. She is frighteningly bright and holds her own on any subject' (Marianne Jones, 1999, p. 32).

It is, of course, quite extraordinary that it is in American society where there is a constant denial of the existence of class, that such a derogatory term as 'trailer-park trash' should be so readily coined and easily used. There could be no more explicit conception as this of the poor as refuse and garbage, of being unintelligent and lacking in culture.

If the othering by conservatives stresses lack of culture, that of liberals moves effortlessly from highlighting the material deprivation, of an underclass supposedly detached from the class structure, to the emergence of dysfunctional families and relationships propelled by the pyrrhic thrust of self-destruction. Dysfunction is immersed in a deficit culture of incivility, of unruly masculinity and of lacking. As I write this (4 January 2006) a 67-year-old youth outreach worker presents his latest despatch from an English sink housing estate. 'The Hunger Within' by Stewart Dakers, is a tale to pull at the heart strings of any *Guardian* reader. It is a story of malnutrition, junk food, chronic fecklessness, belligerent and brutish men spoilt by their mothers and unable to relate to women in any other way but exploitation. Pity and blame is combined in a seductive mix. It is standard fare of the liberal media. A week later (11 January 2006) however, there is a dissenting voice. Professor Harry Ferguson from the University of the West of England points to research by himself and a colleague, Fergus Hogan, which finds, in interviews with vulnerable working-class fathers, that many of them are much more involved than the stereotype of fecklessness allows. He cites Michael, aged 19, who had been homeless and then in prison who talks of his two-year-old son, unplanned but terribly wanted:

> Just take him in me arms at night, if we're watching telly, like, I cuddle and kiss him, like. When he's in bed I tuck him in and all, kiss him goodnight and all this kind of stuff, like. At night, if he needs anything, more times I get up and I go to him, all that kind of stuff.

His partner regards him as a 'brilliant' father yet, as Ferguson points out, professionals have consigned such a class of men as useless and tend to focus solely on the mother. In part this is, as he notes, a reflection of the gross overestimation of the number of single mother households so prevalent in the poverty literature, which is in part a product of an understandable concealment occurring because claiming as single people generates a better income than the admission of co-habitation, and often, even, results in the father's name being excluded from the birth certificate. But more profoundly this is the result of liberal othering, of an optic pointed to the working class which highlights misery and obfuscates all else.

We are bombarded daily in the newspapers and on television with a series of vignettes of the poor: the sullen faces of dysfunctional families looking out at us from both popular and quality press. They are the object of tales of unmitigated depravity and calamity, the subject of political invective: campaigns of 'respect', ASBOs, and vilification. None of these desperate slithers of working-class life carry any sense of warmth, let alone resistance and reflexivity, indeed fun is very hard to find. They are the very opposite of the social realist literature of the 1960s, for instance Alan Sillitoe's brilliant *Saturday Night and Sunday Morning* (1958), there is not even the voyeurism of the nineteenth century, for although Dickens, for example, was no stranger to caricature, he had a poignant sense of the warmth that exists even among the most brutalised sections of humanity.

I have no doubt that stark inequalities produce hardness; socially dysfunctional behaviour if you want, although it is in truth a dysfunctional *system* which has produced such malfeasance. Nor that the individualism of the market place permeates the values of the poor, for indeed they are more exposed to these arbitrary forces than are the middle classes who are, at least to some extent, protected by trade union and professional organisations. Yet this is only one part of the story: it occludes all the rest of what goes on. Nearly 40 years ago Charles Valentine (1968) entered gamely into the heated debate of that time over the nature of the culture of poverty. He surveyed the field, steering adroitly between those who would see the culture of the poor as a heroic site of resistance involving strategies of survival grossly misrecognised by the middle classes, and those who would conceive of it as a pit of dysfunction, disorganisation and brutality where their own lumpen fecklessness holds them back, traps them in poverty. Of course, it is *neither* of these and Valentine created a model which acknowledged both the positive and negative features of poverty but did not exaggerate either. Yet he had the harshest and most perceptive criticism for the denigrators of the poor. He takes Walter Miller's famous characterisation of lower class culture as having 'focal concerns' which centre around trouble with the law, toughness and masculinity, smartness, natural agility over against achievement through routine, excitement and thrill rather than boredom, and autonomy and freedom as against dependence and constraint. He castigates such hyperbole:

The stereotyping and projection in this extraordinary thesis are obvious upon a moment's reflection. Where could one find a better brief inventory of unresolved value conflicts underlying the confusion and anomie of middle-class life in America than the many ambiguities and ambivalences associated with legality, masculinity, shrewdness, boredom, luck, and autonomy? As we college professors construct our theoretical models of poverty culture and our learned images of the poor, the least we can do is to ask ourselves whether these portrayals may not apply at least equally well to our students, colleagues, friends, and neighbors. Since we have a good deal more direct knowledge of these latter groups, this should be useful to the enterprise of determining how the poor differ from the rest of us. (1968, p. 44)

To make such an intervention is, of course, not to insist on an identity of culture, a homogeneity of value. Instead it is to castigate the exaggeration and pathologisation of difference. Yet such a calumny persists to date. The present day 'war against the poor', as Herbert Gans (1995) so famously pronounced it, is a struggle based on stigmatisation and denigration, viewed through a social lens which renders most of their existence invisible while focusing on every blemish and dysfunction of their existence. It is at heart an economic struggle to bring the poor into the legitimate labour market as low paid, taxable, law abiding citizens which has been rendered as a struggle over identity or, more precisely, the presumed lack of it. Further, it is a struggle which unites a wide swathe of middle-class opinion from right to left and is part of a presumed centre ground of current politics and conventional wisdoms.

The use of status denigration to justify gross economic inequalities lies behind this fusion of low status and low income at the very bottom of society. It is here that there is a strange gap in Nancy Fraser's analysis. For, as Axel Honneth points out, the struggles of identity which she concerns herself with are only those which have gained 'official recognition'. He advises the reader to consult a book by Pierre Bourdieu and his fellow scholars; the brilliant yet painful *The Weight of the World* (1999). Honneth writes:

> Here we find a multitude of reports and interviews that make it clear that the overwhelming share of cases of everyday misery are still to be found beyond the perceptual threshold of the political sphere. A few remarks suffice to sketch in broad outline the characteristics of these phenomena of social deprivation: they include the consequences of the 'feminization' of poverty, which primarily affects single mothers with limited job qualifications; long-term unemployment, which goes along with social isolation and private disorganization; the depressing experience of the rapid disqualification of job skills that had enjoyed high esteem at the start of a career and now have been made useless by accelerated technological development; the immiseration of the rural economy, where, despite deprivation and back-breaking work, yields on small farms never seem to be sufficient; and finally, the everyday privations of large families, where low pay renders even the efforts of both parents insufficient to support the children. Each of these social crisis situations – and the list could easily be expanded – goes along with a series of exhausting, embittered activities for which the concept of 'social struggle' would be entirely appropriate. Such tendencies toward immiseration are constantly fought by the afflicted with forms of opposition extending from confrontations with the authorities, to desperate efforts to maintain the integrity of both family and psyche, to the mobilization of aid by relatives or friends. But, as Bourdieu insists in his Postscript, none of these social efforts is recognized by the political public sphere as a relevant form of social conflict. Instead, a sort of perceptual filter ensures that only those problems that have already attained the organization level of a political movement are taken seriously in moral terms. (2003, pp. 118–9)

Honneth believes the 'perceptual filter' makes invisible these widespread ills and, to an extent, he is right, for they rarely register in terms of the identity politics that Fraser describes as the predominant tendency of our

CHAOS AND THE COORDINATES OF ORDER

time. Yet, as we have seen, these people, 'the underclass', the 'poor', whatever, are not invisible. They are regularly portrayed as the epitome of dysfunction in our society, they live, so to speak, in a sort of ASBOland, the scenario and source of all incivilities. The perceptual filter then, is more of a distorting lens than an occlusion and, here, is a further irony. Their invisibility is not because they are outside of the politics of identity because, in fact, they are the recipients of a major exercise in status denigration, an identity politics not of self-discovery and advancement but of stigmatisation and othering. It is this that makes Nancy Fraser's omission of the great strata of the underprivileged as part of the movement in the category towards identity politics all the more poignant.

The meta-humiliation of poverty

At the bottom of the social structure poverty and misrecognition, class and status fuse. Witness Bauman:

Our conversations have pondered the indignity of humiliation. Nothing humiliates more than poverty, and no poverty humiliates more than poverty suffered amidst people bent on fast and accelerating enrichment. To imagine that other forms of humiliation (and there is no shortage of them) can equal the sufferings which are endemic to the prospectless life amidst an orgy of ever more seductive opportunities, the life of miserly handouts amidst the revelry of fabulous made-overnight fortunes and golden handshakes, the sight of children waking up hungry and going to bed famished amidst the opulence spilling out from every shop window, means to grasp a chance of a temporary respite from guilty conscience at the expense of a lie. And it is an illusion which only the well-off can entertain so long as the supply of booze does not run out and the time of sobering-up does not arrive. Poverty is not one humiliation among many socially caused humiliations – and not just because of being the most painful and causing more suffering to its victims than the victims of other kinds of humiliation may live through. It is a 'meta-humiliation' of sorts, a soil on which all-round indignity thrives, a trampoline from which 'multiple humiliation' is launched. (Bauman and Tester, 2001, pp.153–4)

It is here that both the injustice of distribution and the calumny of misrecognition concur. It is where the two strands of justice, distribution and recognition, class and status, come seemingly inextricably together. Poverty is a stigma, because all of the institutions of society say so. The market flaunts its goods but denies you access to all but the most tawdry. It coerces you into work at the very lowest level it can, informing you in very clear monetary terms what you are worth: very little. It is an educational system which brands you as illiterate, a failure; a police force and criminal justice system which treats you blatantly with disrespect and disdain, and a welfare state which, with all its job schemes and back to work agencies, finally individualises you as a shirker, a loser. This is where self-blame and social stigma come together. But even here the institutions of the poor, whether they are progressive political parties and religious groups, or the insistent hedonism and resistance of the cultures of youth all create eddies of resistance which attempt to prise apart the heavy weight of poverty and disgrace. Indeed, even the much maligned solace of the street gang can be seen in a new light. In a dramatic turn around, David Brotherton and Luis Barrios (2004) substitute the lens of social movement for the lens of pathology and survey the New York chapter of the East Harlem based gang, The Latin Kings. The power of resistance, even the poetry of the street, become visible, the retrograde blemishes where they occur become to be seen for what they are, the subject of internal struggle and debate while the lens of pathology is seen in perspective, a creation of moral panic and an instrument of stigmatisation. In a grotesquely unequal society, resistance is always present whether it is fully fledged opposition or the micro-resistance of attitude or style. Some of its manifestations we may not like, some may mirror the othering of the powerful. But resistance is always there.

5

THE DECLINE OF WORK AND
THE INVISIBLE SERVANT

Not a long time ago Jeremy Rifkin, in his bestselling book, *The End of Work* (1996), was heralding a world where vast numbers of people would find themselves outside of the labour market. Automation and outsourcing as part of globalisation would make hundreds of millions of workers permanently idle. Building on the work of Daniel Bell, in his influential *The Coming of Post Industrial Society* (1973), he charted the shift from manufacturing to a service economy revolving around high technology, information-processing, provision of services and the rise of a service class of professionals, scientists and technicians. I want to argue in this chapter that only half of this equation is true, that there has indeed been an increase in scientists, technicians, physicians, researchers, and there has undoubtedly been a shift from the manufacturing to the service sector, but that there has at the same time been a rise in a much lower status service sector, indeed what in many cases might be seen as the re-emergence of a considerable servant class. George Ritzer's justly famous book *The MacDonaldization of Society* (1993) correctly recognises this, but tends to see this as concomitant with the bureaucratisation of service roles. This has indeed happened, from McDonalds itself to low-grade medical assistance, but many more of these roles are the very reverse of bureaucratised. Moreover, much of this work is strangely invisible to the middle-class public, and there is a peculiar contradiction at loose in our society where work is increasingly valorised while tedium is more and more the norm.

But let me first focus on the notion of the declining centrality of work.

The declining centrality of work?

In a brilliantly analysed essay, first published in 1982, Claus Offe argued that work has lost its centrality as an organising feature of modern life. 'What is paradoxical', he wrote, is that while an ever-greater part of the population participates in dependent wage labour, there is a decline in the extent to which wage labour as it were 'participates' in the lives of individuals by involving and shaping them in distinctive ways. This *decentring* of work relative to other spheres of life, its confinement to the margins of biography, is confirmed by many contemporary diagnoses. (trans. 1985, p. 141)

There are two levels to which he pinpointed 'the decline of the work ethic'. Firstly, on the level of *social integration*, work seen as a normatively sanctioned *duty*; secondly, on the level of *system integration*, work as a physical *necessity*. As far as the notion of work giving meaning to life and involving pride in one's job and shame at joblessness, Offe can see little to bind the individual normatively to the workplace. The rationalisation and deskilling of the work process, the patterns of 'Taylorisation', leaves less and less scope for personal satisfaction and autonomy. The disintegration of the bond between the workplace and the local area breaks the way in which work was the major axis of friendship, leisure and family tradition. The steelyard, the mill town, the mining village – all the factors which 'localised proletarian life' are in decline. The discontinuity of jobs, the decline of the lifetime trade, and the vicissitudes of early retirement and unemployment (all of which are the central concern of more recent writers, see for example Richard Sennet's *The Corrosion of Character*, 1998) all militate against the easy identification with work. Indeed, the increasingly common occurrence of unemployment decreases: 'the effect of the moral stigmatization and self-stigmatization ... beyond a certain threshold ... it cannot be accounted for plausibly in terms of individual failure or guilt (ibid., p. 143). Work, therefore, as an unfolding narrative, a secure source of personal identity is, according to Offe, of less and less significance. Indeed:

> taken together, these circumstances make it seem improbable that work, achievement and acquisition will continue to play a central role as a norm which integrates and guides personal existence. Nor does it seem likely that such a reference norm could be politically reactivated or reclaimed. *Recent attempts to 'remoralize' work and treat it as the central category of human existence must therefore be considered as a symptom, rather than a cure, of crisis.* (ibid., p. 143, emphasis added)

I have italicised the last part of Offe's commentary because of its relevance to the present period. The attempted remoralisation of work, for example, a central part of the British New Labour policy, was part of the process of social inclusion. Where work is seen as a source of identity and as a key source of integration into society through financial independence. Which brings us to the second of Offe's modes of integration: the instrumental sanctions which regulate the individual in a morally neutral sense by

THE DECLINE OF WORK

providing positive incentives to work and hardship if work is avoided. Given, Offe argues, that if normative sanctions with regards to work are in decline, then instrumental attachments become all the more significant. But here too he finds a lacking. On the level of positive sanctions, he sees a situation where people experience a rapidly declining marginal satisfaction from any increase of income, this being all more in evidence as work itself becomes viewed as a disutility compared to time spent in leisure and with one's friends. Thus:

speculations about the positive motivating effects of increasing income may, therefore, lose much of their plausibility, at least at the level of wages and saturation with consumer goods attained in Western Europe. (ibid., p. 144)

The carrot, then, no longer coaxes, but what of the stick? Surely reduction in wages or the threat of unemployment will force an adherence to the work system? Here, Offe presents us with his by now familiar thesis that an effective and 'irreversible' Welfare State undermines the brute necessity to work and that to reverse the post-war concordat or settlement achieved between capital and labour would be chronically disequilibriating. Thus he writes:

such a radical cure through a return to 'individualism' and 'market regulation' would possibly seriously endanger the relative social harmony of the work society, which historically was achieved only through a state-guaranteed system of collective distribution and security. In this system, there can be little reliance on individualism and the direct disciplining and legitimating effect of economic distress as one of the integrating means of society. (ibid., p. 146)

Thus the historic compromise between capital and labour which enabled the building of an inclusive society would threaten to tear apart if the safety net of welfare provision were removed. Social inclusion was dependent on welfare provision, welfare benefits inevitably reduced the impact of market discipline and the centrality of work.

Offe then postulates that wherever structural unemployment is concentrated there is built up subcultures based on informal economies which are 'at least passively hostile to the values and legal rules of the "work society", and could easily form themselves into a sub-proletarian "culture of unemployment", a "non-class of non-workers" (ibid., p. 147). Rather than a reserve army of labour which sustains the work culture they represent an opposition or resistance to work. This, of course, looks remarkably like the notion of an underclass as discussed in the current literature. Furthermore, it cannot fail to cross the mind of the reader that Claus Offe, a neo-Marxist, strongly influenced by the writings of Jürgen Habermas, comes to very similar conclusions as right wing libertarians such as Charles Murray and Lawrence Mead, whose extremely influential books, *Losing Ground* (1986) and *Beyond Entitlement* (1986), respectively, were written at about the same time. Thus, if Claus Offe and those on the left (for example André Gorz) saw such work refusal as politically liberating and a product of a major contradiction inherent in advanced capitalism, those commentators on the right were in precise agreement and conceived of this as the key problem.

Of course all of this is history, both the decline in the instrumentality of work and its normative centrality were fiercely and explicitly combated by politicians across the First World. The forces of neo-liberalism, the advocates of a more flexible and 'efficient' labour force intervened both to reduce 'dependency' on welfare and to re-valorise work as a central ideal of citizenship. The class struggle was not abandoned, far from it. The class struggle was fought, as David Harvey put it, and the powerful won. And we have the 'paradox' that just as wages and stability of work fell, the welfare net was trimmed back and withdrawn, just as work became more tedious and less a trusty prop of identity, it became all the more rigorously advocated as a responsibility rather than as a right.

Getting the poor to work: the US experiment

Just as Communists, radicals and progressives travelled to Moscow in the 1920s to see socialism being built in one country, so are politicians, policy analysts, and journalists today arriving in Wisconsin to see the welfare state being dismantled.

(Massing, 1999, p. 22)

The paradox that European politicians and journalists travel to the United States to learn about crime control and not the other way round, given the gargantuan nature of the American crime problem, has been frequently commented upon. What has not been sufficiently highlighted is the even more surprising attraction of the United States to European social democrats, including New Labour, who travel across the Atlantic in order to learn about what to do about the Welfare State. Opinion about the American welfare system has changed dramatically. Whereas it was widely regarded as a textbook exemplar of inadequacy which systematically neglected the poor, it is now increasingly caricatured as a profligate institution which generated dependency among the poor and created an urban underclass. The goal became, then, not to emulate the rich welfare structures of Europe but for Europe to follow the lead of America in stripping down and dismantling provisions and benefits.

Wisconsin led the way in welfare reform with its rigorous programme of time limits to welfare and strict work requirements. In the last ten years its welfare roll dropped from 100,000 to 9,000; in 1997 Wisconsin Works (or W2 as it is popularly known) was introduced, which insists that everyone must work and has entirely replaced its welfare programme with an employment assistance programme. The preferred workplace is in the private sector, those judged not quite ready for work are expected to do community service jobs and those with particularly serious problems attend compulsory education and training classes. Similar programmes occurred throughout the United States; for example, the Wisconsin model was introduced in New York City by Mayor Giuliani and in Michigan 'Project Zero' aimed to eliminate unemployment in the State.

On a comparative level what should be stressed is the particularly miserable nature of the US welfare system. Thus the paradox: that the industrial nation with the least developed welfare state views its interventions in the lives of its citizens as most insidious and develops the most draconian plans to dismantle it.

In the inclusive society of the post-war period, the Welfare State, particularly in Europe, was seen as the main instrument of the state to *include* citizens. It reached out to those who were marginal and ensured that they had the minimal benefits of economic citizenship. In the 1980s and early 1990s a critique of this position occurred from libertarians and neo-liberals of the right. They completely reversed the social democratic nostrum. For they argued that the Welfare State generated a dependency culture which, far from ensuring the integration of the marginal into society, was the prime force in creating an underclass who excluded themselves from society (see, for example, Murray, 1984).

In their analysis the benefits system was a disincentive to entering the world of work and normal economic behaviour. Furthermore, the dependency culture created a situation where those permanently on benefits were not only unwilling but eventually unable to meet the disciplines and punctualities necessary to function in the workaday world. By the 1990s the administrations of Clinton and of Blair took on board much of this thinking. In particular, the change in direction of New Labour was most astonishing because, instead of returning to some new Fabianism bent on seeking out the poor and bestowing upon them welfare rights, benefits and empowerment, they began to argue that the Welfare State 'as we know it' did not correspond to present day realities, and compounded the problems of the poor while the poor themselves, because of welfare dependency, lost their sense of responsibility as citizens.

Redemption through labour

Work is central to the Government's attack on social exclusion. Work is the only route to sustained financial independence. But it is also much more. Work is not just about earning a living. It is a way of life ... Work helps to fulfil our aspirations – it is the key to independence, self-respect and opportunities for advancement ... Work brings a sense of order that is missing from the lives of many unemployed young men. ... [The socially excluded] and their families are trapped in dependency. They inhabit a parallel world: where income is derived from benefits, not work; where school is an option not a key to opportunity; and where the dominant influence on young people is the culture of the street, not the values that bind families and communities together. There are some estates in my constituency: where the common currency is the giro; where the black economy involves much more than moonlighting – it involves the twilight world of drugs; and where relentless anti-social behaviour grinds people down ...

(A speech by Harriet Harman, then Minister for Social Security, at the opening of the Centre for the Analysis of Social Exclusion at the London School of Economics, 1997)

> The worker ... feels only outside of work, and during work he is outside himself. He is at home when he is not working and when he is working he is not at home. His work, therefore, is not voluntary, but coerced *forced labour*. It is not the satisfaction of a need but only a *means* to satisfy other needs. Its alien character is obvious from the fact that as soon as no physical or other pressure exists, labour is avoided like the plague. ... Finally the external nature of work for the worker appears in the fact that it is not his own but another person's, that in work he does not belong to himself but to some one else ... It is the loss of his own self.

(Karl Marx, *Economic and Philosophic Manuscripts,*1967 [1844], p. 292)

Being a member of society, being *included*, means being in work and *useful* work means paid work, labour sold in the market place (Levitas, 1996). It is here we encounter one of the 'magical' qualities of work. For work in this usage does not mean the work of a painter who paints for himself and his friends and does not put his canvasses in the market place; it is not the work of the person who looks after an elderly relative. It is not identical with creativity, labour of love, contribution to the community or even simply effort, sweat and tears. No, it is that labour which is a commodity in the market place. For, as André Gorz puts it:

> It is, unambiguously, the specific 'work' peculiar to industrial capitalism: the work we are referring to when we say 'she doesn't work' of a woman who devotes her time to bringing up her own children, but 'she works' of one who gives even some small part of her time to bringing up other people's children in a playgroup or a nursery school. (1999, p. 2)

To suggest that any work is better than no work and that work has this essential redeeming quality is bizarre in the extreme. Work, as John K.Galbraith so wryly commented in *The Culture of Contentment* (1992), is largely repetitive and demeaning, the use of 'work' by the 'contented classes' to describe their highly paid, creative and self-fulfilling activities in the same breath as the low paid, oppressive chores of the working poor is a fraud of the first order. And to add to this the notion of the majority of work as an act of redemption, a liberation of the self and a role model to one's children, as our New Labour politicians and their American cousins would maintain, is to add insult to injury.

Even for the working majority, the main virtues of work are the coffee break, the wage packet and the weekend. In fact the inherently boring and tedious nature of work seems to many people to be precisely the reason that one is paid to do it. It is what you *definitely* would not do if you were not being paid. Yet providing the hours are not too long and the wages high enough, a deal of some sort is being made based much more on the perceived obdurate, difficult and unchanging nature of reality rather than any ideas of redemption. There is always the teenagers' Saturday night, the forty-somethings' house and car, the 'real' world of home, kids and television. But such a *realpolitik* of desire is far from redemption. The confusion arises of course, as Galbraith points out, that for the contented classes work is indeed precisely that: it is

enjoyable, socially reputable and economically rewarding. Those who spend pleasant, well compensated days say with emphasis that they are 'hard at work' thereby suppressing the notion that they are a favored class. They are, of course, allured to say that they enjoy their work, but it is presumed that such enjoyment is shared by any *good* worker. In a brief moment of truth, we speak, when sentencing criminals, of years at 'hard labor'. Otherwise we place a common gloss over what is agreeable and what, to a greater or lesser extent, is endured or suffered. (1992, p. 33)

The élite workers of stage, screen and song, the sportsmen and women and the sizeable segment of the contented middle classes for whom the day is never long enough – for all of these, their identity is based upon work. Take work away from them and they flounder hopelessly: their ontology *is* work. But if one part of society defines work as what they are: the other very definitely defines it as what they are not.

Below the contented top of society, the broad mass of people who are, if anxious about job security, reconciled to the wage deal. But below that for the working poor the deal breaks down, the equivalence of selling time and buying leisure is frayed and insubstantial. To take family life as an example: the politicians' rhetoric about work sustaining the family and providing role models for the children is hollow if not downright cruel. For, in fact, the type of work available to many of the poor leaves little time for stable family relationships either to partners or to children, and has wide repercussions for community instability. As Elliott Currie puts it 'less often discussed [than lack of work] but not less important, is the effect of *overwork* in poorly-paid jobs on the capacity of parents to provide a nurturing and competent environment for childrearing and on the capacity of communities for self-regulation and the maintenance of networks of mutual support and care' (1997, p. 155).

To force people to work long and anti-social hours undermines the very 'basic' morality of family and community which the politicians of all persuasions are constantly harping on about. The way in which, for example, single mothers are forced into work at rates which scarcely makes affordable the childcare which long hours necessitates, suggests ideology is at work rather than any genuine care for people. The single mother looking after her children is dependent, the same mother paid to look after your children is an angel who by some miracle has become independent and resourceful. The true motive, the reduction of the tax burden of the well-off, is as Galbraith suggests, thinly concealed by the rhetoric. Furthermore, the notion that such work provides role models for the children of the neighbourhood is implausible: much more likely is that they make crime and the illicit markets of drug dealing all the more attractive. If there are indeed 'seductions of crime', as Jack Katz (1988) suggests, then these seductions are all the more sweet given the misery of the alternatives.

Including the excluded

What I am suggesting is that both the unemployed and the working poor – what one might call the over-employed – experience exclusion from social citizenship. The first because they are denied the basic economic substratum concomitant with the widespread expectations of what citizenship implies, the second because they experience the nature of their work, the hours worked and the remuneration as unfair, as being outside of the norms of the wage deal – a fair day's work for a fair day's pay. They are, of course, part of the labour market but they are not full citizens. The dragooning, therefore, of people from one category of exclusion to another ('getting the people to work', as the British Social Exclusion Unit (1999a) put it with its cheerless *double entendre*) is experienced all too frequently not as inclusion but as exclusion, not as the 'free' sale of labour, but as straightforward coercion. The 'New Deal', therefore, is not the solution it is the problem, it is not inclusion it is palpable exclusion, the solution to the New Deal is engaging in the hidden economy, wheeling and dealing, becoming a single mother – the solution is what the aptly named Social Exclusion Unit sets out as the problem (see Willis, 2000, pp. 89–91).

We have thus a paradox: just as manufacturing industry across the First World goes into decline, just as industries are re-engineered and many thrown out of their hitherto lifetime jobs, just as work insecurity rises and it becomes more and more difficult to find the stable building blocks of identity in one's work, *just at this point* work becomes hailed as a great virtue. This, as André Gorz trenchantly puts it:

> … is an enormous fraud. There is not and never will be 'enough work' (enough paid, steady, full-time employment) for everyone any longer, but society (or, rather, capital), which no longer needs everyone's labour, and is coming to need it less and less, keeps on repeating that it is not society which needs work (far from it!), but you who need it, …

THE DECLINE OF WORK

Never had the 'irreplaceable', 'indispensable' function of labour as the source of 'social ties', 'social cohesion', 'integration', 'socialization', 'personalization', 'personal identity' and meaning been invoked so obsessively as it has since the day it became unable any longer to fulfil *any* of these functions ... Having become insecure, flexible, intermittent, variable as regards hours and wages, employment no longer integrates one into a community, no longer structures the daily, weekly or annual round, or the stages of life, and is no longer the foundation on which everyone can base his/her life project.

The society in which everyone could hope to have a place and a future marked out for him/her – the 'work-based society', in which he/she could hope to have security and usefulness – is dead. Work now retains merely a phantom centrality: phantom in the sense of phantom limb from which an amputee might continue to feel pain ... (1999, pp. 57–8)

Work, in the sense of that which involves self-realisation and creativity is not, of course, dead but secure, paid, full-time employment for life is considerably diminished and where it exists does not have this quality. The jobs that grant stable income and identity are, of course, still there at the top of the structure, among the professional middle classes and even lower in the sturcture, but this 'contented class' has shrunk much more than Galbraith calculated. For the bulk of the population this is not so and, as for those at the bottom of the pile, there is little to be gained in terms of secure income or identity. Indeed the very opposite is true, their low incomes and insecurity generate feelings of marginalisation and their stigmatisation as an underclass provides negative rather than any positive building blocks of identity.

Welfare: from relief to irresponsibility

Let me just recapitulate the situation of the working poor, the target of welfare reform. First of all, they are typically in a position backwards and forwards between welfare and work, or with welfare supplementing work: the long-term unemployed in a small minority. Secondly, the actual cost of benefits is comparatively small. Thus Joel Handler points out that at its height in the United States the AFDC (Aid to Families with Dependent Children) absorbed $23 billion in Federal and State expenditure. This is, he notes, 'a trifling amount compared with the budget for Social Security (pensions) at more than $300 billion, or Medicare at $280 billion. Welfare has been a lightning rod because the term has operated as a code-word over race, gender and ethnicity, focusing overwhelmingly on young African–American women, allegedly breeding a criminal underclass' (2000, p. 117). And this is echoed, in a British context, by Jayne Mooney (2002) in her analysis of the moral panic over single mothers and delinquency which I will return to in the next chapter.

All of this is redolent of ideology and, as I have already outlined, is a clear manifestation of resentment. Even the names of the legislation have a whiff of moral indignation. Witness Clinton's 1996 Personal Responsibility and Work Opportunity Reconciliation Act which abolished AFDC outright. Handler notes how welfare, once seen as a relief to poverty, has now become the opposite of self-sufficiency and asks about welfare to work:

> there is also a more widespread sense that technological changes make it unlikely that the labour markets of the twenty-first century would ever provide enough jobs anyway. Furthermore, should the creation of lower-end jobs even be encouraged, if they involve degrading conditions and harmful consequences for families – above all, women and children? Wouldn't it be better to expand social benefits for people who are already excluded from the labour market – instead of forcing single mothers into low-wage work, to reward their home-care properly? (2000, p. 135)

Early morning in Harlem

Katherine Newman, in the preface of her book *No Shame in My Game* (2000), a study of the working poor in the inner city, describes a taxi ride early one Monday morning from her New York home, at that time, on the Upper West Side near the University of Columbia, to La Guardia Airport in Queens. She was on the way to a meeting, pondering the fact that she had promised to write a paper for a conference on urban poverty and jobless neighbourhoods, and travelling through Harlem. The taxi got mired in the traffic down 125th Street and she had a good chance to look out on the main thoroughfare of central Harlem. What she saw surprised her:

> Standing at the bus shelters were lines of men and women dressed for work, holding the hands of their children on their way to day care and the local schools. Black men in mechanic's overalls, women in suits – drinking coffee from Dunkin' Donuts cups, reading the *New York Post,* fussing with their children's backpacks – tapped their feet on the ground, waiting for the buses trying to manoeuver toward them, caught in the same maddening traffic. The portals of the subways were swallowing up hordes of commuters who had given up on the buses. Meanwhile, people walking purposefully to work were moving down the sidewalks, flowing around the bus shelters, avoiding the outstretched arm of the occasional beggar, and ignoring the insistent calls of the street vendors selling clothing and videotapes from tables set up along the edge of the sidewalk. It was Monday morning in Harlem, and as far as the eye could see, thousands of people were on their way to work. (2000, p. ix–x)

Let us pause for a moment to reflect upon the fact that an experienced and talented social scientist can be surprised to discover that the poor actually work. How else could one expect them to live in a city with such a minimal and tardy welfare provision? But very much to her credit Newman points out quite correctly that social scientists, preoccupied with urban poverty and the flight of manufacturing jobs from the urban centres – and here she is thinking particularly of the work of William Julius Wilson and his associates – simply do not focus on the working poor. Yet, as she points out, 69% of families living in central Harlem has at least one worker – and in the same family one has police officers and felons, drug users and diligent workers. Indeed Wilson's own study, *When Work Disappears* (1996), conducted in the poorest parts of Chicago found that over half the respondents are in work. And, of course, these numbers are clearly underestimates, there are many reasons – taxation being the most obvious – why people should conceal their work habits and income sources. There is not a binary of work/non-work but work is of necessity part of the regimen of nearly every family: whether it is formal employment which is picked up in the survey statistics or informal legal work – which is definitely not – or informal illegal work (which is the one-sided focus of criminological inquiry). Further such work of any variety may involve a drifting in and out from one to the other – it has no stasis, which does not, of course, mean that it is not there. Newman, herself, astutely points to the existence of a huge concealed informal economy. Thus she talks of one of her respondents, Rey:

If we were to look at an official government census for Rey's household, we would find that the adults within it are classified as out of the labor force. Indeed, it would be deemed a single-parent household supported by the welfare system. Harlem is populated by thousands of families whose official profiles look just like this. Yet there is a steady income stream coming into Rey's home, because most of the adults are indeed working, often in the mostly unregulated economy of small-scale services and self-employment, including home-based seamstresses, food vendors, gypsy cab drivers, and carpenters. Most of this income never sees the tax man.

Much of what has been written about this underground system focuses on the drug world. But for thousands of poor people in New York who cannot afford a unionized plumber or electrician, unlicensed craftsmen and informal service workers (who provide child care or personal services) are more important exemplars of the shadow economy. Men like Rey and his father provide reasonably priced services and products, making it possible for people who would otherwise have to do without to get their cars fixed, their leaking roofs patched, or their children looked after. Immigrants who lack legal papers find employment in this shadow world, and those who are legal take second jobs in the underground economy.

It has proved extremely hard to estimate the size of this alternative system, but it is so widespread in poor communities that it often rivals the formal economy. The multi-purpose shop Rey's father runs from the living room and the street corner is the mainstay of the family's income, and in this they are hardly alone. The thoroughfares of Harlem have, for many years, had an active sidewalk market trade that is largely invisible to the Internal Revenue Service. (1999, p. 201)

Yet both the formal and the informal work of the poor is invisible, but not all. Note how Katherine Newman points to the focus on the drug economy. The illicit economy of the poor is a major focus of sociological inquiry and media interest. Newman's driver finally gets fed up of trying to get down the main boulevard of Harlem and turns off 125th Street in order to try and out-manoeuvre the jam; here in the back streets there are the broken down houses, the litter of crack vials – the face of the ghetto that we readily recognise. It is like the image of Spanish Harlem which we find in Philippe Bourgois' *In Search of Respect* (1999), one of crack dealers, the permanently unemployed, despite the fact that very many of the East Barrio are at work. For, however brilliant Bourgois' ethnography, it must not be forgotten that he focuses only on a tiny minority: his lens focuses on the atypical and gives it an image of normality.

Michael Harrington, writing in the 1960s, famously notes in *The Other America* (1963) that the poor in the United States had become invisible. Nowadays, the poor are only too visible: they are forever in the searchlight of condemnation, the object of stigmatisation, surveillance and blame. But the searchlight only picks out certain features, the exotic, the dangerous, the derelict, and these it highlights, stereotypes, distrusts while it ignores the humdrum, the prosaic, the core basis of being poor in an intensely affluent society. In doing this it reinforces the late modern binary which I outlined earlier. Indeed the fabrication of the underclass and the invisibility of the working poor are part and parcel of the same process of othering. The polit-ical implications of this are evident for, as Newman points out:

> Having convinced ourselves that welfare dependency and joblessness repre-sent the true face of American poverty, the policy agenda of the 1990s ... became very easy to sell. If the inner city is a mess because no one wants to work, we need to aim all our efforts at making it much harder to get on wel-fare and much easier to push people off of state support. (1999, p. xi)

Add to this that such supposed shiftlessness is tied up with the informal economies of drug dealing, the mean streets of muggers and the gang, and we have the basis not only of welfare to work but the shift from welfare to the criminal justice system as a means of achieving social order. None of this is to romanticise the poor parts of town as places of crime-free utopias where informal economies daily solve the problems of poverty. Far from it, crime is an endemic problem of poverty and day-to-day existence involves a hardship and struggle. Rather it is to realise that the focus on crime is a partial vision attractive to criminologists and urban anthropologists alike. To view the community through this lens is to bring out the exotic and the deviant at the expense of much of the everyday life of the community (see Wacquant, 1997). To this extent Newman provides us with a corrective, a focus upon hardworking Harlem and an awareness of the wide range of work which occurs. Yet her own lens has its own particular bias and agenda. The focus on the fast food industry or, for example, Burger King serving the people of Harlem and beyond this on the informal economies from child care to motor repair which service the community, presents the work of the poor as if it were a thing that occurs out there in the slum or the ghetto, not as work that has any relationship to *us*, the wider middle class society. It maintains both distance and hiatus in common with much urban ethnography.

I want to turn now to discuss this relationship. But first let us note that the creation of the ideological category 'underclass' necessitates the invisibility of the working poor, the notion of a group outside of the economy and wider society and that 'working poor' itself is an oxymoron to a politics which revolves around the palliative and redemptive qualities of work.

Others call this 'the betrayal of work', witness the title of Beth Shulman's (2003) trenchant description of how low-wage jobs fail to provide either a material living or any dignity in labour for 30 million Americans and their families. The harrowing descriptions of people with two jobs, long days and minimal wages which simply do not cover the rent and food costs, makes bitter reading. But they are not exceptions, they are not a residuum of poverty, they are not marginal to the economy, they are central to it: part of essential and vital economic circuits. The jobs are not the stereotype – which Katherine Newman in part plays into – of fast food workers. As Shulman puts it:

> Contrary to the dominant myth that most low-wage jobs are the ones you see in your neighborhood McDonald's, fast-food jobs constitute less than 5 percent of all low-end jobs. Then where do we find the people working in these low-wage, low-reward jobs? They are all around us: security guards, nurse's aides and home health-care aides, child-care workers and educational assistants, maids and porters, 1,800 call-center workers, bank tellers, data-entry keyers, cooks, food-preparation workers, waiters and waitresses, cashiers and pharmacy assistants, hairdressers and manicurists, parking-lot attendants, hotel receptionists and clerks, ambulance drivers, poultry, fish, and meat processors, sewing-machine operators, laundry and dry-cleaning operators, and agricultural workers. (2003, pp. 45–6)

Most of these jobs, as Shulman points out, involve interaction with the public, they require knowledge, patience, care, commitment and are essential to the economy, to the prosperity of the United States and other First World countries. They are a growth sector, the new economy has not, as I noted, decreased the level of low-paid jobs, it has increased them. In the United States, for example, the two lowest paying sectors of the economy, retail and service, increased from 30% to 48% of all production and non-supervisory employment between 1965 and 1998 and this proportion is expected to grow (ibid., p. 105). But despite this key role in the economy these workers remain strangely invisible. It is this 'invisibility' that I would like to further explore.

The invisible worker

David Rieff is a connoisseur of invisibility, the very title of his book *Los Angeles: Capital of the Third World* (1993) captures the irony of a city where the white Angelinos forget that they are a minority. People, he notes, often assume that Los Angeles is a green and verdant place – a place where anything grows, lushly and easily. But it isn't so: the Los Angeles basin is, in fact, a desert ringed by the Pacific and the mountains. The green crispness of lawn, the luxuriant variation of plant and shrubs is all achieved by invisible helpers. He describes taking a friend's dog for a walk one morning:

> When I would go out in the early morning, the streets would be empty, but by the time the dog and I would begin pantingly to make our way home, we would pass those tell-tale beat-up old station wagons and pickup trucks. Slowing to a halt, these vehicles would disgorge their cargoes of small, brown-skinned men. In silence, they would set to work, mowing the lawns, trimming the opulent hedges, seeing to the sprinkler systems, and sweeping up the natural debris – palm fronds, eucalyptus leaves, and the like ... But if, by 8:00 a.m., the streets of Brentwood were filled with these gardeners ... by noon they had vanished. Sometime in the interim, it appeared, the men had either walked to the bus stop on San Vicente Boulevard to begin the hours-long trek back to East Los Angeles by RTD, or else they had been collected by the same beat-up old jalopies that had delivered them to the Westside in the first place. (1993, p. 101)

But it is the area of domestic service that is most illuminating. People want to have children, to have domestic pets, to have spotless houses, but the professional couple does not have the time for childrearing, walking the dog, or domestic work. What is more important, neither do they have the inclination. Their dream of late modernity is one of self-discovery, of enjoyment detached from these sorts of worries. Many of the people Rieff interviewed would, in his estimation, find life impossible without a maid, or perhaps it was that they could not even conceive of life without servants.

> It was one thing to work long hours at something you cared about, or devote yourself to a sport or a hobby. But there was no way as long as they could afford it that a generation that had grown up thinking of life as, essentially, fun was going to be reconciled to mopping their own floors or cleaning their own toilets. Somebody had to, though, usually somebody whose last name ended with a *z*, an *a*, or an *o*. (ibid., p. 100)

Not that these people are real servants, they are not, after all, the starched people who appeared in the early British imports 'Upstairs Downstairs' or 'Brideshead Revisited' and many of these rich Angelinos, coming from impoverished immigrant backgrounds, saw themselves as giving these new immigrants a help up. Language aided the invisibility, Spanish becomes either the language of service or of incomprehension. Now and then the smoke screen parted, but not for long. Witness this lovely passage:

Once, as I chatted with a friend of Allegra's about her new baby, and asked her how her life was different, she replied, 'Oh, it changes your life, all right.' Then, pausing for a moment and shaking her head ruefully, she added, 'I mean, it changes some-one's life; I mean it changes some Guatemalan's life.' She meant the remark as a joke, of course, but, after she had delivered it, she shifted uncomfortably, as if its truth had only then become clear to her, and swept off into the kitchen to pour herself another cup of coffee. When she returned, we talked about German reunification. (ibid., p. 102)

The invisible servants were the bit actors who provided the backdrop for real life, for self-discovery and enjoyment. There would 'always be some unknown person to take care of the "dirty bits" of life'. Certain physical activities were obviously part of these 'dirty bits, yet other physical activities were part of self-development and realisation. Rieff is exquisite in his description of the Angelinos in their extraordinary bright spandex outfits with their self-disciplined jogging, dedicated to burn up calories and build up tone, who would not be seen dead working in their own gardens where they would have got a considerably better workout. For, as he puts it, 'in West LA … sweat and labor had bifurcated' (ibid., p. 108).

It is this differential of work between that which is self-developing, the very stuff of life, and that which is soul destroying which is a key component of the late modern Dream. One might also note that there is beneath this a division between dirty work (scrubbing floors, cleaning toilets, changing nappies, digging ditches, shovelling leaves) and a world which is crisp, clean, creative and unencumbered by the material. All of this might find easy resonance with Mary Douglas' *Purity and Danger* (1966) but it all adds up to what Ehrenreich calls the *solipsis* of middle-class life. That is, a world that believes that its existence is self-created, is detached from material reality. In short, the invisibility of the working poor, the denial of our dependence (and the ironic projection of dependency upon them) is part of the process of othering, of creating distance and hiatus. And it also involves a belittling, often an infanticisation, a notion of the servant as less than us, of being in deficit.

The invisible servant

To be unaware that the poor work out there in those areas of poverty where the well-off never venture is one thing. To be unaware of the poverty of the shelf-fillers, busboys, telemarketers, and the sanitation providers who one glimpses or glances at the nether regions of restaurants or speaks to on the end of telephones, is on the edge of comprehendible. But to be somehow unaware or directly conscious of those one directly employs, and the fact that they are often badly off, is strange and paradoxical. To understand this one has to grasp the power of solipsis, the almost feudal nature of such employment and the gendered and often racist nature of the work relationship itself.

Barbara Ehrenreich, in her investigation of the world of the working poor, describes her work as an employee of Maids International, a world of endless scrubbable floors. Graphically she describes how she is nearly invisible, not unlike the servants of the nineteenth century:

> It's a different world down there below knee level, one that few adults voluntarily enter. Here you find elaborate dust structures held together by a scaffolding of dog hairs; dried bits of pasta glued to the floor by their sauce; the congealed remains of gravies, jellies, contraceptive creams, vomit, and urine. Sometimes too you encounter some fragment of a human being: a child's legs stamping by in disgust because the maids are still present when he gets home from school, or, more commonly, the Joan and David-clad feet and electrolyzed calves of the female homeowner. Look up and you may find this person staring at you, arms folded, in anticipation of an overlooked stain. In rare instances, she may try to help in some vague, symbolic way, by moving a cockatoo's cage, for example, or apologizing for the leaves shed by a miniature indoor tree. Mostly though, she will not see you at all, and may even sit down with her mail at a table in the very room you are cleaning, where she will remain completely unaware of your existence – unless you were to crawl under that table and start gnawing away at her ankles. (2002, p. 86)

The most fundamental reason for invisibility is that we do not see poorly paid work, often done by immigrant women, as a key part of the economy. Their work is simply an add on, a bit of help, it is random, non-institutionalised, not a proper sector of the economy. Saskia Sassen powerfully takes issue with this. The usual narrative of post-industrial society which only emphasises the emergence of a highly skilled, information rich workforce is wrong, she maintains. It also necessitates a very large unskilled workforce. Thus she writes:

> Low-wage workers accomplish a sizable portion of the day-to-day work in global cities' leading sectors. After all, advanced professionals require clerical, cleaning, and repair workers for their state-of-the art offices, and they require truckers to bring them their software and their toilet paper. In my research on New York and other cities, I have found that between 30 and 60 percent of workers in the leading sectors are actually low-wage workers.
>
> The similarly state-of-the-art lifestyles of professionals in these sectors have created a whole new demand for household workers, particularly maids and nannies, as well as for service workers to cater to those professionals' high-income consumption habits. Expensive restaurants, luxury housing, luxury hotels, gourmet shops, boutiques,

French hand laundries, and special cleaning services, for example, are more labor-intensive than their lower-priced equivalents. To an extent not seen in a very long time, we are witnessing the reemergence of a 'serving class' in contemporary high-income households and neighborhoods. (2002, p. 252)

She talks of 'professional houses without wives'; that is, whether they consist of a man and a woman, two men or two women, they work at time-consuming, high income jobs and rely on the market place to cater for their domestic work and, of course, meals eaten out, clothes cleaned at laundries, etc.

Thus a sizeable yet relatively invisible workforce has emerged to support the professional élite. The current narrative of globalisation then, for Sassen, focuses only on the upper circuit and not the lower circuit. Further, the lower circuit is fuelled by the deepening misery of the global south and its circle is completed by the considerable funds which are sent home to subsidise the relatives of the immigrant workers. Let us add a further refinement to this, as much labour as is possible is outsourced, from telephone information services to medical diagnosis based on e-mailed X-rays (see Friedman, 2005). What is left in the First World is highly skilled, innovative design work and that unskilled labour which physically cannot be outsourced. That is, you can out-source the restaurant booking, but you can't outsource the act of putting the steak on the restaurant table, you can outsource children's clothes, and old people's diapers, but you need someone to put them on your children or your grandparents. Thus, as we outsource manufacture and services to the Third World, we *insource* from the Third World a whole series of caring jobs from nannies to sex workers. You can outsource pornography, but you have to insource sex. The subtitle of Ehrenreich and Hochschild's book, *Global Woman: Nannies, Maids and Sex Workers in the New Economy* says it all. Indeed, Arlie Hochschild talks in her essay 'Love and Gold' (2002) of a new form of imperialism: of a First World which once extracted minerals now imports care, where 'love and care become the new gold'.

The brutality of that era's imperialism is not to be minimized, even as we compare the extraction of material resources from the Third World of that time to the extraction of emotional resources today. Today's north does not extract love from the south by force: there are no colonial officers in tan helmets, no invading armies, no ships bearing arms sailing off to the colonies. Instead, we see a benign scene of Third World women push-ing baby carriages, elder care workers patiently walking, arms linked, with elderly clients on streets or sitting beside them in First World parks.

Today, coercion operates differently. While the sex trade and some domestic service is brutally enforced in the main the new emotional imperialism does not issue from the barrel of a gun. Women choose to migrate for domestic work. But they choose it because economic pressures all but coerce them to. That yawning gap between rich and poor countries is itself a form of coercion, pushing Third World mothers to seek work in the First for lack of options closer to home. But given the prevailing free market ideology, migration is viewed as a 'personal choice'. Its consequences are seen as 'personal problems.' In this sense, migration creates not a white man's burden but, through a series of invisible links, a dark child's burden. (2002, p. 27)

Entering the zone of humiliation

The tardy material circumstances of the working poor carry with them a heavy irony, the knowledge that one is working harder than most people in society, often with two jobs and different times and shifts, and yet still is unable to make ends meet. The irony extends further for, as David Shipler points out in his book *The Working Poor: Invisible in America* (2004), it manifests itself in the guy working at the car wash who can't afford a car, the medical book copy editor who can't pay for a visit to the dentist, the accounts clerk at the bank with only $2.02 in her own account, and to this one might add, as we shall see later, the nanny pushing the buggy in the park who has not the time to look after her own children.

But it is not just material deprivation, to be poor is to enter a world which few middle-class professionals can comprehend. This is why Barbara Ehrenreich's justly celebrated *Nickled and Dimed* (2001) is such an eye opener. Ehrenreich did what few social scientists would naturally do, for instead of studying the poor, she attempts to survive, albeit temporarily, on the wages of the poor doing the jobs of waitressing, shop assistant, cleaning houses. What is striking is not only the day-to-day difficulty of being poor, it is paradoxically more expensive in terms of housing and food, but the day-to-day put downs and petty rules and restrictions which dominate this zone of humiliation. The drug testing demanded by most of the major supermarket chains, the employment on precisely the minimum wage – which basically tells you that your boss would pay you less if it were only legally possible, the strict rules for going to the bathroom, the forced enthusiasm demanded by management, and the strict prohibition on trade unions.

The humiliation is bestowed not only by employers, customers, the well contented public but, of course, also by the government agencies of neo-liberalism set up to maintain the core of work behaviour and market values. Let me give you an example. Michelle Kennedy writes about this in her harrowing *Without a Net* (2005). She is a young woman from a middle-class background who, after a series of mistakes and worse luck, finds herself homeless with three kids. She gets a job waitressing at $2.12 per hour plus tips, but is unable to find affordable housing so she and her children sleep in their car. Indeed, while she works at the restaurant, she leaves the children in the car park, popping out regularly to check on their well-being. She reckons that she must be a prime candidate for some sort of assistance and dutifully goes along to the local Job Center. She is told that she did not qualify, that 'according to the computer you and your children should be fine on the income you currently provide'. But help is at hand: 'If you like, I can set you up with a financial counselor and she can help you budget your money better' (2005, pp. 94–5). She fights back the tears, exits with one child on her hip the other two following her.

Service as a feudal relationship

Bridget Anderson, in her brilliant and moving book *Doing the Dirty Work* (2000), charts the great economic circuit of migrant workers, their emigration out and the money they send home, and the increasing feminisation of this process. She notes also their invisibility in line with all the commentators we have discussed. One of the aspects of their invisibility is, she argues, that the servant relationship is not seen by the employer as a contractual relationship of normal wage employment but something more. It involves an exchange not just of money and time, but material comfort, personal attention and intimacy, whether it is looking after the children, or old people, or the meals, the access to a comfortable home and, often with live-in servants their room and board. They become not like an employee, far from it, more like 'one of the family', or at least that is what the employer likes to believe. One of the interviewees is Zenaida, a Moroccan woman working in Barcelona, whose situation as part of the family exposed her to vulnerability and revealed what Anderson sees as the act of killing the self, a predicament of deep depersonalisation.

She had cared for an old woman for five years, doing domestic chores as well as caring work. She lived in, was 'part of the family', and felt she was treated with respect by her employing family. She was paid by the woman's sons, who even took a holiday in her house in Morocco. Yet she could spend only one night a week with her five children, who lived in Barcelona, and the rest of the time had to leave them to fend for themselves because she lived in. Although he could have obtained a residence permit for Spain, the father of her children remained in Morocco because the first two children were too old to be admitted to Spain under family reunification. The youngest child was six, and she had left her when she was only a baby for six days a week in order to be the old woman's carer. There was no question of her being allowed to sleep with the baby: 'You can't do these things. No. Everyone thinks, I don't know, about themselves. You can't do that'. (2000, pp. 124–5)

Furthermore, a relationship of 'maternalism' frequently emerges between the female help and the mistress of the house (see Rollins, 1985). The servant is often younger, nearly always poorly educated, frequently an immigrant. The role becomes to help her out – the help becomes helped out, the dependency of mistress on maid becomes perceived as the dependency of the maid on the mistress. With immigrants, almost always the low wages and long hours of the job are seen as part of the necessary first step in coming to North America or the European Union. In the case of coming to the United States or Canada, immigrant societies, it is seen as almost a rite of passage which the employees' own forbears went through.

This maternalism allows grossly unequal relationships to be conceived of as acts of kindness. And acts of kindness not fully recognised are perceived as attitudes of ingratitude. Witness the employer, Nina, interviewed by Bridget Anderson:

> But there is no feeling for what I offer. I give you an example of the last woman from Bulgaria ... I had a bright thought, 'she needs to see her friends'. Because I was tired of all the girls changing so many times I gave her Sunday off. Now, every morning, including Sundays the girl wakes, helps grandmother to the toilet and changes her pamper ... Then she goes, but she must be back for seven pm ... Then, after all I do for her, the girl says every Sunday she would like to be back at midnight and not to do any work – that is not to change the pamper in the morning. (2000, p. 144)

Nina had employed dozens of domestic workers to care for her mother offering, in her terms, comfortable circumstances and a loving home but her perception was that she had faced a whole series of gold-diggers.

The mistress-servant relationship then has consequences both for the servant and for the mistress. Ehrenreich and Hochschild are very forthright about this. The feminist debate about gender inequality and the politics of housework has been 'resolved' but it has done so at the expense of the poor:

> ... the globalization of child care and housework brings the ambitious and independent women of the world together: the career-oriented upper-middle-class woman of an affluent nation and the striving woman from a crumbling Third World or postcommunist economy. Only it does not bring them together in the way that second-wave feminists in affluent countries once liked to imagine – as sisters and allies struggling to achieve common goals. Instead, they come together as mistress and maid, employer and employee, across a great divide of privilege and opportunity.
>
> This trend toward global redivision of women's traditional work throws new light on the entire process of globalization. Conventionally, it is the poorer countries that are thought to be dependent on the richer ones – a dependency symbolized by the huge debt they owe to global financial institutions. What we explore ..., however, is a dependency that works in the other direction, and it is a dependency of a particularly intimate kind. Increasingly often, as affluent and middle-class families in the First World come to depend on migrants from poorer regions to provide child care, homemaking, and sexual services, a global relationship arises that in some ways mirrors the traditional relationship between the sexes. The First World takes on a role like that of the old-fashioned male in the

family – pampered, entitled, unable to cook, clean or find his socks. Poor countries take on the role like that of the traditional woman within the family – patient, nurturing and self-denying. A division of labor feminists critiqued when it was 'local' has now, metaphorically speaking, gone global. (2002, pp. 11–2)

The invisible poor in a classless society

Let us put the strands of this argument together. I have been concerned how certain aspects of the lives of the poor have been rendered invisible while others, their crime and deviance, are highlighted. Indeed, quite commonly, the triptych of underclass, immigrant, and criminal are elided together into a gross stereotype of the poor. This perception is facilitated by a lens which casts the world into binaries. The binary middle class/underclass is a strange construct, lumping together – particularly in the US – nearly everyone with a regular job as middle class, ignoring the rich and placing the rest of the population strangely 'below', 'beneath', out of the class structure altogether. It is an imaginary? which revolves around the notion of a classless society. Such a binary is seen to correspond to those in work and those who are supposedly fairly permanently out of it. Hence Katherine Newman's surprise at the workers of Harlem. But the binary further insists that those who work are reasonably well-off and that poverty is associated with worklessness. The existence of the working poor negates this supposed oxymoron, it breaches the borders. Their invisibility stems from the binary; it is a powerful critique of neo-liberal faith in the inclusive qualities of the market place. Employment: legal, illegal; formal, informal is much more ubiquitous than is frequently supposed. Further, contracy to the inclusionary/exclusionary categorisation of the binary, it involves relationships between the poor and the well-off, class relationships of a regularised nature, part of important, key economic circuits within our society which are frequently global in their reach.

The rise of an élite of highly skilled experts and professionals in the service sector, concomitant with the rapid decline of manufacture because of automation and out-sourcing to the Third World, was heralded as the emergence of a new class, a harbinger of a post-industrial age. This group increased, it is to be sure, as did the service sector as a whole, but what was ignored was the emergence of a considerable body of workers in the downmarket part of the sector whose jobs were to service the work 'rich', dual income professionals and marginal families. That is, just as a considerable portion of manufacturing slipped away overseas and working class institutions went into decline, a large segment of labour emerged poorly paid and ignored, whose very invisibility enabled the imaginary of classlessness to be propagated and believed in.

Such a lower class services a wide array of tasks from the repair and maintenance of buildings in the regentrified city, to the host of restaurants serving the needs of the professional élite, to direct domestic service within the home. It exists very often within the informal economy, it has a large proportion of immigrants and is increasingly female. As such it is part of major economic circuits which have a global compass.

Guilt and middle-class solipsism

What effect does such a service class have on the middle class they serve? At the very least, as Barbara Ehrenreich points out, it produces a sense of solipsism: a feeling of detachment, of self-absorption, of existing separately and independently of the rest of society. Thus, in a famous phrase, she writes:

> A servant economy may provide opportunities, however limited, for poor and immigrant women. But it also breeds callousness and solipsism in the served, and it does so all the more effectively when the service is performed close up and routinely in the place where they live and reproduce. (2002, p. 103)

And, in an earlier work, Ehrenreich notes how we excoriated the poor for living off welfare but now we have them self-sufficient yet living on the edge of poverty. In an extraordinary act of othering we have become dependent on those we stigmatised as suffering from dependency. And how should we feel?

> Guilt, you may be thinking warily. Isn't that what we're supposed to feel? But guilt doesn't go anywhere near far enough; the appropriate emotion is shame – shame at our *own* dependency, in this case, on the underpaid labor of others. When someone works for less pay than she can live on – when, for example, she goes hungry so that you can eat more cheaply and conveniently – then she has made a great sacrifice for you, she has made you a gift of some part of her abilities, her health, and her life. The 'working poor', as they are approvingly termed, are in fact the major philanthropists of our society. They neglect their own children so that the children of others will be cared for; they live in substandard housing so that other homes will be shiny and perfect; they endure privation so that inflation will be low and stock prices high. To be a member of the working poor is to be an anonymous donor, a nameless benefactor to everyone else. As Gail, one of my restaurant coworkers put it, 'you give and you give.'
>
> Someday, of course – and I will make no predictions as to exactly when – they are bound to tire of getting so little in return and to demand to be paid what they're worth. There'll be a lot of anger when that day comes, and strikes and disruption. But the sky will not fall, and we will all be better off for it in the end. (Ehrenreich, 2001, p. 221)

6

SOCIAL INCLUSION AND REDEMPTION
THROUGH LABOUR

I have attempted to draw an outline of the social terrain of late modernity. The decline of manufacturing in the First World, the automation of many jobs, and the outsourcing of many others, has sent a massive shiver through the class structure. The élite of celebrity and wealth at the top and a slightly augmented professional class exists in a world secure both materially and ontologically. But beneath that there is a vast middle class from bank clerk to financial consultant, from aero-engineer to accountant, insecure and uncertain, better off than before but uncertain for how long, who must at times renegotiate both their lifestyles and life narratives. Immediately below is a working class decimated by the loss of manufacturing jobs, the drive against the trade unions, with a palpable, everyday fear of falling. And below that … here, of course, there is great controversy. For some an underclass has formed detached from society, irrelevant, distant, dysfunctional and costly in tax pounds and dollars. I have been critical of such a notion of residuum – of a late modern binary which casts the lower part of society outside of the social structure, whose impact is seen only as a liability and as victims of the disease of dependency, whom we are better off without. That is, I have criticised what has been characterised by Goran Therborn (1986) and many others as the 'Brazilianization' of advanced capitalism with its threefold design of society into the rich, the insecure middle and the excluded poor (see Byrne, 1999). Rather I would argue that the lower class has reconstructed itself as a service class which provides service, servants and security for the rest of society. It is far from dysfunctional, it is essential for the reproduction of labour and the maintenance of the cost of consumer goods, whether in shops or in restaurants, at a low cost. It is an integral part of society, the lower terraces of the wider structure. Joel Nelson, in his *Post-Industrial Capitalism* (1995), comes to a somewhat similar conclusion, but stresses the rationalisation of such delivery systems from food outlets to childcare, to specialised shops in highly managed organisations and franchises which cater for the new consumption habits and services by employing low-paid workers in dead-end jobs. I would hesitate at such a closure – a *fait accompli* extension of neo-liberal policies and management strategies to incorporate and envelop all levels of the class structure. It is too systematic, too total, too successful. Instead, I have presented a world of work which is sometimes part of the formal economy but often informal and below the radar of tax authority and census, sometimes legal, sometimes illegal, sometimes paid work, sometimes unpaid, sometimes there, sometimes not – what Ulrich Beck (2000) calls 'a patchwork of activities'. It is, after all, this ducking and diving which characteristically makes the working poor invisible. The informal economy alone is enormous, from carpet laying to childminding, and is characteristically a collaboration – although on very unequal terms – of the middle and lower classes to avoid taxes and regulations. And such a patchwork involves both services rendered to the middle classes and, as Katherine Newman points out, services rendered by the poor to each other.

So, although the lower class workplace of Wallmarts and MacDonald's is only too evident, it is not all there is by far. And it is this lack of closure which is the target of government policies of social inclusion. I would maintain that these initiatives are not so much to socially include the excluded – although this may well be the legitimation, or the rationale which aids such an illusion, but rather initiatives to regiment, to bring within the system, to eliminate the hidden economies, to minimise unpaid work (quite explicitly in terms of teenage mothers), to bring the poor fully within the market economy. That is, to avoid the satisfaction of Claus Offe or the warnings of Charles Murray. For it is not so much an act of social inclusion (for they already are included), as an attempt to include all within the market economy aided by the elision that only those active in legitimate work are fully social beings and tolerable citizens. In short, it seeks the deliverance of the poor by the delivery of the poor to the market place.

In this task the aim is to reform the poor, that is, through the agency of work, to render them taxable, rid them of benefit dependency, and, here the task is more redemptive than mere reform, to transform them into responsible and *independent* citizens, and as a consequence to reap the benefit of a reduction in crime and anti-social behaviour.

In this chapter I will largely focus on the notion of inclusion in its economic dimension. That is, of the inclusion of a posited underclass into the market economy. This is the Anglo-Saxon model well rehearsed in the United States' numerous Welfare to Work programmes and most elaborately detailed in the interventions of the British Social Exclusion Unit. Not until the end of the chapter will I touch upon the problem of political inclusion, particularly as seen as incorporation into citizenship which is best exemplified in French and Continental European discussion of social inclusion. Often these are cast as oppositions in thought. I shall argue to the contrary.

The problem of social exclusion is a central concern within the European Union, it is a key term in the policies of New Labour and, although less frequently used in North America, parallel discourses are present in the major arenas of social policy. The discourse emerged out of the economic and social problems of late modernity, the increasing pressures on the Welfare State and the debate with neo-liberalism. It is a term which is flexible and somewhat amorphous in use, yet there are core features which separate it out from previous notions such as poverty or marginalisation. Firstly, it is multi-dimensional: social exclusion can involve economic, political, and spatial exclusion as well as lack of access to specific areas such as information, medical provision, housing, policing and security. These dimensions are seen to interrelate and reinforce each other: overall they involve exclusion in what are seen as the 'normal' areas of participation of full citizenship (Percy-Smith, 2000a). Secondly, that social exclusion is a social not an individual problem. It contrasts with earlier post-war notions which viewed marginality as a problem of isolated dysfunctional individuals. Rather, it is a collective phenomenon, hence its association with a posited underclass. Indeed it has more in common with the dangerous classes of Victorian times than the dysfunctional families of the Welfare State of the 1950s and 1960s. Thirdly, that such exclusion has global roots rather than being a restricted local problem. It is a function of the impact of the rapid changes in the labour market, the decline of manufacturing industries, the rise of a more fragmented service sector, the creation of structural unemployment in particular areas where industry has shut down. It is thus a *systemic* problem: global in its causes, local in its impact. Fourthly, the concept of social exclusion carries with it the imperative of inclusion, it is not happy with the excluded being outside of the ranks of citizenship and seeks to generate opportunities, whether by changing the motivation, capacity or available openings for the socially excluded.

This being said, there are important differences and politically divergent interpretations of social exclusion. There are three major issues: that of agency; that of the extent and distribution of exclusion; and that of the mode of exclusion, whether it is basically passive and economic or has an active social dimension. The issue of agency revolves around whether social exclusion is seen as self-imposed or structurally imposed. John Veit-Wilson (1998) makes the distinction between 'weak' and 'strong' conceptions of social exclusion. The weak version emphasises the individual's self-handicapping characteristics which inhibit their integration into society, the strong version emphasises the role of structural change in exclusion. The issue of extent and distribution centres around whether social exclusion is a minority problem within society or whether it is an endemic problem affecting the whole social order. The issue of economic or social exclusion concerns whether social exclusion is brought about simply by economic isolation from the wider society or whether there is active misrecognition and stigmatisation. That is, in Fraser's (1997) terms, whether the problem is simply one of distributive justice or whether it also involves the injustice of social denigration. This relates closely, as we shall see, to whether social exclusion is seen as a problem of economic integration, as it were, vertically up into the class structure, or whether, in more Durkheimian terms, it is more a problem of horizontal integration into society as a whole. Veit-Wilson's conception of the weak thesis focuses on structure and agency. I wish to widen this out and use the weak thesis to refer to the discourse on social exclusion which focuses on agency rather than structure, sees exclusion as a limited problem of residuum rather than an endemic problem of structure, and which sees exclusion as a passive rather than active process of rejection.

Let me finesse this further. There would seem to be three basic notions of social exclusion:

Type one That which basically blames the individuals concerned for their lack of motivation, their self-exclusion from society as a whole, although the ultimate responsibility for this is placed at the doors of the Welfare State which is seen as engendering a state of 'dependency' where, for example, even if the jobs are available out there, the underclass does not want to take them. The classic example of this position is the work of Charles Murray (1984, 1990).

Type two That which sees the problem as a sort of hydraulic failure of the system to provide jobs which leads to a situation of 'social isolation' wherein people lose, not the motive to work, but the capacity to find work because of lack of positive role models. Direct exclusion, for example because of racism, is explicitly ruled out as a primary reason for social exclusion. The classic texts here are the work of William Julius Wilson, *The Truly Disadvantaged* (1987) and *When Work Disappears* (1996).

Type three Finally there is a commentary which stresses the active rejection of the underclass by society: through the downsizing of industry, the stigmatisation of the workless, and the stereotyping of an underclass as criminogenic and drug-ridden, with images which are frequently racialised and prejudiced. The work of Foucauldians, such as Nikolas Rose (1999), fits this bill, as does *Lockdown America*, the brilliantly written neo-Marxist account of Christian Parenti (2000), and as does the prolific critical work of Zygmunt Bauman (see particularly 1998b; 2000). Unlike the two previous models, it sees social exclusion as an endemic problem within society, symptomatic of a wider social malaise and that it is the creation of a market society which is the core problem rather than neo-liberalism and the market being the cure for the disease.

In the first instance, then, there is self-exclusion, in the second the structure unintentionally excludes by leaving behind pockets of incapacitated actors. In the last instance it is the structure which actively excludes. In the first instance agency refuses opportunity, in the second opportunities are few and far between and the agent does not have the capacity to take them up, and in the third, opportunities are actively blocked. The weak thesis is the realm of the first, and the strong of the third, whereas the notion of social isolation involves the arena between them. Let me say at this juncture that, although all these elements – motivation, capacity and opportunity – are necessary part of the process of social exclusion – they are, after all, the fundamental components of the relationship between agency and structure – the weak thesis which puts almost total emphasis on inadequacies of motivation and capacity is palpably ideological in nature. To put it bluntly, it blames social exclusion on the excluded. As Bauman maintains: 'In the process of exclusion, the excluded themselves are cast as the principal, perhaps the sole, agency. Being excluded is presented as an outcome of social *suicide*, not a social *execution*' (2000, p. 25). Thus structure and agency have been reversed and what starts out as a problem *of* society becomes a problem *for* society (see Colley and Hodkinson, 2001). Furthermore, it should be noted that it is the weak thesis which has by far the widest political currency. I want to illustrate this by first describing the use of social exclusion by New Labour. I do so because the formulation and implementation of social exclusion policies by the Labour Party in Britain, elected on a landslide in 1997 and now in its third term, are by far the most elaborate and thought-through of any government. But let me first put the new policies in their historical context.

New Labour: new inclusionism

At the very heart of the British Labour Party's thinking is the notion of social inclusion. Thus we have a Welfare to Work programme, a New Deal for teenagers, lone parents and communities, and a core think tank, the Social Exclusion Unit, established by Peter Mandelson in the summer of 1997, whose task has been to tackle the problems of bringing truants back into school, single mothers to work, reduce dole queues, rescue sink estates and rehabilitate teenage mothers (see Mandelson 1997; Social Exclusion Unit 1999a, 1999b). In the area of crime control the focus on inclusionism is most marked: The Crime and Disorder Act of 1998 crucially views crime and all sorts of sub-criminal disorder (noisy neighbours, vandals, teenagers on the street late at night, etc.) as the very antithesis of community and their reduction as a central aspect of the process of inclusion. Curfews are, therefore, to be set by local authorities to control local youth, 'hotspots' of crime are to be identified, focused upon and eliminated, crime audits set up across the country by local authorities and backed by an intricate system of performance indicators (see Hough and Tilley, 1998).

The inclusionary project of New Labour represents a response to the new and difficult social terrain of the late twentieth century. It directly acknowledges the exclusionary problems on the level of the market and community: the rise of structural unemployment, the decay of community, the breakdown of family, the fears of crime and the intrusions of disorder. Yet its attempts to counteract the emergence of an exclusive society are, ironically for a party committed to modernisation, surprisingly nostalgic. Father (and mother) is at work, the children are at school, the truant officers scour the streets, the teenage curfew begins at dark, the nuclear family is shored up (the positive virtues of marriage are introduced to the national curriculum), the criminal effectively punished and disorderly individuals curbed and neighbourhoods tidied up. Every now and then the images of the old Labour Party, the paternalistic world post-1945 of Herbert Morrison, Clement Attlee and Sir Stafford Cripps seems to peep through the veneer yet the problems are distinctly late modern and the emergence of a politics of nostalgia, or backward looking discourse, at the end of the twentieth century is perfectly understandable in terms of the new times that we find ourselves in. A comparison with the neo-liberal responses of the Conservative Administrations which preceded New Labour underscores this, for here we have a contrasting response to the same newly emerged problems. For, at risk of exaggeration, if New Labour attempts to roll back the exclusive society, neo-liberalism accedes to or even encourages it. Famous of all the pronouncements – a *frisson noir* to the ears of all progressive commentators the world over – was Thatcher's 'there is no such thing as society, only individuals and their families'. The atomisation of society into a series of exclusive units was in this axiom elevated to an accurate depiction of reality and, by implication, the inclusive society portrayed as an illusion, an interference in the market relations between free-standing individuals. And the divisions between people are augmented by the divisions between classes. The economic divisions within society were actively widened during the Conservative administrations, partly by tax-benefit policies, so that between 1979 and 1994/5, the poorest 10% had a cut of 8% on real income whereas the top 10% had an increase of 42% (Lister, 1998). Unemployment soared casting whole neighbourhoods into a limbo of poverty and worklessness while the recorded crime rate more than doubled between 1979 and 1991. In one year alone, 1991, the increase in recorded crime was one and a quarter times that of all the total rate in 1950. The response to this far from inclusion was, if anything, a defensive exclusion. The central ethos, for example, of the Home Office moved from notions of rehabilitation to that of 'situational crime prevention'. Seeking to understand the causes of crime and the motivation of the offender was deemed a nonsensical task: almost

SOCIAL INCLUSION AND REDEMPTION

anyone would commit crime if the opportunities arose. What was necessary was to prevent crime, by interposing locks and bolts, physical barriers and closer surveillance to cut down the opportunities for offending (Clarke, 1980; Young, 1994). The Home Office produced booklets on crime prevention strongly reminiscent of the civil defence booklets of two decades earlier: a middle class, detached house where arrows marked possible weaknesses, and points of entry, targets to be hardened, doors and windows to be made safe: the enemy was without and the family home a place of safety and tranquillity (see Radford and Stanko, 1991).

Thatcher's neo-liberalism, then, involved a deregulation of industry, a further commodification of labour, the advocacy of self-sufficiency and individualism, the emergence of structural unemployment, the notion of defence against crime rather than the rehabilitation of the offender. All in all, a programme which went with the tide of exclusion and actually egged it on. But New Labour has reacted, on one level, in the opposite direction. It is intent on reversing the trend, and of achieving an inclusive society; it engages in an almost postmodern bricollaging of the past in order to depict its ideal, yet the past is somehow just around the corner and the means to get there a mere change of management or effort of will.

Yet the move from neo-liberalism to New Labour is not as revolutionary as might seem, for paradoxically the core mechanism which is identified as creating the problem was shared by both neo-liberals and New Labour: that is the notion of an underclass of weak and dysfunctional families immersed in a dependency culture generated by an over generous Welfare State.

The Welfare State: not the solution but the problem

As noted in the last chapter, in the immediate post-war period the Welfare State was seen as being the major instrument of social inclusion. It was the means of achieving, in T. H. Marshall's famous formulation (1950), full citizenship. That is not only legal and political rights but the right to sufficient income to avoid poverty and to provide decent housing, health care and education. In short, the basic needs by which active citizenship and engagement in society would be possible. Further, it was explicitly recognized that the market was unable to provide the basics for very many citizens. That is, the Welfare State was a key corrective to the defects of a market economy and the necessary basis of an inclusive society? (See J. Young, 1999, Chapter One). The neo-liberal ascendancy of the Reagan and Thatcher years simply reversed this argument. Drawing on the work of writers such as Charles Murray (1984) and Lawrence Mead (1986) they vigorously pursued policies which viewed the Welfare State as the problem and the Market as the solution. That is, far from the Welfare State ameliorating the problems of a maket society, it carried the diseases of 'welfarism' and depedency. Thus, it undermined the inclusionary nature of the marketplace in jobs and created both an economic and psychological propensity to withdraw from full citizenship. As we have seen, Clinton's Democrats in the United States adopted these ideas and New Labour while in the political wilderness of the Thatcher years looked enviously on their American cousins' success, particularly in the fields of welfare reform and law and order politics, both areas which were seen as a political liability for 'Old Labour'.

The will to win

Tony Blair's first speech after coming to power in a landslide victory in 1997 was in the Aylesbury Estate in South London (Southwark, 2 June), selected for its poverty and exclusion from the mainstream of British society. Let us imagine for an instant Blair at his moment of electoral triumph, standing in this wretched estate and delivering a lengthy speech which promised the tenants deliverance from social exclusion. At the very beginning of the speech he exhorts them in an almost Nietzchean fashion to bring back the 'will to win'. For it is not poverty alone which is the problem, but 'fatalism', 'the dead weight of low expectations', from the outset it is conceived as a problem of agency as much as structure, of will as much as predicament. He then goes on to outline, in a most prescient way, all the major themes of New Labour's project which would be constantly revisited in the coming years.[1]

Tony Blair's speech was to incorporate the *leitmotif* of New Labour – a core theme which has resonated throughout its first three terms of office. He talked of the decline of old industries, the shift in the economy which left some behind and created a new class, 'a workless class': these were the people who were either forgotten by society or, as by the previous (Conservative) government, became the object of blame. There would, he insisted, be 'no forgotten people' under New Labour and that the greatest challenge for government was 'to bring this new workless class back into society and into useful work'. On the 8 December 1997 the Social Exclusion Unit (SEU) was set up by Peter Mandelson with a strategic relationship to all government departments. It is located in the Cabinet Office 'putting it at the heart of government'. Since that time it has characteristically focused on a wide range of issues, for example, deprived neighbourhoods, unemployment, drug use, teenage pregnancy, truancy, school exclusion, and reintegration of ex-offenders into society.

It is important to stress the underlying dimensions of this concept of social exclusion. Firstly, it sees it as a global problem of social and economic change which has impacted considerably on Britain. As Blair later put it,

SOCIAL INCLUSION AND REDEMPTION

We came into office determined to tackle a deep social crisis. We had a poor record in this country in adapting to social and economic change. The result was sharp income inequality, a third of children growing up in poverty, a host of social problems such as homelessness and drug abuse, and divisions in society typified by deprived neighbour-hoods that had become no go areas for some and no exit zones for others. All of us bore the cost of social breakdown – directly, or through the costs to society and public finances. And we were never going to have a successful economy while we continued to waste the talents of so many. (2001, p. 1)

This text illustrates both the centrality of social exclusion to his thinking, but also that its amelioration is seen as the radical project of New Labour: for exclusion is the way in which poverty and inequality is seen to config-ure in these new times. Note also that the problem is seen as one that impacts not only on the excluded, but also on the included in terms of taxes, economic inefficiency and incivilities.

Secondly, social exclusion is seen as a series of linked problems. It is a 'shorthand term for what can happen when people or areas suffer from a combination of linked problems such as unemployment, poor skills, low incomes, poor housing, high crime, bad health and family breakdown' (Social Exclusion Unit, 2001, p. 1.1). Further, 'only when these links are properly understood will policies really be effective' (ibid., p. 3).

Thirdly, corresponding to this across-the-board, linked, nature of the problem is the necessity of a response which is 'joined up'. The Social Exclusion Unit works across departments, it demands multi-agency inter-vention, it was, at that time, overseen by the Deputy Prime Minister, John Prescott, whose role is co-ordinating cross-departmental issues. As he put it at an address to the Fabian Society, 'Departments cannot ignore social exclusion any more – it is part of their everyday work. It is the day-to-day business of every Secretary of State' (2002).

Fourthly, social exclusion is seen in the context of rights and responsibil-ities. This 'makes Government help available but requires a contribution from the individual and the community' (Social Exclusion Unit, 2001, p. 3). Benefits can be withdrawn if job opportunities are not taken up, educational maintenance depends on regular attendance, neighbourhood funding depends on community involvement. And here we have the notion of The Third Way: neither to the left nor to the right, neither a philosophy which stresses rights nor responsibilities, but both as part of a social contract (see Corrigan et al., 1988).

Lastly, crime and incivilities are seen as a key reason for tackling social exclusion. The SEU quite clearly posits that 'social exclusion is a key driver' (2001, p. 2.3) in the genesis of crime, and indeed that crime and fear of crime are part of the complex of problems that indicate social exclusion.

To explain the UK's high level of social exclusion the SEU points to two sets of factors: economic and social changes, and weaknesses in Government policies. On the economic level the emphasis is on globalisation – on the rapid change in industry, higher competition, the decline of manufacturing and rise of knowledge-based industries: in short, the demands for a flexible labour force and the inequality that results from some being left behind. At the same time, on a social level, there have been changes in the wider society which weakened or removed the support systems that helped people to cope in the past. These involve the breakdown of the family and the community.

Finally, it is acknowledged that Government policies – by this the SEU presumably refers particularly to previous Conservative administrations – have not coped well in helping people come to terms with these changes. They list a series of managerial problems (insufficient emphasis on partnership, on sustained change rather than short-term programmes, top-down initiatives, etc.) but also a 'passive welfare state that sometimes trapped people on benefits rather than enabling them to help themselves' (2001, 3.7).

What problems constitute social exclusion?

Social exclusion is seen as a series of problems which are 'linked and mutually reinforcing [which] can combine to create a complex and fast-moving vicious circle' (Social Exclusion Unit, 2001, 1.4). The list of problems is extensive and almost eclectic: drug use, educational under-achievement, truancy, child poverty, rough sleepers, ill health, inadequate housing, alcohol dependency, unemployment, poor access to services and to information sources, having a criminal record, sink estates, teenage pregnancy and, of course, crime and fear of crime. In order to illustrate this approach I will focus on the latter two – crime and teenage pregnancy – which, as we shall see, are central concerns of the SEU.

Globalisation, insecurity and crime

Let us first note that the SEU clearly recognises the global background to economic and social problems. The cause of crime is not located in the individual *per se*, however such individuals may be harmed by the wider social factors. It is thus distinctly different from the notion of crime being a product of isolated dysfunctional individuals (as with 'Old' Labour's positivistic notions of crime and delinquency) or of opportunistic, voluntaristic individuals (as with the neo-liberalism of Margaret Thatcher, with its classicist ideas of criminal motivation). The approach thus distances itself from the analytical individualism of the past. Further, it locates these global processes in the production of social and economic inequality. Thus, if we are looking for the causes of crime, we can find them in the inequalities engendered by globalisation. The concept of social exclusion is, in this sense, an advance. Further, it sets the local in the context of the global; just as it does not presume criminal behaviour stems from the characteristics of an individual, it does not locate the criminogenic within the delineated limits of a geographical area. Its emphasis on the role of flexible labour markets, global competition and the decline of manufacturing industry begins, at least, to embrace the notion of the transition to late modernity as the key to understanding the transformation and problems of contemporary society. Indeed, the Scottish Social Exclusion Network, in its report *Three Nations: Social Exclusion in Scotland* (Scottish Council Foundation, 1998), adopted the categories 'Excluded Scotland', 'Insecure Scotland' and 'Settled Scotland', which echo the well-known '30:30:40' divisions of the liberal commentator Will Hutton (1995).

The linked nature of crime as a problem and the response to it

Crime is not seen as a separate problem, but as part of a matrix of problems and the result of interrelated causes. There is not a separate criminology nor a hermetic aetiology, but the various manifestations of social exclusion are linked together – and their causes reside at the level of the family, the community, and the economy. Further, interventions must occur on all these levels and be part of a linked and co-ordinated response; indeed this is the *raison d'être* of the Social Exclusion Unit itself. If one looks across the array of interventions which the SEU suggests, it would not look out of place in the repertoire of interventions suggested by radical criminology. Indeed, there is very little here with which one would not find resonance in, say, Elliott Currie's *Crime and Punishment in America* (1998).

Crime, then, is seen as both a product of social exclusion and a cause of social exclusion. All interlinking factors outlined above are seen to lead to crime just as crime creates disorder and fear, and thus promoting social exclusion in its own right.

Many's the slip 'twixt cup and lip: New Labour's obsessional neurosis

All of this so far would seem promising. As noted by John Pitts, New Labour might well claim 'that its deliberations on crime and justice have paid due attention to "background" socio-structural factors and that it is precisely these factors that its social exclusion strategy is designed to address. Indeed, in *Bringing Britain Together* (Social Exclusion Unit, 1999a) ... there is a clear acknowledgement of the structural origins and the interrelatedness of crime, poverty and inequality.' (Pitts, 2001, p. 136). Yet, as Pitts notes, the discussion of structure ends up being seen as a problem of lack of joined-up administration: 'Suddenly the problem is reduced from one of social structure to one of social administration. Like the victim of an obsessional neurosis, incapacitated in the face of real problems they revert to an obsessive preoccupation with the detail of that which they can control.' (Pitts, 2001, p. 136).

The structural causes of crime are clearly delineated, but that is as far as it goes; rather than these being located in the deep structures of society, and its inevitable divisions of class, the concept of social exclusion carries with it the notion that the problem is that of inadequate management of society. The solution becomes managerial rather than transformative. Thus, a constant theme is that Britain performs less well than its European equivalents. Thus, 'In the mid-1990s, this country was distinguished from its EU competitors by high levels of social exclusion' (Social Exclusion Unit, 2001, p. 1). To demonstrate this, a series of tables are presented by the SEU showing that the United Kingdom has the worst record in terms of percentage of children living under the poverty line, children living in households without an adult in employment, and levels of adult illiteracy, teenage births, drug use, crimes, etc. By this simple presentation tactic the SEU suggests that good practice *already exists*, out there in Europe, and all we have to do is replicate it.

Furthermore, the crime problem rendered managerial is given a precise social and spatial focus within the posited underclass. Here all the problems of othering, of using the binary lens of late modernity, is writ large. The SEU's 2001 publication, *Preventing Social Exclusion*, points to the fact that 'there is no agreed way of measuring overall social exclusion' (2001, p. 1.5), but gives a range of figures from 'a fraction of one per cent' who suffer the most extreme forms of multiple deprivation to 'as many as a third or more [who] are in some way at risk' (ibid.). The authors are, however, much more precise as to the numbers with regard to crime, noting that 'about ten percent of all active criminals may be responsible for half of all crime: about 100,000 individuals. Of this 10%, half are under 21 and nearly two-thirds are hard drug users' (2001, p. 5.71).

It is obvious also that the government adopted both intensive inclusionary and exclusionary strategies towards crime. The two seemingly contradictory processes – the source of the frisson in Tony Blair's 'tough on crime, tough on the causes of crime' couplet – make sense in terms of the position of crime in the discourse. Crime is a product of exclusion; it must, therefore, be tackled at a fundamental level by policies of inclusion which will, in time, bring down crime rates. But crime *in the here and now* disintegrates

SOCIAL INCLUSION AND REDEMPTION

communities, it undermines the forces of inclusion; it must therefore be combated strongly where it arises. Let us summarise at this point the posited relationship between social exclusion and crime:

1 Although crime is widespread, a small number of offenders commit a large proportion of these offences.
2 These offenders are clustered within a socially excluded underclass.
3 The social disorganisation and drug use endemic in these areas permit and sustain crime.
4 The cause of social exclusion lies in lack of motivation and capability, itself a product of a dependency culture.
5 Such disorganised communities produce and perpetuate inadequate families, particularly those with a high proportion of single mothers, often in their teenage years.
6 Such inadequate families are criminogenic, reproducing disorganisation over generations and perpetuating delinquency.
7 The policy solution is inclusionary, back-to-work programmes to tackle the 'causes', backed up with a forceful criminal justice system to deal with the problems of the present.

The suggestion that one half of all the crime in England and Wales is committed by a relatively small number of what John Dilulio (1995) notoriously termed 'super-predators' clearly illustrates this. Furthermore, it severely stretches credibility to believe that this problem is located in the childcare practices of single mothers. As Jayne Mooney puts it, the '5 million crimes reported to the police every year in England and Wales, with an estimated 10 million or more unreported, cannot be blamed on the fraction of single mothers who are on state benefits and have adolescent sons' (2003, p. 107).

The analysis of crime, therefore, emphasises agency over structure, and management and the administration of life's difficulties over the structural inequalities which generate those difficulties. No more is such an approach better illustrated than in my second example: teenage pregnancy.

The moral panic over teenage pregnancy

Teenage Pregnancy (Social Exclusion Unit, 1999b) is a remarkable document. It displays in full the anxieties, the stereotypes and the tensions which permeate the discourse around social exclusion. It touches, in particular, the nerve surrounding fears with regard to teenage sexuality. It goes further than any of the other documents in prioritising agency over structure. Note that it was one of the first reports produced by the Social Exclusion Unit: thus reflecting Blair's priorities in his 'Will to Win' speech, where he highlighted that the problem of young men was the loss of jobs in manufacturing whereas for 'part of a generation of young women, early pregnancies and the absence of a reliable father almost guarantee a life of poverty'. It is noteworthy for its construction of a major social problem out of a situation which was on the whole unproblematic, and doing so by the evocation of medical and epidemiological language, phrasing human decision-making in the language of risk, vulnerability and pathology.

It set off an extraordinary flurry of policy initiatives including the setting up of a national 'teenage pregnancy strategy', the creation of a network of 'teenage pregnancy coordinators' across the country (an irony of title obviously missed by the policy-makers, a situation only, as we have seen, surpassed by the advertisements for 'anti-social behaviour coordinators', a little later) and, lastly, in line with New Labour's obsession with performance indicators, a schedule of targets to complete (teenage conceptions down by 50% by 2010). It galvanised the energies of the great and the good. Witness the Queen Mary and Westfield College Public Policy Seminar on 'Effectively Tackling Teenage Pregnancy' on 18 November 1999 which started off its blurb with '12 year old pregnant girls in Rotherham', and promised attendance of 'the Minister and key players' all for £265 per person plus tax, luncheon thrown in, at the Royal Over-Seas League, in St. James's, London, 'just behind the Ritz Hotel'.

Let us look at the problem as viewed through the lens of the Social Exclusion Unit. Teenage pregnancy is seen as a frequent 'cause and consequence of social exclusion' (Social Exclusion Unit, 1999b, p. 17). It results in poverty, low birth weight, ill health of child and mother, high infant mortality and relationship breakdown. It is a deviance which leads to further deviance: one effect is to have daughters who themselves are more likely to be teenage mothers. And of course, the discourse has close affinity to that which links single mothers to adolescents who supposedly contribute considerably to the crime rate: indeed the document explicitly notes how delinquent teenagers are more likely to be teenage parents. Lastly, there is the cost: 'The United Kingdom cannot afford high rates of teenage conception and parenthood at the end of the 20th century.' (ibid., p. 7). All of this discussion is cast, as I have noted, in the language of epidemiology and pathology, of risk rates and unfortunate consequences. The tone of this approach to teenage pregnancy is set at the onset by the first sentence in Tony Blair's introduction: 'Britain has the worst record of teenage pregnancy in Europe. It is not a record in which we can take any pride' (1999, p. 4).

What are the problems with this approach?

1 *Prevalence and constancy*   Years ago, when discussing the mass media and formation of moral panics, I noted how the 'atypical, is presented in a stereotypical fashion and then posited against the overtypical' (Young, 1971). The overtypical is the presumption of the normal, it is the stereotype of the normal just as the atypical forms the stereotype of the deviant. Thus

we have a notion of the *normal* age of pregnancy, the *normal* mother having her first child at this age which is, of course, identified with the *normal* and most propitious timing, medically, socially and psychologically. This is seen as obvious and somewhat 'natural' and eternal. Against this we have the atypical where, as in any moral panic, extreme instances are presented as *increasingly* the norm. Let us look at what the figures actually tell us.

First of all one has to get the size of the phenomenon in proportion. Only 7% of all births in the United Kingdom are to teenagers, the vast majority of these are to 18 and 19-year-old women; 0.5% are under 16, and less than 0.1% under 14. The 12-year-old girl in Rotherham (a poor city in the North of England) who figured greatly in the British tabloid press and prompted the blurb introducing the Queen Mary's College Conference, is a rarity. In fact, not only is the 12-year-old mother extremely atypical, the age of teenage childbearing in the United Kingdom has not changed to any great degree over the period. Thus, from 1981 to 2001, the rate of live births per 100,000 women under 20 had a very slight deviance of 0.01%. It was para-doxically stable during the period of anxiety about teenage pregnancy, with a very slight bump in the early 1990s which soon rectified itself.

The atypical is in fact not changing, but wait a minute, the typical, the so-called 'normal' is! For the overall trend has been for later and later child-birth. Thus the decline in births to those in their twenties is over 30% between 1981 and 2001, whereas the significant rise is those over thirty: 27% of those in the 30–34 age range, and an extraordinary 84% rise for those in the 35–39 range. Indeed, by 2003 the rate of birth in the older range had doubled (*Social Trends*, 2005).

Now this is a strange thing. Usually in social science one is concerned first of all to explain change and then turn to phenomena which are stable. But in this instance it is the other way round. We have cast with causal suspi-cion that which is unchanged and ignored that which is rapidly changing.

What can this be about? Well, of course, all the most obvious things which we have discussed spring to mind. Middle-class women entering the labour market are postponing the age of their first child birth in order to not threaten their careers. And this is part and parcel of the trend towards the dual income family and its necessity to maintain middle-class living standards. Herbert Gans points his finger directly at the problem when he writes:

today's poor teenagers are in the unfortunate position of becoming mothers when America's culturally dominant female role models – upper-middle-class professional women – postpone motherhood as long as possible in order to put their careers on a secure footing. Thus what may be rational behavior for poor young women is decidedly irrational according to cultural norms these days. Teenage motherhood does not thereby become desirable, but once more, the fundamental problem is the poverty that helps to make it happen. (1995, p. 72)

Thus middle-class behaviour is seen as normal (however much it has changed) while the behaviour of the poor becomes, from that stance, pathological (however much it is unchanged).

2 *International comparisons*   Such a misconception of pathology is underscored in *Teenage Pregnancy* by making international comparisons with other European countries which indicate that the British rate comes out highest. What is relatively ignored in comparison is the United States (where the rate is much higher), New Zealand, and Canada (where the rate is somewhat higher) and Australia (where the Australian rate is a little higher). Let us pause for a moment to consider that many of the European countries have a more traditional family structure with, in some instances, a large Roman Catholic population, factors which may greatly contribute to the differential rates, but which are ignored by this polemic of comparison where the countries chosen to make comparison all score 'better' than the United Kingdom. And to this, let us add, the overriding assumption that those countries with the lowest rates are indeed somehow 'better' in their standards of teenage sexual behaviour and education. The assumption of pathology is thus underscored by this artifice of comparison.

3 *The poverty tautology*   Such a depiction of pathology necessitates showing a series of negative consequences. As teenage pregnancy is supposedly a deviation from the healthy norm, its consequences are seen as ill health, higher infant mortality, slower infant development and, in terms of worldly success, poverty, low educational achievement and, perhaps worst of all, the likelihood of having children who are likely to become teenage mothers! (the 'disease' transmits itself intergenerationally).

The problem here is obviously that of spurious causality, as poor women are more likely to experience medical problems, have low educational achievement, eventual income, etc. and to give birth as teenagers, then a correlation is being confused as a causation. As it is, if class factors are factored in, whether a young woman from a poor background is a teenage mother makes very little difference to the outcome in terms of, for example, educational achievement, qualifications, employment or pay at the age of 30 (Ermisch and Prevalin, 2003). The major negative effect is that she is more likely to partner men who are unemployed, and this will have an effect on the family income. Similar findings have been made in terms of perinatal mortality, revolving around the conundrum that, in the general population, teenage pregnancies show an elevated rate of mortality than those of women in their 20s, whereas university hospital studies (American and Danish) show that teenage pregnancies have a *lower* rate than any other age groups. The researchers (Mednick et al., 1979) found that the reason for this was the high quality of medical care in the university hospitals. Teenage mothers coming disproportionally from low in the class structure had less access to such facilities and, therefore, had higher rates of perinatal mortality than in the general population. Thus, if medical treatment were equally available, teenage mothers in general would have the lowest rate of mortality. Furthermore, it should be pointed out that for poor women the safest time *for them* to have children is when they are younger and physically more resilient.

All of this points to the situation being socially structured, it is not inevitable; social intervention by providing medical and educational opportunities for teenage mothers, good childcare, and flexibility of education and work could ameliorate any negative consequences. Of course, the very fact that society becomes chary of giving welfare payments to the single, unmarried mother stacks the cards against her moving out of poverty. That is, the very belief in the dangers of welfare dependency among the underclass serves to perpetuate an underclass. Let me add, as an aside, one of the major problems that Western European countries have in terms of their social structure is an aging population which is a product of low fertility rates. Part of this problem can be solved by immigration, for immigration is not a problem but a solution – and the cultural diversity which this results in is a great bonus to the quality of life in the great cities of late modernity. A further major contribution would be pro-natal policies which encouraged childbirth and heightened fertility rates, not ones which regard early childbirth and likewise large families as something of a personal failure, or even a pathology.

There is a fundamental paradox here. Biologically there can be little doubt that early childbirth is safer and, in terms of our evolutionary history, more natural, while late childbirth is fraught with medical difficulties. Yet we have socially constructed a situation which in terms of social approval inverts what is historically and biologically most natural. As Alison Perry put it, in a midwifery journal:

Teenage pregnancy itself is perceived by our society as a deviation from normal. It has been placed alongside drug abuse and crime on Government initiative agenda. This overt pathologisation reinforces a culture of disapproval of teenage pregnancy; having babies when you are young is seen as a bad thing. It is ironic that having babies during the time that doctors insist is the optimal time physiologically ... no longer coincides with society's more modern priorities and expectations. (2002, p. 2)

4 *Risk factors*   Once cast as a pathology, teenage pregnancy is seen in an epidemiological light, it is a danger engendered by risk. Cause then becomes risk, effect becomes danger. The risk factors which the report enumerates are a very strange collection of categories:

The effect of multiple risk factors can be quantified in longitudinal surveys. Analysis of the 1958 United Kingdom birth cohort found that women with all the following characteristics had a 56 per cent chance of becoming a teenage mother, compared with a 3 per cent chance for those with none of them:

A emotional problems at 7 or 16;
B mother was a teenage mother;
C families who experienced financial adversity when they were 7 or 16;
D a preference for being a young mother;
E a low educational attainment at 16.

(Social Exclusion Unit, 1999b, p. 18; source of study: K Kiernan, 1995)

It is evident that two of the factors, experience of financial adversity (C), and low educational attainment (E) are strongly associated with being lower working class. Now there are all sorts of reasons why poor people should wish to have children earlier. One is there is often a considerable backup of kin, grandmothers and mothers in particular, who will provide some child-care support, particularly as they are likely to be younger having had their own children earlier. Another is that definitions of youth vary by class and ethnicity and, as Herbert Gans points out, 18 or 19 years old is 'already young adulthood in the chronological world of the poor' (1995, p. 3). It is almost certainly the most healthy time to have children if you are living in poverty. For later child birth is considerably riskier the poorer you are. And last, but not least, the alternatives of humdrum and tedious work do not compete well with the pleasures of motherhood. Early parenthood and larger families are valued more. Hence the rather unsurprising factor (B), that the woman's mother was a teenage mother. As for one of the most potent predictors: wanting to be a teenage mother (D), the mind boggles as to the scientificity of such studies. That the major risk factor of doing an action is wanting to do it takes obviousness to new heights. Presumably further research studies will show that the major factors causing people to smoke marijuana will be a desire to do so, and drinking light ale liking it!

But there is a serious side to this casting of the debate in terms of risks. The delay in childbirth among the middle classes is fraught with medical risks: miscarriage, infertility or multiple fertility because of drug treatment, hopes risen, hopes dashed. Here the problem is seen not of choice but of the lack of it, here the setting is seen as the *chances* of giving birth not the *risks* of being pregnant. Thus a strange reversal of reality has occurred where that which is a real social problem is occluded whereas that which is innocuous is problematised.

5   *Then why do they do it?*   Given that teenage pregnancy is cast in the language of pathology there obviously arises the question of why any young

woman would want to get pregnant. This devolves into the question of why teenagers have sex. The list of reasons for sexual intercourse uncovered by survey and interview is of interest in its startling omissions:

young people, parents and those working with young people give a variety of reasons for starting sex, including:

- curiosity;
- opportunity;
- real or imagined peer pressure;
- the wish not to be left behind;
- being in a relationship;
- fear of losing boy or girlfriend;
- the need to feel loved and the belief that sex equals love;
- media influences that glamorise sex; and
- alcohol.

(Social Exclusion Unit, 1999b, p. 45)

Look at the above list: what is missing is desire! A feeling, I daresay, which any-one who has been a teenager has experienced. *Teenage Pregnancy* is thus a strange document, it takes desire out of sex and humanity out of having a baby. It casts the poor in the role of irrationality and places the middle class fair and squarely on the path of reality. Social inclusion becomes, therefore, the process of bringing the actor into the world of reason. It does not suggest changing the structure to ameliorate the problems of poverty, but changing the actor so she can act 'rationally' like her middle class counterparts.

Rationality and the middle classes

Let us examine for the moment this notion that rationality can be defined as the behaviour of middle-class women and irrationality the activities of the lower orders. As I have noted, even in terms of income, infant mortality, job satisfaction etc, that is rationality by middle-class standards, there is no blatant irrationality here. But we can go a little further than this, for the assumption behind such thinking is that the maximisation of income and career are the necessary prerequisites (or perhaps even preferences) to the process of having children and setting up a family, together presumably with the successful middle-class marriage. Behind this there is an assumption of rational choice theory where both means and ends are seen as somehow obvious. But are they? Why shouldn't having children be a priority that eas-ily overrides career? Why is the nuclear marriage a necessary means? What makes one immediately suspicious is that the norms and values of middle-class women have changed in quite a short time (they privileged childbear-ing over career not so long ago) and they might change again, who knows?

Further, even within the stratum of middle-class women there are many differences of opinions, a multitude of doubts, even different lifestyles and rationalities. Just read the magazines, listen to the chat shows.

The errors of inclusion

Let us now return to looking at the larger picture. First of all let us look at an overview of New Labour's policies in Social Exclusion.

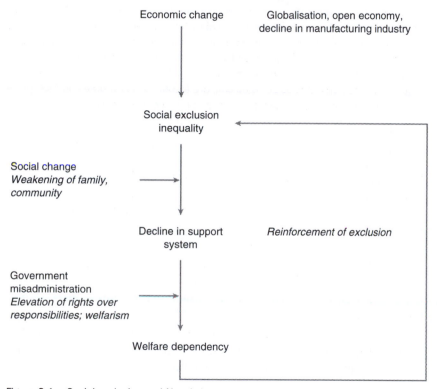

Figure 6.1   Social exclusion and New Labour

Blaming the actor

What is interesting is that this discourse on social exclusion takes the stronger structural version of liberals such as William Julius Wilson (1987) and bolts on to it the right-wing notions of exclusion of writers such as Charles Murray (1984) and Lawrence Mead (1992, see Pitts, 2003). Thus it fuses together Type One and Type Two models of social exclusion: it does not even countenance the radical Type Three. Furthermore, in terms of actual policies in the two areas examined: crime of extremes and teenage pregnancy, it quickly proceeds to discard the more liberal Type Two interpretation and focuses on Type One.

The false binary of exclusion

Let us recapitulate the problems of a binary division:

- *Homogeneity* It suggests a homogenous group of people in the category of excluded, whereas in fact the socially excluded incorporate the young, the old, the temporarily poor, etc. (see Gans, 1995).
- *Social immobility* The presumption of a fairly static underclass is misleading. There is, in fact, a great deal of social mobility across narrow categories, although substantial social mobility is limited (see Hills et al., 2002).
- *Fixed locality and separate morality* The concept harbours the notion of a group of people outcast, spatially cut off from the rest of society, with perhaps different values and motivations. In fact, no such spatial segregation occurs (physical mobility in and out of the ghetto, for example, is frequent) and values are shared with the wider society.
- *Focus of problems* The notion of a socially excluded underclass gives the false notion that the majority of social problems are located in these areas. In fact, problems exist across the city, the majority outside of the poorest areas.

Losing class

Thus the opposition of, say, 20%, the 'excluded', to a wider society of 'included' massively underestimates the economic and social problems of those in the wider society. It suggests that the included do not suffer the problems of class – indeed that if they make the transition from the zones of exclusion to the inclusive world of mainstream society, the rest of their problems would vanish. Most importantly, this notion of social exclusion carries with it the implication that the problem is a Durkheimian one of a failure of integration, rather than a socialist one, which would emphasise problems of class. That is, globalisation is seen as having resulted in problems of social cohesion – those left behind by change – rather than as an exacerbation of existing class divisions (Levitas, 1996). Indeed, John Andersen argues that this notion of social exclusion involves a major conceptual transformation:

Theoretically, the notion of social exclusion points to a shift in the conceptualization of poverty from extreme class inequality and lack of resources in the Townsend tradition … to a broader insider-outsider *problematique* – that is, a change of focus in the poverty and inequality discourse from a vertical to a horizontal perspective. The shift of focus can to some extent also be described as a shift from Marxist and Weberian tradition of class and status analysis to a Durkheimian 'anomie-integration' discourse. (1999, p. 129)

From RED to SID

Ruth Levitas (1996) notes how the concept of social exclusion became popular after the publication of Peter Townsend's book *Poverty in the United*

Kingdom (1979). At that time it was used in tandem with the notion of relative poverty where people's *relative* (rather than absolute) impoverishment does not allow them to take part in the normal social and political activities associated with citizenship. Here is, of course, a loud resonance with the work of T.H. Marshall and the argument that without greater economic equality, full citizenship cannot be achieved. But the present discourse is, according to Levitas, distinctly different:

> The original popularity of this term does therefore derive, like the 'outcast poverty' version of the 'underclass', from a concern with inequality, even if it always contained a tendency to present an overly homogeneous view of the situation of those included in society. But the way it is currently being used actually obscures the questions of material inequality it was originally intended to illuminate: it has been co-opted into a different discourse, with different purposes and different effects. It is a discourse unable to address the question of unpaid work in society (work done principally by women), or of low-paid work, and completely erases from view the inequality between those owning the bulk of productive property and the working population, as well as obscuring the inequalities among workers. It presents 'society' as experiencing a rising standard of living by defining those who have not done so, who have become poorer, as 'excluded from' society, as 'outside' it.' (1996, p. 7)

Levitas (1997) famously describes this transition as from a 'Redistributive, Egalitarian Discourse' (RED) to a 'Social Integrationist Discourse' SID).

It cannot be overstressed that to include people into a market system which allocates them to work which is menial, mindless and uncertain, without granting the possibilities of substantial mobility, is not social inclusion but merely a recasting of the lines of social exclusion within the market economy. As Loic Wacquant puts it:

> A 'reinvigorated escalator' that would lift a select subgroup of low-wage workers into more stable and better-paid position on grounds of 'merit' does nothing to alter the flawed design of a social edifice in which the vast distances between floors condemns the residents of its lower tier to a life of material misery and social indignity by leaving them and their families at the permanent mercy of the whim of unreliable employers, the vagaries of business cycles, and the hazards of the life course. Facilitating mobility up the occupational ladder does nothing to remedy the fact that the minimum wage puts a full-time, year-round employee well below the official poverty line; ... In short, the 'employment problems of urban ghettos' are due not to a penury but to a surfeit of slave-like jobs. They pertain not to the hoary and ideologically consensual issue of *opportunity* but to the broader, and politically as well as intellectually more troublesome, question of the new *inequality* spawned by an 'apartheid economy' in which the state has allowed the bottom rungs of the workforce to collapse by both omission and

commission. The remedy for precipitous inequality redoubled by the foundering of labor is not – and has never been – to 'open up the opportunity structure'; it is to *alter that very structure* so as to raise its lower tier and thwart the spread of work insecurity and 'flexibility' that now threatens not only the livelihood of the working class as a whole but growing segments of the middle class as well. (2002, p. 1519)

Or, as Elliott Currie simply puts it:

If the reduction of extreme poverty is our goal, what most needs reforming is the labor market itself, and particularly the spread of low-wage, unstable work. We will not sever the links between poverty and crime by increasing the number of poorly paid, stressful jobs and forcing low-income parents to take them. If anything, the research tells us that diminishing the time available to parents to nurture and supervise children could make the crime problem worse, not better. A far more rational approach is to boost both the rewards and the stability of work, in order to strengthen families and stabilize communities. (1998, p. 149)

Furthermore it is necessary to ask the fundamental question as to whether such a change in opportunity structure is, indeed, wanted; whether actual change is seen by many as desirable. Let us put the problem as clearly as possible. The notion of the inclusion of the socially excluded through the provision of education and job training is dependent on the requirements of the labour market. Often, as has been frequently pointed out, there are no such jobs, particularly in certain areas, to provide such opportunities. But the problem is more severe than this; it goes beyond the binary jobs/no jobs. For there is, as I have argued, a considerable labour market in the lower part of the service sector which has been largely unacknowledged and invisible. The wages here are low, they are often below poverty level and the tedium and length of hours are considerable. The dragooning of people into these jobs is not perceived as being inclusion but *ipso facto* exclusion. They are jobs that no one else wants to do, at the wages no one else would work for, they are the support roles for those in jobs that are valued, that enable people to feel included, to be part of society. The simple fact is that many people in the more well off part of the class structure want to get their lives serviced cheaply. They want to pay these workers low wages: *they want the poor to be poor*. An acknowledgement of the actual nature of the labour market is rare. The very invisibility of these jobs makes it all the more possible to imagine that a whole class of people can be somehow upwardly mobile, whereas to achieve this would necessitate a fundamental change in the class structure. However, every now and then commentators will come out with the unpalatable truth. Elliott Liebow in the final chapter of *Tally's Corner* (2003 [1997]) cites this interesting remark of Walter Miller:

The fundamental questions are: How large a low-skilled laboring force does our society require? ... From what sources are we to get the incumbents of these jobs, and where are they to receive the socialization and training needed to execute them? Under existing circumstances, the female-based child-rearing unit is a prime source of this essential pool of low-skilled laborers. It brings them into the world, and it furnishes them the values, the aspiration, and the psychic make-up that low-skill jobs require (e.g., high toleration of recurrent unemployment; high boredom tolerance; high flexibility with respect to work, residence, relational patterns; capacity to find life gratification outside the world of work). (Miller, 1964, p. x)

Charles Valentine, in a blistering critique of Walter Miller and other writers on the culture of poverty, points to the starkness of this admission:

So it appears that the lower-class milieu generates something more than delinquency, indeed something that seems to be regarded as valuable by people who are not poor. The cause-and-effect relationships stated in these lines remain to be demonstrated. Nevertheless, it would be hard to find a statement that more starkly reflects the conflict between the interests of the poor and the interests of those who feel that their comfortable life depends on maintaining a 'pool of low-skilled labourers.' This passage is like much of the writing reviewed here: while demonstrating little about the cultural patterns of the poor it nevertheless implies a good deal about the values and perceived self-interest of the non-poor. (1968, p. 45)

As Liebow himself comments, wryly, writing as he explicitly acknowledges in the wake of the 1965 Watts Riots:

These are, indeed, fundamental questions, and the maintenance of the lower classes as they are presently ordered is one way of answering them. This solution, however, in which those who are to be at the bottom of our society are selected while they are still in the womb violates every hope and promise this nation has held out to its people.

Moreover, if 'high boredom tolerance ... flexibility' and 'capacity to find life gratification outside the world of work' are understood to mean that people at the bottom of our society are content with their lot, even happy with it, this understanding represents a grave misreading of history and recent events and leads to the assumption that the impetus to change their life circumstances comes not from the lower classes themselves but from moralists, humanitarians, politicians, and others on the outside. Persons involved in poverty programs may even congratulate themselves on their humanitarian work, claiming to be helping people who have not even asked for it. ...

Self-deception ... simply will not do. It is precisely the discontent of the poor, and their expression of it, which lie behind recent attempts to change the life conditions of the poor. The refusal to see clearly and state frankly the self-serving character of recent efforts to assist those at the bottom of our society is a disservice to everyone concerned and stands in the way of real progress. (2003, pp. 147–8)

From structure to agency: beyond the weak thesis

As we have seen, John Veit-Wilson (1998) makes the important distinction between 'strong' and 'weak' versions of social exclusion. The strong versions of this discourse emphasise the role of those excluding, whereas the weak versions involve focusing on the qualities of the excluded, where 'the solutions lie in altering those excluded people's handicapping characteristics and enhancing their integration into dominant society' (Veit-Wilson, 1998, p. 45). David Byrne, in his key book *Social Exclusion* (1999), stresses his intention to focus on the strong version, emphasising, as he does, 'that exclusion is not a property of individuals or even social spaces. Rather it is an inherent characteristic of an unequal post-industrial capitalism founded around a flexible labour market and with a systematic constraining of the organizational powers of workers as collective actors' (1999, p. 128). Here the underclass are a reserve army of labour, who shift in and out of work, and who interface in terms of upward and downward mobility with a more traditional working class that has a higher standard of living but also a new degree of insecurity characteristic of late modernity.

Note that Byrne's formulation involves a more robust discourse around social exclusion. It emphasises the strong thesis with its focus on exclusion, it tackles the criticism of the dualistic notion of the discontented underclass and the contented majority by pointing to the widespread insecurity occurring throughout society, and places this within the context of a reserve army of labour, the surplus population which the market cannot incorporate. He points to the political process of social exclusion, where there has been a systematic undermining of the power of trade unions and the elevation of neo-liberal notions of the individualistic contract between employee and employer. Lastly, he places this process in the transition from modernity to late modernity, contrasting it with the Fordist deal between worker and employer in the 'golden years' of Keynesianism, where work was relatively secure and well paid. Here the post-war consensus on wages, the compromise negotiated between capital and labour, although not involving genuine economic equality, at least granted the notion of a fair day's wage for a fair day's work, security of employment and some shift towards the decommodification of labour. This inclusiveness of the wage deal was lost in the process of globalisation and economic liberalisation.

As to New Labour's version of social exclusion, Byrne has no doubt that it is the weak version, and, echoing many other writers, he dismisses the discourse 'as a method of closure in relation to challenges to inequality as a general social issue' (1999, p. 5). Indeed, Helen Colley and Phil Hodkinson (2001) point to the reversal of structure and agency in the discourse of the Social Exclusion Unit, focusing particularly on its analysis of youth in *Bridging the Gap* (1999c). Thus:

> ... the young people we meet in this report are at best passive victims of inevitable processes ... sponging off society as a whole in their costly benefit dependency. At worst they are deviant perpetrators of criminal behaviour and drug abuse who pose a sinister threat to the rest of society. Somewhere in the middle are the pregnant teenagers reproducing future non-participants at alarming rates, ready to pass on their misconceived negativity about education, training and employment to perpetuate the cycle of social exclusion. (Colley and Hodkinson, 2001, p. 341)

Further it must be noted that the impact of such governmental interventions with the wider range of work programmes and schemes, far from reforming the character of the people concerned, are frequently likely to self-fulfil such posited feelings of failure. Thus Paul Willis laments the lack of widespread opposition to those schemes and adds:

> This may be explained in part by some bleak, in-turned and individualistic additions to the reproduction repertoire whereby individuals blame themselves for their lack of work and for the lack of success that scheme attendance brings. Individualizing and internalizing a structural problem, they reproach themselves, one by one, for their inability to find work. Having been given so many training opportunities to develop their own individual employability, and having been told repeatedly that finding work is a question of permanent individual job searches, it must be their own *individual* fault when they cannot find work. Quite apart from the institutional encouragement, self-blame is always an insidious and treacherous possibility .... (2000, pp. 89–90).

In this sense the weak thesis which substitutes agency for structure self-fulfils itself.

Ignoring stigmatisation and criminalisation

Byrne's critique of the 'weak thesis' tackles the problems of the loss of class (it sees globalisation as having an impact across the class structure) and the rigid dualism of underclass and mainstream society. I made a parallel argument concerning the fluid nature of the underclass and the post-Fordist nature of exclusion in *The Exclusive Society*, also written in 1999. However, in this latter text, written from a more sociological point of view, it became clear that the discussion of social exclusion even in the 'strong version' did not go far enough. That is, there is a tendency for writers on the impact of globalisation (such as Byrne himself, but see also William Julius Wilson, 1987) to view the process of exclusion as occurring solely on an economic level and involving simply a hydraulic withdrawal of labour markets. Work disappears elsewhere, or becomes more complex, particularly with regard to information technology, so that the excluded are, so to speak, *non-intentionally* stranded.

This view ignores the processes of social exclusion that occur on the level of civil society and the criminal justice system. That is, parallel to the process of economic exclusion, there occurs the *active* social exclusion by stigmatisation and the 'othering' of the poor as inadequate, criminogenic and troublesome. Frequently this involves, as we have seen, the blaming of single mothers, and the invocation of the sins of welfare dependency, an accusation which is often racialised, and particularly associated with immigrants. Such a social process of moral panic and stigmatisation is captured well in Herbert Gans's *The War Against the Poor* (1995), and by Zygmunt Bauman in *Work, Consumerism and the New Poor* (1998b). Such a phenomenon of scapegoating and blame is a major component of social exclusion, yet is scarcely touched upon in the discourse. Indeed, it may well be argued, as Colley and Hodkinson (2001) imply, that the discourse of the SEU, with its obsession with dependency, teenage pregnancy (see Social Exclusion Unit, 1999b) and anti-social behaviour, contributes volubly to this process of 'othering'.

Similarly, a staple of criminological discussion is the manner in which the criminal justice system discriminates against the poor, both in a heavy-handedness of suspicion as offenders and in inadequate provision when victims of crime. Such a palpable force for social exclusion is ignored in this discourse (see Mooney and Young, 2000). Indeed, what is remarkable when one compares the crime audits, set up by New Labour on a borough-by-borough basis under the remit of the 1998 Crime and Disorder Act, with the radical crime and policing surveys conducted by Labour boroughs in the 1980s (see Jones et al., 1986; Painter et al., 1989) is the absence of any public assessment of police illegalities and lack of accountability. Thus, the 'strong' thesis could be strengthened even further by adding to the non-intentional exclusion by market forces, the intentional exclusion exerted within civil society or by the criminal justice system.

Social and political exclusion

'It is interesting to reflect', Janie Percy-Smith notes, 'that, while there is an increasing literature on social and economic exclusion, there is relatively little on political exclusion'. And she adds that the first annual government report on poverty and social exclusion, *Opportunity for All: Tackling Poverty and Social Exclusion* (Department of Social Security, 1999), 'despite being extremely wide-ranging, reporting progress on all the myriad initiatives which are being developed to address social exclusion, makes no mention of political exclusion' (Percy-Smith, 2000b, pp. 148–9). And the same situation exists today. Let us examine the subjects in *Preventing Social Exclusion*, intended to measure trends in levels of social exclusion: Long-Term Unemployment; Workless Households; Income Inequality; Exclusion from

School; Drug Addicts; Crime; Children living in Low Income Households; Adult Literacy; 18-Year Olds in Learning; Teenage Births (see Social Exclusion Unit, 2001, pp. 1.6–1.12).

What is of interest here is what is omitted. For there is no mention of any measures of political inclusion, for example: voting levels; membership of political parties; community participation; social capital; tenants' organisations; trade union membership; participation in local community decision-making; candidature in local political forums; or participation in pressure groups.

Now, of course, all studies of the lower part of the class structure have indicated that political involvement is extremely low (see Burchardt et al., 2002). Such a situation creates an extremely unequal relationship between powerful interests and a local community. This is clearly revealed in the massive inequalities in urban regeneration schemes between the interests of capital and those of local working-class communities. As Byrne points out:

> This is not simply because the interests of development capital have been given absolute priority. That has been possible only because in 'partnership' there has been no real countervailing power from the 'community' precisely because the 'community' is so fragmented and disorganized. Given the fragmented nature of 'community' and the logic of personal mobility in space, the proposals contained in the Cabinet Office Social Exclusion Unit 1998 White Paper *Bringing Britain Together: A National Strategy for Neighbourhood Renewal* (Cm 4045) can be described only as vacuous. The authors of this piece seem simply not to know how people actually conduct their lives in the divided city. It is plain that organization is the key to any kind of re-empowerment of the dispossessed. That is the issue to which we now turn in the conclusion of this book. ... It is process which matters most when we are dealing with issues of power. (Byrne, 1999, p.123)

And, however much the Third Way politicians talk about a new contract between the citizen and the state, based on rights and duties, and modernisers argue for a *reciprocity* between the state and citizens (Corrigan et al., 1988), the old Welfare State, which bestows problems and grants rights to its citizens, remains very much to the fore (see Young, 1999, pp. 197–199). As such it becomes more understandable how progressive discourses about social exclusion are undermined by those that stress the faults of actors. Indeed, as Mooney (2003) indicates, the social democratic emphasis on the dysfunctional family in relation to crime present in 'Old' Labour is replicated by New Labour, but this time read in the context of welfare dependency. There can be little doubt that the individuals themselves, if they had some political input into the debate, would not describe themselves as inadequate, nor would *they* stress lack of ability over lack of opportunities.

Let us turn now to what is the likely effect of political exclusion on levels of crime and disorder. The most prominent of all symptoms of social exclusion are riots (see Percy-Smith, 2000b). The background to large-scale civil disturbances in the last 30 years have involved situations where populations have been both economically *and* politically marginalised; where people have felt left out of the economic success of the wider society, and have had no obvious means of political change in the near future. The spark for such rioting has most frequently been some gross example of police malpractice, preceded by a history of corrupt, violent and non-effective policing. Indeed, police malpractices represent very palpably the lack of political power of marginal groups – the inability of localised politics to deliver basic legal and civil rights and keep policing within the rule of law (see Power and Tunstall, 1997; Lea and Young, 1993). Urban riots, such as those in England in 1981, 1984, 1991 and 2001, and the French riots of 1981 and 2005, represent dramatic expressions of failure of inclusion. Indeed, one commentator, John Pitts (2003) has indicated that the most recent English riots of 2001 in the northern cities of Burnley, Bradford and Oldham represent the major setback for the social inclusionary policies of the New Labour Government, a theme I will return to in the next chapter.

The origins of civil disorders and of crime are similar in many ways. A major source of endemic criminality is economic marginalisation coupled with a feeling of political and social marginalisation. And, as with rioting, this latter marginalisation is made evident to a group or locality by them being the disproportionate focus of police attention and malpractice (see Mooney and Young, 2000). Riots differ in that they are more collective and, to some extent, more targeted; but the background of economic despair and hostility to the police is common.

Pitts, in *The New Politics of Youth Crime* (2001), makes an illuminating comparison between the responses of the British and the French to the riots that occurred in 1981 in both their countries. The response of the former gave rise to *The Scarman Report* (1982); the latter produced the report of Henri Bonnemaison (1983), the result of an inquiry set up by the new socialist administration of François Mitterand following nationwide riots in the multiracial *banlieues*. Pitts' conclusion is that while both reports recognised the problem of economic marginalisation as a core part of the problem, the Bonnemaison report went further in pointing to the key problem of political alienation.

Thus, if Scarman emphasised economic exclusion, Bonnemaison affirmed this, but placed it in the context of a problem of citizenship, of political exclusion. And here, of course, we return, ironically, to earlier commentaries on the concept of social exclusion, which distinguish a 'Durkheimian' concept of inclusion, that is concerned with horizontal integration, and that which is more social democratic and class-based in its emphasis and which focuses on vertical integration. This, as we have seen, is the basis of the argument of critics such as Ruth Levitas, who castigates New Labour's formulation of social exclusion as being too integrationist (SID) and not sufficiently redistributionist (RED).

The truth, however, is that *both* an integrationist and a redistributionist element of policy is necessary if a more egalitarian, social-inclusionary policy is to be achieved. A 'strong' thesis must not only strengthen its economic policies with a greater emphasis on structure than agency, but it must pay attention to the empowerment of the excluded. That is, it must have *policies* of political inclusion and *politics* which are inclusionary. Thus the economic and the political, the two models of social inclusion, that of the Anglo-Saxons and that of the French, are both a necessity if radical and significant changes are to be achieved. As we shall see, in the wake of the riots both in the northern towns of Britain in 2002 and in the banlieues of France in 2005, the automatic enactment or primacy of either model is obviously in doubt. It is not a question of simply voicing a policy, it is a matter of implementing it. Further the advocacy of policies which stress meritocracy but do not actually offer it, or idealise political equality but deny it on the streets and in the estates, merely fans discontent rather than offers cohesion.

Social inclusion, as it has been widely formulated, merely reproduces the exclusions it attempts to remedy and in doing so replays the resentments which underlie the deep social divisions within late modern society. In short, in Nancy Fraser's terms, they merely affirm the existing order rather than serve to transform it. I will, at the conclusion of this book, outline a transformative politics which would allow us to move beyond the repeated reaffirmation of the status quo. But for the moment let me turn to those exclusions which are associated with immigration and the controversies which surround it.

Note

1 It is perhaps significant that eight years after this speech plans are in motion to demolish the Aylesbury Estate. It seems that after these long years of New Labour the solution to the problems of the estate were not so much social inclusion as physical destruction.

7

CROSSING THE BORDER: TO THESE WET AND WINDY SHORES

UNWELCOME GUESTS

One of the drawbacks of efficient intercontinental travel is that sometimes plants and animals hatch or land in the ballast of boats, in people's belongings, in imported products or other ways, and take up residence in a new eco-system. These biological invaders are changing the nature of acquatic and terrestrial ecosystems around the globe. Some of these alien acquatic species in the United States waters include European zebra mussels, walking catfish and South American redbellied piranhas. In some areas, these introduced species are posing serious problems by choking waterways and eating the natural plants and animals, throwing off the natural balance of the ecosystem.

WHY ARE EXOTIC SPECIES A PROBLEM

Invasive species by competing with them for space and food, consuming them, introducing pathological genes and parasites that kill them, mating with them and decreasing their genetic diversity. If these invasive species do not have natural predators in their adopted environment they can grow quickly, out of control.

FIGHTING BACK

The major goal of the US New Indigenous Acquatic Nuisance Prevention and Control Act of 1990 is to prevent non-natural species from entering the United States and its territorial waters ...

(Giant Ocean Tank, New England Aquarium, Boston, 2003)

When the *Sun* and its readers protest that asylum seekers are making mugs of us, the chattering classes have a standard response. 'You're prejudiced because you're ignorant of the facts' ... The [beggars] ARE taking us for a ride. They earn more in an hour's begging on the streets of London than the average Romanian makes in a week. And they're using it – and their social security which is paid for by YOUR taxes – to build marble palaces for the rest of the scroungers back home ... This is not an extreme country.

Just the opposite, in fact. But even the fairest-minded nation has it breaking point. And Britain has reached it.

(From the *Sun*, 14 March 2000)

The pool of potential beggar criminals – call them what you will – is deep. A generation ago it was just the Republican Irish and the West Indians. They have been joined by the West Africans ... East Africans, too, are coming in growing numbers. There are potentially millions more from the Balkans, the Caucasus, Ukraine and Russia. Then there are Pakistan, Bangladesh, Sri Lanka and, above all, India, with a billion people. Some of them have not yet even heard of Britain. But they will, they will.

(Paul Johnson in the *Daily Mail*, 11 March 2000)

The social construction of the immigrant

In March 2000 the British media were greatly exercised by the problem of 'gypsy' beggars. Prompted by the sentencing of a Romanian woman for begging with her child and the police promise of a zero tolerance policy towards 'aggressive begging' the tabloids had a field day of demonisation, a veritable feast of othering. London is a city of great wealth and poverty; it is a city with a myriad problems: health, housing, education, transport, employment, to name a few, the list could go on forever; it is difficult to see where women with children 'aggressively' asking for money, palms 'threateningly' forwards in supplication, would come in this list. A hundredth or thousandth – perhaps not at all?

No other group than the immigrant has the power to mobilise prejudice and the magical ability to explain away problems inherent in the host society. For he or she is an alien other, a *carrier* of problems into the First World rather than a group who are most blatantly exposed to the problems *inherent* in the First World. Even the term 'immigrant' is subject to intense social construction. It is rare that Britons abroad ever think of themselves as immigrants, émigrés perhaps, but immigrants certainly not! A recent survey of immigration into the UK, carried out by the Institute of Public Policy (Kyambi, 2005), revealed that Americans were the sixth largest immigrant group, ahead of Bangladeshis – a finding which created great media surprise and, indeed, one rarely hears of Americans over here described as immigrants or their numbers noticed or commented upon. In 2002 I attended a large conference on immigration at the Centre de Cultura Contemporania in Barcelona. To my knowledge the existence of the British, by far one of the largest immigrant groups in Spain – over 674,000 at the last estimate – was not referred to. No, because 'immigrants', of course, are from the South, from India or Columbia, sometimes from the former Soviet bloc countries, often with dark skins, from Africa, Albania, Algeria.

The irony of English immigration to Spain is manifold. Many of these immigrants, far from adapting to their host country, reconstitute or reinvent a Britain of yesteryear, somewhere north of Malaga. That is, as *The Observer* journalist Jason Burke comments, 'one with no crime, cheap property – and no one who is not white'. Or at least almost no one. He describes a British community living on the outskirts of a Spanish town serviced by 'British bars, a shop selling English newspapers, a Chinese takeaway and an Indian restaurant'. One couple he interviews explain their reasons for immigration: 'I am not racist...' began Timms 62 before correcting himself. 'Actually I am racist. Britain has gone to the dogs. There's just too many foreigners. They're all coming from Somalia, Czechoslovakia and Bangladesh. It's all wrong' ... 'There are so many immigrants, it's black Britain now', said Jay, his Irish-born 52 year old wife' (9 October, 2005). As for the Spanish, they call their new English compatriots the '*por favores*' for despite being in Spain for many years all they can say is *por favor*.

The social construction of the immigrant is perfectly conveyed by a front page article in the British *Daily Express* of 26 February 2004:

> EXODUS: *As we face a flood of immigrants ... thousands of fed-up Britons like this teacher are making a new life in Spain.*

And next to it a picture of a white mother with her two lovely children seemingly forced to live in Spain as it is their only hope of a decent standard of living. And we are told they go there because of Spain's excellent national health service, its firm attitudes to crime, its family values. Meanwhile, inside the newspaper on page 5, there is a picture of Abdikadir Muse, an immigrant *into* the UK from Somalia under the heading *Benefit of Being British*, who 'has not worked for months', receives £100 a month in State Benefits, a flat provided by the local council, while his children receive child benefits. It is peculiar how in the tabloid press the British emigrating abroad are seen as resourceful and seeking a better life wherever in the world their adventurous spirit takes them, while the immigrants coming into the UK are frequently portrayed as lazy, benefit-seeking scroungers who bring crime and disorder into our towns and cities. It is a contrast reminiscent of the famous pictures of the New Orleans flood disaster where two photos of victims provided an illuminating contrast in captions. A black man up to his chest in water dragging a black bag was described as wading through water 'after looting', whereas a white couple similarly disposed in the floodwater were described as 'finding bread and soda from a local grocery'.

When we turn to official documents and discussions of immigration such a discourse is seldom as blatant. I shall argue that here, also, one finds othering but it is in the terms we have discussed, liberal rather than conservative othering, at least in its foremost presentation. That is, instead of the image of the immigrant as essentially different and something of a scoundrel, the image is differentiated into two categories: the 'deserving' and the 'undeserving' immigrant. The major focus is on the deserving: here liberal othering prevails; immigration is portrayed as a passage of becoming, the immigrant is materially deprived and lacks the civilities of citizenship, ideally the immigrant improves him or herself both materially and in the acquisition of the trappings of citizenship. As for the undeserving immigrant, here the more conservative image of the incorrigible, the alien, the threat, comes into play. But such imagery is not spelt out directly, rather it is implicit, what is explicit is the differences in terms of border controls, customs and policy which are couched quite clearly in terms of protective devices against an alien other and in the language of personal and national security.

To these wet and windy shores

Four events have shaped recent British immigration policy. The first concerns the repeated attempts by illegal immigrants to board the freight and passenger trains at Sangette on the French side of the Channel Tunnel, the second is the extremely hostile reception to the dispersal of immigrants in disturbances in towns such as Dover and Southampton, the third is the riots which occurred in the North of England, in Bradford, Oldham and Burnley in the Summer of 2001, the last, and most recent, is the terrible events in July 2005 – the terrorist attacks on London. The first concerns problems of the entry of immigrants, the second and third with the problems of inter-communal relations and the dispersal of immigrants, the fourth represents acts not only of great tragedy but of considerable significance. For the terrorist attacks reveal a level of intransigence and of fightback, however brutal and indiscriminate, of at least a portion of immigrants 'settled' in the UK. And all four episodes convey the gamut of crossing the borderline from the clamour to gain entry into the country, the hostility of certain sectors of the indigenous population, the outbreak of extensive hostilities between the white and immigrant poor (two segments of the socially excluded) and the links to the fateful tragedy in London of the 7 July. For it was no coincidence that the suburbs of Leeds, where three of the bombers lived and grew up were no great distance, both spatially and socially, from the Northern towns in which the riots occurred.

The riots in the Northern towns which involved police and public injuries and considerable property damage, where there was a great deal of inter-racial tension as well as conflicts with the police, were pivotal. They were the culmination of the conflicts between immigrant and indigenous populations, an indication of a major failure of policies of social inclusion and a foreboding of the outbreak of terrorism in July 2005. They were the worst riots in England in 20 years, involved many hundreds of young people, ten million pounds of damage and, most seriously, in the majority of instances involved conflicts across ethnic lines, predominantly between white and people of Pakistani and Bangladeshi origin and arose out of months of racial tension. These not only were the most sizeable disturbances in 20 years but indicated unrest, not merely at the initial dispersal points but in communities which had settled for two or more generations. A whole series of official documents arose out of this, the most important of these being the White Paper *Secure Borders, Safe Haven: Integration and Diversity in Britain* (2002a), which is concerned largely with entry criteria and citizenship and the two Home Office reports, *Community Cohesion* (2002b) and *Building Cohesive Communities* (2002c) which, as their titles suggest, focus on problems of integration in terms of the disturbances in the Northern towns. The then Home Secretary, David Blunkett, appointed in Labour's second term in office, was transparently clear as to the economic and cultural aims of immigration policy. Thus, in the foreword to *Secure Borders, Safe Havens*, he writes:

There is nothing more controversial, and yet more natural, than men and women from across the world seeking a better life for themselves and their families. Ease of communication and of transportation have transformed the time it takes to move across the globe. This ease of movement has broken down traditional boundaries ...

But the tensions, as well as the enrichment, which flow from the inward migration of those arriving on our often wet and windy shores, must be understood, abated and addressed. Migration is an inevitable reality of the modern world and it brings significant benefits. But to ensure that we sustain the positive contribution of migration to our social well-being and economic prosperity, we need to manage it properly and build firmer foundations on which integration with diversity can be achieved. ... This White Paper sets out ... a nationality, immigration and asylum policy that secures the sustainable growth and social inclusion that are an essential part of our core principles ... (2002a, pp. 1 and 3)

Immigration is seen as generating benefits both to the economy and in terms of cultural diversity but it must be controlled to ensure that disturbances among the indigenous population are minimised and this is to be done through a process of 'integration with diversity'. And here, once again, the key *leitmotif* of New Labour is invoked, *social inclusion. Secure Borders, Safe Havens* is a fascinating document because it quite clearly represents the application of such inclusionary principles to the problem of immigration. Thus the stress is on the propelling forces of globalisation, the economic gains of incorporation, and the need for inclusion. The White Paper first of all talks of cultural inclusion and then economic inclusion. I will follow this order. What form does this cultural inclusion take? It is here that the concept of integration with diversity holds sway. The document is thoroughly multiculturalist rather than assimilationist. Here the contrast is made with 'other democracies' in their response to immigration and its 'challenge' to concepts of national identity and citizenship:

> All major democracies have had to face up to these changes in different ways in recent decades. In important respects, the UK has responded successfully to diversity. Unlike many other countries, British nationality has never been associated with membership of a particular ethnic group. For centuries we have been a multi-ethnic nation. We do not exclude people from citizenship on the basis of race and ethnicity. Similarly, our society is based on cultural difference, rather than assimilation to a prevailing monoculture. This diversity is a source of pride, and it helps explain our cultural vitality, the strength of our economy and our strong international links. (Home Office, 2002a, p.10)

And again:

> Common citizenship is not about cultural uniformity, nor is it born out of some narrow and out-dated view of what it means to be 'British'. The Government welcomes the richness of cultural diversity which immigrants have brought to the UK – our society is multi-cultural and is shaped by its diverse peoples. We want British citizenship positively to embrace the diversity of backgrounds, cultures and faiths that is one of the hallmarks of Britain in the 21st Century. (ibid., p.29)

Let us pause to examine this. It is, of course, a non-compromising commitment to multi-culturalism, underpinned by a notion of common citizenship. It purposely does not equate mono-culture with citizenship. This being said, it paints a completely unrealistic picture of Britain in terms of tolerance, either in the past – witness the widespread Anti-Irish and anti-Semitic prejudice – or in the present where racism is palpably widespread. Indeed, for many people nationality is associated with ethnicity – 'white British' to use the ethnic category now used in the Census and in official documents (despite, of course, its inappropriateness as an *ethnic* classification rather than a remark about the relative absence of melanin in the skin).

After congratulating the UK on its diversity, the White Paper proceeds to note that some failures have occurred and points to the riots in Bradford, Oldham and Burnley. These, it notes, were the result of 'fractured and divided communities lacking a sense of common values or shared civic identity'. They signalled 'the need for us to foster and renew the social fabric of the communities, and rebuild a sense of common citizenship, which embraces the different and diverse experiences of today's Britain' (op.cit, p. 10).

It is at this juncture that the White Paper patently links the problem to social exclusion but it is not just the social exclusion of the immigrant but also that of many indigenous working-class communities:

Citizenship is not just for those entering the country – it is for all British citizens ... The Government will initiate and open constructive debate about citizenship, civic identity and shared values ... This dialogue will form a central part of our drive for civil renewal in all our communities. Community cohesion and communality is weak. Too many of our citizens are excluded from meaningful participation in society. This is true of white working class communities whose alienation from the political process, along with their physical living conditions and standards of living, leaves them socially excluded from the increased wealth and quality of life which they see around them. In the same way, those who have entered this country and joined friends, family or ethnic groupings may find themselves experiencing relative economic disadvantage and sometimes overt racism. (ibid., p. 10)

This section is worth quoting in full, it sees social exclusion occurring to both the alienated and poor white working class with their relative deprivation to the wider more wealthy inclusive society and among the immigrants both in their comparisons with the wider society and in the racism they experience from the excluded whites. Further, it sees the need for citizenship, shared identity and a sense of shared values. That the *combination* of economic and political marginalisation is a potent source of discontent which can *in extremis* result in riots is a well rehearsed argument, indeed this is precisely the combustive formula which John Lea and myself uncovered when analysing the widespread riots across Britain of 1981 (see Lea and Young, 1982). There are, however, considerable differences between the riots of 1981 and 20 years later in 2001, both in the composition of rioters and the targets of discontent. Further this account is somewhat confused in its notion of relative deprivation. I will return to this in a moment, but let us for now briefly examine the role of 'citizenship' as a policy solution to the problem of exclusion.

The acquisition of British citizenship, the White Paper notes, has in the past been a mere bureaucratic exercise. Instead it proposes the promotion of language training, citizenship ceremonies, and elementary education in British civic institutions centring around the notion of rights and responsibilities. Here, again, the motif is social inclusion: lack of English language is seen as a major cause of social exclusion (ibid., p. 32) and the notion of rights and responsibilities is a key element of New Labour's thinking on the basis of social inclusion.

The second 'challenge' is seen as economic. For not only do diverse cultures enrich Britain but migrants, with their skills, ambitions and energy, enrich the economy. The aim is to encourage economic immigration where it meets the requirement of the labour market, while retaining the right to asylum for those who are the subjects of political persecution in their home country. Here the White Paper attempts to tackle the problem of illegal immigration via the request for asylum by providing a legal method of entry on an economic basis and thus removing from the asylum category the 'bogus' applicants who are actually propelled by economic motives. Thus it distinguishes two modes of entry, economic and asylum seeker, and while welcoming these immigrants, is concerned about both the immigrant who has not the requisite skills or the refugee who has insufficient grounds for asylum. The latter part of the White Paper details elaborate ways of maintaining 'secure borders' around the 'safe haven' that the first part of the report concentrates upon. It thus makes a distinction between the deserving and undeserving immigrants, albeit considerably widening the deserving category (see Sales, 2002). The 'safe haven' thus refers rather neatly to the deserving immigrants (the object of liberal othering) whereas the 'secure borders' represents the protection from the undeserving immigrants (the implicit object of conservative othering), who threatens to penetrate our borders and create insecurity.

Let us sum up the position of the White Paper. It is multi-culturalist and advocates both economic and refugee immigration, yet this is a 'managed immigration' in contrast to the free, unregulated immigration of a libertarian or neo-liberal sort. It welcomes the cultural and economic contribution to Britain of the immigrant communities. The underarching discourse is that of social inclusion, indeed it sees the problems that have arisen as a product of the conflict between excluded immigrant and indigenous populations. The White Paper's policy solution is, therefore, social inclusionary: it seeks a diverse population with a common citizenship and sense of civil virtue and responsibility. It is thus integrationist rather than assimilationist, indeed its position, although unstated, is undoubtedly that of Amitai Etzioni's communitarianism – a key influence on New Labour thinking. That is, it seeks a diverse mosaic of cultures with a 'thick' common framework of citizenship (see Etzioni, 1997). And just as it is not assimilationist, neither does it propose a diverse, relatively unintegrated population with a 'thin' framework as advocated by libertarians such as Paul Hirst (1994) or neo-liberals, who would view the State as having no right to intervene in the self-regulation of communities.

Two modes of entry

It is overall a significant change in policy from that of the 1980s and 1990s as well as differing from that of the 1950s. The immigration policy of the

1950s was motivated by labour shortages, it was economic immigration within a culturally assimilationist politics – compared to the multiculturalism of today. The period following this, up to the present day, was overwhelmingly negative concerning immigration compared to the 'managed immigration' advocated in the White Paper, with a stress on the economic and cultural advantages of immigration. Contrast this to a commentator during the 1980s who wrote: 'Insofar as Britain can be said to have an immigration policy, it is a policy designed to contain the social problems of past immigration by eliminating virtually all future inwards flows.' (Rees, 1982, p. 95).

My criticism of the White Paper revolves around a more general critique of New Labour's underlying doctrine of social inclusion, both in its economic and cultural dimensions. As I have argued earlier, New Labour's privileging of paid work of any sort as the key process expediting the passage to social inclusion severely misunderstands the nature of relative deprivation and the discontent it gives rise to. To shift individuals from unemployment to the lowest levels of employment structure, with long hours, poor pay and intense job insecurity, is not experienced as inclusion in the ranks of the 'contented majority' but simply being reclassified in the ranks of exclusion. The problem both for the immigrant and indigenous communities in these depressed regions of the North is connecting up with the economic developments within the wider society rather than being perpetually marginalised. Social inclusion, on an economic level, is only viable where education and opportunity allows meritocratic advance, otherwise its potentiality is exceedingly geographically varied and dependent on the local labour market (see Peck, 1999).

But, of course, the aims of the White Paper are manifestly to avoid the 'sort' of immigration that has given rise to such economic marginalisation in the Northern towns. For the answer on the level of citizenship to the problems of social exclusion is to grant citizenship overwhelmingly to those people who *are* meritocrats – who have already the capabilities and the opportunities. Thus the high fliers of the refugee circuit (and, of course, there are very many of them) are to be admitted in as economic migrants. Such supposed liberalisation is accompanied by the *quid pro quo* of tightening even further on the asylum mode of entry – to ensure only the most bona fide of refugees are allowed entry. It is difficult to see how such cherry picking of skilled immigrants will solve either the wretched attempts to jump the freight trains at Sangette or, indeed, to genuinely respond to the future labour needs of the UK. The massive movement of people seeking to better their lives is worldwide and will scarcely be halted by an international competition for skilled labour. Further, as we have seen, the UK, like so many European countries, has a declining fertility rate and an ageing population. Work on *all levels* will be necessary if the country's economic viability and social support systems are to be maintained. If this is so, immigration must be much more widespread and the problems of economic inclusion cannot be obviated by concentrating on the admission of high fliers.

In the case of cultural inclusion there is considerable evidence that multi-culturalism in the form of a mosaic of distinct cultures held together by a frame of citizenship (i.e. that advocated by Etzioni) does not achieve a friction free situation of social integration. In fact, all the evidence is to the contrary: the United States being the prime example, where inter-ethnic dispute and competition is commonplace, where rioting has occurred on an unprecedented level in Western societies and where social and spatial segregation is exceptional. But let us turn now to look at the actual processes which lie behind the sort of discontent that can bubble over into a full-blown riot.

Over 20 years ago: the riots of 1981

First of all let me return to the earlier analysis of the 1981 Riots, the prime sites of which were Brixton, Moss Side and Toxteth (see Lea and Young, 1982). The rioters were predominantly African–Caribbean with a significant white minority and were directed against the police and accompanied by the looting of shops. An explanation in terms of poverty alone was insufficient – in so far as historically there has been worse poverty and unemployment in the UK without rioting and, further, it does not explain why at this time in the early 1980s certain sections of the population, particularly African–Caribbeans, were involved and not others such as Asians, or the absence of riots in areas such as Glasgow with a predominantly poor white population.

The conservative thesis – most strongly advocated at the time by The *Daily Telegraph* correspondent, Peregrine Worsthorne – was that there had been a failure of race relations because of a lack of assimilationist policies. Successive governments because of pluralist, multi-cultural policies had allowed immigrant cultures to remain which were essentially 'alien' and did not identify with British culture. Thus when the pressure of poverty and unemployment occurred, this loose pluralism had simply fallen apart. Here the contrast was made with the United States in the 1950s where assimilationist policies were vigorously pursued: where the flag was displayed in classroom and public building, and recitations of the constitution and a celebration of citizenship were *de riguer*.

Our critique of this was that the explanation of events was not discontent because of lack of assimilation but rather discontent *because* of the degree of assimilation. That the reason why discontent was highest among second generation immigrants was that they had incorporated notions of citizenship: in all its economic, social and political aspects. This was a riot of citizenship *thwarted*, not of failure to understand the meaning of citizenship. It involved a generation of African–Caribbeans who had experienced lack of jobs where their expectations were employment, racism where their beliefs were in equality and harassment from the police where they had learnt to expect the rule of law. Let us now put this in a more general perspective.

Crime, immigration and the demonisation of the other

All over the Western world the process of economic globalisation has been associated with the mass migration of labour from the Third World and from the countries of the Second World: the ex-Soviet nations of Eastern Europe. In every instance a social and spatial process of exclusion has occurred in the 'host' country and, concomitant with this, the cultural 'othering' of the immigrant population. That is a designation of the immigrant as an Other, an alien group as opposed to the supposed cultural normality of the indigenous population. A series of binaries are set up: us–them, majority–minority, pure–impure, and with a seeming inevitability law-abiding–criminal, normal–deviant. The immigrant population is seen as a source of crime, of drugs, prostitution and violence. Let us make the facts clear: the research, in Britain indicates quite unequivocally that first generation immigrants have lower crime rates than the indigenous population. Indeed, as Dario Melossi (2000) points out, such a finding is part of the history of immigration in the US with both the Immigration Commission of 1911 and the Wickersam Commission of 1931, and in Britain was a crucial finding of the 1972 Select Committee on Race Relations (see Lea and Young, 1993, pp. 135–8). As we argue in *What is to be Done About Law and Order?* (1993), it is the second generation immigrants who have become more assimilated to the values of the wider society who most acutely feel relative deprivation, the discontent of which frequently leads to higher crime rates. Furthermore, this is not a product of any racial essence but of subcultures which have adapted to the new country and which transmute rather than replicate the original culture of origin (ibid. pp. 124–9). Similarly Ineke Haen Marshall, in her survey of crime rates amongst minorities in the US and Europe, notes:

> There appears to be a general consensus that, if there are any marked differences between the criminal involvement of immigrants and natives, these are manifested in the criminal involvement of the children of immigrants (second – and third – generation immigrants). It is argued that children of immigrants will have higher expectations; they will have changed life aspirations. (1997, pp. 237–8; see also Karydis, 1996)

Add to this the predicament and hardships of residence either in inner cities or peripheral estates and you have a formula for disaster.

Furthermore, the type of crimes which occur are predominantly those associated with the demographics of youth and the predicaments of poverty. Over and over again the determinants of class are confused with the propensities of 'race' or ethnicity (see Mooney and Young, 2000).

The roots of othering

How does one explain this process of cultural 'othering'? Attempts are frequently made to explain such tendencies utilising the psychoanalytic theories of Melanie Klein, Erik Erikson and more latterly Julia Kristeva. These, in the tradition of object relations theory, trace parallels between the infants' development of a sense of self in distinction to the external world and the cultural demarcations of 'us' and 'other'. An alternative explanation rooted in cultural anthropology and the work of Mary Douglas locates such exclusions in the need for social groups to maintain boundaries and details how rules about purity and the fear and loathing of others strengthen the security of the entrenched majority.

The problem about such theorisation, most eloquently advocated in David Sibley's book *Geographies of Exclusion* (1995), is that it tends to depict such othering or demonisation as a cultural universal, a product of ever-present problems of human psychology or group formation. Instead I wish to locate such a process in time and social context, to specify who is more likely to demonise, to explain the context of the labels applied to outsiders, to understand the mechanisms of exclusion and describe the likely outcome of such othering. In short, to know the when, why, who, what, how and whither of demonisation.

I have attempted in this book to locate sociologically the roots of othering. The disembededness of late modern society, the shock of pluralism, the fear of the ever possible loss of status or of downward mobility generates a vertigo of insecurity. One solution to such a loss of firm identity is nationalism, fundamentalism, racism (and for men, hypermasculinity) – that is to construct – or as Hobsbawm and Ranger (1983) would have it, 'invent' – a fixed identity based on the notion of a cultural essence which is reaffirmed, rediscovered and elaborated upon. This essentialising of the self, the allocation of oneself and one's kith and kin, firm virtues rooted in ones culture, is inevitably accompanied by the essentialising and denigration of the other. The process of constituting the devil thus proceeds apace. The simplest notion of what constitutes a demon, a folk devil, an enemy for any particular culture is that it is what they are not. It is the embodiment of all they stand against, a violation of their highest principles, ethics and values – it is, in short, constituted by negativity – it is the black and white of moral photography.

Let us try to develop our understanding of the role of the immigrant in the process of othering a little further. Up until now I have discussed the genesis of othering but it is important to stress also how blaming the immigrant is a very useful addition to the insidious public narrative which centres around crime and disorder. As I have argued elsewhere, if one starts from the position that First World societies are characterised by gross inequalities and widespread stigmatisation (unfairness in the justice of distribution and recognition), then the existence of disorder is scarcely surprising. This is the position of critical criminology. However, if one starts from a more establishment position: that our social world, however imperfect, is the best of all possible worlds, then disorder, however understandable in the Third World, becomes problematic in the First. For this reason the narrative of the 'war against crime' must explain deviance without indicting order. It must achieve what Berger and Luckman (1966) call an exercise in the 'maintenance of the symbolic universe'. The technique of solving this problem is two-fold: Firstly *distancing*: blaming factors or groups which are seen as unrelated to the normal functioning social order. An example of this would be the almost magical invocation of 'the gang' in the American media and, rather disgracefully, in academic criminology (for a critique of this see Kontos, Brotherton and Barrios, 2003). Secondly *inversion*: instead of the problems of society giving rise to crime, crime is seen to be an autonomous problem for society.

A key example of both of these is the rhetoric of the war on drugs. Drug use is seen to give rise to crime which creates problems for society, not that a problematic social order gives rise to crime and deleterious drug use. The war against crime becomes the war against drugs, that is:

Drugs → Crime → Social Problems

rather than:

Now the immigrant other is a very useful addition to such a narrative of denial. As an outsider, an alien, the immigrant (Albanian, Jamaican, etc.) brings in crime to society, it is obviously not a problem of the social order but a problem group imported into society, that is:

Immigration → Crime → Social Problems

or, even better:

Immigrants → Drugs → Crime → Social Problems

In this process of othering, then, the immigrant, rather than facing the full brunt of the social problems of our society (e.g. poor housing, inadequate education, second rate health facilities, high rates of crime and incivilities) is conjured up as the cause of these problems.

The final phase: the irony of assimilation

The grand irony of cultural 'othering' is that as migrant groups become more like the majority culture, they experience higher levels of relative deprivation and discontent in response to their poverty, and their level of crime increases. Thus, second generation African–Caribbeans in Britain have a higher level of crime. Similarly, as we have seen, the ethnographic studies of Carl Nightingale of African–Americans in Philadelphia (1993), and Philippe Bourgois of Puerto Ricans in East Harlem (1995), indicate that discontent and crime occurs not because of simple exclusion but the reverse, widespread cultural inclusion followed by structural exclusion: what I have called the bulimia of later modernity. Finally, of course, some minority groups take up the negative characteristics projected upon them, while others evolve cultures of difference and fundamentalism to cope with and make sense of their rejection. Having summoned forth false demons we find, in front of our eyes, real demons arising.

The roots of the disturbances

The interpretation of the disturbances amongst immigrant groups is, therefore, one of 'othering'. Incivilities, crime, rioting are seen as a product of lack of assimilation to the values and civic virtues of the host country. It is a product of their unreconciled 'alienness'. The policy response in the case of conservatives, involves a stress on assimilation per se, in the case of New Labour, with its key discourse of social inclusion and its commitment to multiculturalism, the stress is on integration and social inclusion. For conservatives assimilation is the equivalent of social exorcism, the dispelling of alien qualities: the conversion of the folk devil into a civilised being. For the liberal it is inclusion by the remedying of deficit. In both political instances, the roots of the disturbances are 'out there', rooted in unadapted difference. What I am arguing is the very opposite of this: disturbance occurs because of the degree of assimilation, it is a function of becoming more 'like us' rather than being unlike us. It is assimilation or integration which allows structural exclusion and lack of opportunities of work or acceptance as citizens to be experienced as unfair. The Asian youths who rioted in the Northern towns had the same accents and expectations as the white youths who rioted on the other side of the ethnic line. They scarcely needed teaching citizenship or English – they knew full well that bad policing was a violation of their citizenship just as was their considerable exclusion from the national job markets.

How did such a process of assimilation into Western values and aspirations occur? It occurs without the need for any government intervention by the exposure, particularly in the second generation, to the mass media, to mass education with its national curriculum, to the vast apparatus of the consumer society in advertisement, shopping mall and the images of success, and status, as embodied in clothes, motor cars and fashion accessories. Against this overwhelming cultural barrage, global in its dimensions and intense in its impact – the ability of any immigrant group to stay separate in its identity is extremely limited. The paradox, then, is that as the second generation immigrants become culturally closer to the 'host' and their economic and political aspirations concur with the wider society, at that point, they face both cultural exclusion because of racism and prejudice and become aware of the limits of economic opportunities. As I will argue in the concluding section, this discontent rather than finding political expression – a realisation of the common predicament of poor and socially excluded people of whatever ethnic origin (including the indigenous population) becomes transformed in a situation of segregation into conflict between socially excluded groups. In this instance, cultural differences although narrowing are grotesquely exaggerated and economic differentials although narrow are perceived as being grossly unfair and disproportionate.

The riots in Bradford, Oldham and Burnley

The riots which occurred in Bradford, Oldham and Burnley in 2001 were of a different nature than the widespread disturbances which occurred throughout Britain in 1981 and 1985. The riots of the 1980s were riots of inclusion, they were a fight back *against* the whole catalogue of social exclusions: police racism, unemployment, political marginalisation and impotence. They were not propelled by racism but against racism. In contrast those which have occurred more recently in our Northern cities have a more sinister aspect; sections of the community have become pitted against each other, racist stereotypes and ethnic prejudice have been mobilised and the aim on both sides has, at times, been to exclude, separate and divide. Thus, whereas the uprisings of the 1980s were never remotely race riots, those of today teeter on the edge of this category. Such events create dangerous opportunities for the parties of the far right, but they are the beneficiaries rather than the causes of such inter-community conflict. Of course unemployment and economic exclusion lies behind both the events of the 1980s and today. But the shape of the disturbances is very different and it is here that problems of identity and multiculturalism have had their impact.

Loic Wacquant, in his celebrated study of the comparison between Woodlawn in South Chicago and La Courneuve in the outer ring of Paris, notes the dramatic contrast between the extreme segregation of Chicago and the mixed population of Paris. 'Racial enclaves', he notes, are 'unknown in France and in all of Europe for that matter' (1996, p. 560). The diverse populations of the great European metropolises are one of the most significant achievements – however unintended – of late modernity. Indeed I write this in Stoke Newington, in the London Borough of Hackney where, if you take class and ethnicity into consideration, there is probably not a majority population – it is a constituency of intermixed diversity, an enclave of minorities. But Wacquant's observations, however true of great sections of our cities and reinforced by high rates of intermarriage and friendship, are not true of certain areas where housing provision, schools and the fears of racism have begun to create segregation and mono-culturalism. Bradford and Oldham are examples of this, as are the more exceptional situations in Belfast and Derry.

In the United States the exceptional degree of spatial segregation has been underscored by an ideology of multiculturalism and communitarianism. As writers as diverse as Zygmunt Bauman, Robert Hughes, Paul Gilroy and Tod Gitlin have pointed out, conventional notions of multiculturalism, however liberal in their intent, have potentially reactionary consequences. In a late modern world where people increasingly create their own sense of identity and culture, multiculturalism encourages exactly the opposite, to go to your roots and find your 'true' self. Such a fixed essence is then contrasted with 'Others' (Catholics against Protestants, Islam against non-Islam, White against Black) and allows prejudice to be based on notions of fixed differences. A multiculturalism which seeks tolerance paradoxically creates the conditions for prejudice and intolerance.

One solution to this problem is communitarianism, a mosaic of separate communities, each homogenous in their own values, and secure in their own identities. But as the US experience has shown the mosaic constantly frays at the edges, there is, in Tod Gitlin's haunting phrase, a 'twilight of common dreams' (1995), each community sets itself up against each other, competitive, exclusive and prejudiced in their attitudes.

What can we do about this? First of all we need to solve the problem of economic exclusion which fuels the antagonisms between the communities. As we have seen, such economic inclusion must involve genuine possibilities of education and economic and social improvement, it cannot merely involve, in the name of flexibility of labour, the shifting of a whole category of people into the bottom end of the labour market. Secondly, we must tackle the very notion of multicultural communities which underscore so much of conventional thinking – left and right – and which facilitates such antagonisms. The rational solution to dividing the world into binaries – them and us – as the New York radical philosopher Nancy Fraser (1997) has stressed, is to deconstruct the binaries – *not* to shore them up. This involves setting our goal on a new sort of multiculturalism – a multiculturalism of genuine diversity. A diverse society is one where there is genuine choice, where there is a mix of traditions, where the stress is on the ongoing creation of culture rather than the inheritance of a weighty tradition. A diverse society is not Oldham or Bradford or Burnley, where fixed and monolithic cultures confront one another, nor is it the neo-tribalism of Northern Ireland where tradition is glorified and the problems of identity are seemingly solved by consulting the fixed geographical contours of an atlas. In contrast, genuine cultural diversity is about creating new lifestyles and values, it is about bricollaging bits from here and there, it is the hybridisation of culture rather than the pursuit of a fake authenticity. It is, in fact, the actual lived culture that young people in schools which recruit from a wider range of ethnic and class backgrounds create everyday of the week. The enemy of this diversity is segregated housing policies, single faith schools, backward looking community leaders, and, above all, the glib allocation of people to fixed ethnic categories.

This is not the old story of assimilation where the 'host' country absorbs the immigrant minority. It is not *Daily Mail* columnist Melanie Phillips' prescription for the riots: a new assimiliationism – a melting pot – where everyone comes out culturally 'white' and terribly English. In the politics of diversity everybody changes and the hallmark of progress is a multiculturalism which overlaps, blurs and merges, which does not constantly reinvent the past but looks forward to the future.

It is not lack of knowledge of citizenship which generated the riots in the Northern towns but the very reverse: a strong, learnt sense of economic, political and social citizenship thwarted. What is necessary is a notion of social inclusion which tackles both the alienation of immigrant communities and the racism of the indigenous population by providing the education and jobs necessary to overcome the economic and geographical isolation of such towns and policies which ensure fair policing and political integration. Further, conventional multiculturalism which stresses a separate, static, communitarian mosaic must be replaced by a multiculturalism which puts emphasis on interaction, change and diversity by choice. All of this, whether in terms of jobs, policing, politics, opposition to social segregation – spatially and in schools – requires not merely citizens who realise their responsibilities but *also* the responsibility of government to provide structures which will facilitate citizens' rights and genuine social inclusion.

The riots in France, which started in the banlieus of Paris and spread throughout the country, evoked harsh responses from within the Republic and strange commentaries abroad. The interior minister, Nicolas Sarkovsky, the ex-Hungarian aristocrat who is a leading contender for the presidency of France, talked of 'Karcherising the scum'. Karcher is a sandblaster one might use to remove bird droppings from the wall; the phrase is reminiscent of ethnic cleansing. The commentaries from across the channel were largely self-congratulatory. The *Guardian*, in its editorial column, maintained that France should learn from Britain just as Britain had learnt from the US. They cite the riots in Detroit and Brixton and the subsequent inquiries as evidence. It points to the failure of the social market model and that: 'France has never had any time for Britain's multicultural approach. ... But what has been happening in France reinforces the correctness of our current goals.' (9 November 2005).

Let us note at the outset that such comparisons border on the preposterous. Detroit, the poorest large city in the US, with poverty levels worse than New Orleans, can scarcely be held as an example to instruct the French social model of the welfare state. Further, to argue for the success of British multiculturalism is astonishing given the recent past. Thus Jonathan Freedland (The *Guardian*, 9 November) presents us with an interesting analysis of the French riots, but his conclusions simply baffle me. To argue that 'British multiculturalism' is 'still the best model we have' ignores the fact that six years ago, as outlined, we experienced intensive rioting in Bradford, Oldham and Burnley, that this was based on racial division, greatly exacerbated by a racist and aggressive policing, and that such discontent continued and festered, culminating in the July bomb attacks in London of which he has written so vividly and perceptively. As we have seen, conventional multiculturalism of the Anglo–American variety has come under widespread radical criticism. It encourages differences which often initially do not exist and insists on ethnic, nationalist and religious pigeonholing which ignores the multi-faceted experience and identities of people living in the real world. It over-stresses differences and occludes the actual overlaps and blurring: the hybridisation of cultures as well as the common cross-cutting interests which people, particularly those in poverty, share. A genuine culture of diversity would not engage in binaries (Muslim/Christian; Black/White, Protestant/ Catholic) but would encourage a pluralism of cultures which borrow and bricollage from each other: cultures of innovation rather than of tradition. It would neither make an edifice of difference nor engage in denial: it would celebrate diversity and seek to achieve common values.

The irony is that these British riots were characterised by explicit ethnic conflict between poor whites and those of Muslim background, whereas the

French riots involved joint action against the police and the authorities by second-generation kids from varied backgrounds, many of them Muslims in background, and some Christians if you want, but in fact religion was not a factor. The closest British parallel would be the Brixton riots of the early 1980s. As the French sociologist Akim Oualhaci (2006) pointed out, the 'rioters' were severely misrecognised in the world's media. They were not immigrants or foreigners but second generation or more, French citizens, they were not homogenous ethnically but a heterogeneity of North African, Sub-Saharan, Italian, Portuguese, Spanish, Asian. They were not all Muslims – although religious community leaders attempted to muscle in on the act. What they had in common was class – they were the alienated poor – *culturally integrated but socially non-integrated* because of lack of jobs and police prejudice.

This being said, the emphasis in the two rival models of social inclusion – Anglo–American and French – on economic and political inclusion respectively – are not alternatives for both dimensions but are a democratic necessity. They fail not because of their ideals, but because of their failure to deliver. The kids in Paris, Lyons and Toulouse were not rioting because of their lack of assimilation, but because they had absorbed and taken seriously the ideals of the Republic. But instead of Liberty, Equality and Fraternity they have encountered police harassment, lack of jobs, poor schools and gross stigmatisation. Riots or uprisings, if you will, are the most poignant indicators of the contradictions in our society: the ideals of inclusion and the bulimia of rejection. We did not learn much from Detroit, Brixton or Bradford. We should attempt to learn from them now.

8

TERRORISM AND ANTI-TERRORISM
TERRORISM: THE BANALITY OF EVIL

When we ingest the anodyne of war we feel what those we strive to destroy feel, including the Islamic fundamentalists who are painted as alien, barbaric, and uncivilized. It is the same narcotic. I partook of it for many years. And like every recovering addict there is a part of me that remains nostalgic for war's simplicity and high, even as I cope with the scars it has left behind, mourn the deaths of those I worked with, and struggle with the bestiality I would have been better off not witnessing. There is a part of me – maybe it is a part of many of us – that decided at certain moments that I would rather die like this than go back to the routine of life. The chance to exist for an intense and overpowering moment, even if it meant certain oblivion, seemed worth it in the midst of war – and very stupid once the war ended.

(Chris Hedges, *War is a Force Which Gives us Meaning*, 2003, p. 5)

Implicit in the idea of terrorism is the contrast with what is seen as normal patterns of war hinged with the notion that terrorism itself has become the major justification for war. The conventional notion of terrorism carries with it a simple dualism of violence:

The West	The Other
Rational	Irrational
Justified	Hysterical
Focused	Wanton
Response	Provocation
Defensive	Offensive
Generating security	Inspiring terror
Modernity	Anti-Modernity

Such a binary of violence is – all the more so in the context of the conflicts in the Middle East – reminiscent of Edward Said's (2003 [1978]) notion of Orientalism. In Said's formulation, Orientalism is a discourse about the East which carries with it notions of the chaotic, the violent, the disorderly, the treacherous, and the irrational. It creates an Other in a binary mode which, by contrast, serves to define the West, the Occident. It is an 'imaginary geography' wherein 'The Orient ... seems to be not an unlimited extension beyond the familiar European world but rather a closed field, a theoretical stage affixed to Europe' (2003 [1978], p. 63). Such a discourse is a legitimation of power, it can be seen as a rationale for intervention, for resolving the 'clash of civilisation' (see Huntingdon, 1993). Against this, Said stresses the imaginary notions of the discourse around Orient and Occident: '[they] correspond to no stable reality that exist as a natural fact. Moreover, all such geographical designations are an odd combination of the empirical and the imaginative' (2003, p. 331). Instead, 'rather than the manufactured clash of civilisations, we need to concentrate on the slow working together of cultures that overlap, borrow from each other, and live together in far more interesting ways than abridged or inauthentic mode of understanding can allow' (ibid., p. xxix).

It is apparent that such a binary conception of violence carries with it:

- A denigration/beatification which ignores blurred lines and similarities in the use of violence.
- A justification for violence on the part of a counter terrorism even though this may be wildly disproportionate and mis-targeted.
- A rationale for military and/or economic intervention in which it evokes Western modernity as delivering democracy, rationality and the rule of law.

It is when one comes to look at Western definitions of terrorism that suspicions as to their objectivity and the distinctive nature of such violence immediately arise. There are two institutions which seek to define terrorism: law and social science. A fairly typical legal definition is that of the US Code and the FBI, here terrorism is: 'unlawful use of force or violence against persons or property to intimidate or coerce a government, the civilian population, or any segment thereof in furtherance of political or social objectives' (FBI, 1998, p. ii).

Of course, if one removed the word 'unlawful', such a definition would easily fit, say, Dresden or Hiroshima in the Second World War. The word 'unlawful' merely allows a tautology to be perpetrated. Nor do social scientific definitions come off any better. In search of the positivistic, the scientific, social scientists would eschew words like 'unlawful' for they make the pretence of focusing on the 'objective', the behavioural: that to be discovered out there, irrespective of fiat or law. Thus Holmes and Holmes in their standard text, *Murder in America*, define terrorism as: 'premeditated, politically motivated violence, perpetrated against non-combatant targets by subnational groups or clandestine stage agents usually to influence an audience.' (1994, p. 130).

What country, one might ask, does not utilise clandestine stage agents, commit premeditated politically motivated violence, and in late twentieth/early twenty first century wars inflict violence on non-combatants? (see Kaldor, 2003). What could be more terrifying than an AC-130 gunship at the siege of Falluja going backwards and forwards in what they call a 'lazy arc' with its 105mm cannons blazing? Is this not wanton in its savagery, collateral in its civilian casualties let alone property damage, and terrifying in its impact? Here again the use of 'subnational' in the text facilitates tautology. Or to take these authors' definition of the 'serial killer': 'someone who murders at least three persons in more than a 30-day period' (ibid., p. 92). They are surely not talking of a sniper in the Marine Corps on active duty?

Indeed, Martin Shaw in his *War and Genocide* traces the change in the nature of warfare from the notion of violence being targeted specifically at combatants and the rules of war being applicable in such struggles to what he calls the 'degenerate' warfare of modern times, where the definition of the enemy is extended to civilians as well as the military, where the civilian population is deliberately targeted, and where the means of destruction are immensely augmented and killing is increasingly indiscriminate (see 2003, pp. 23–6). In this light one might point to one major distinction between conventional warfare and terrorism as being the more limited aspirations of the latter.

The truth is that there is little to objectively distinguish between normal warfare and terrorism except for the level of power and legitimacy which state agents have over their less powerful opponents: the worry is that it is the imaginary difference that is used to justify 'normal' warfare.

Proxy wars and the defeat of the Soviet Union

The line between conventional warfare is further irrevocably blurred by the advent of proxy wars as a common mode of armed intervention for political reasons during the Cold War. Both the United States and the Soviet Union, rather than face the nuclear dangers of direct confrontation, or the political embarrassment of overt intervention, funded guerrilla groups in every major conflict zone of the globe. An illustration of this was the covert US funding of the Contras in Nicaragua in order to overturn the left wing administration, conducted interestingly via the Saudis, which led to the well known 'contra scandal'. But undoubtedly the climax of proxy warfare was the funding of the Taliban in order to overthrow the Communist government of Afghanistan. This was the most successful covert programme in the whole of the CIA's history, it was ridiculously cheap, costing $3 billion of American taxpayers' money, and hardly any US casualties. The low cost, both in money and in men, was the great attraction of the proxy war – the allure of terrorism to the Western powers. The support for the fundamentalist Mujahideen was intended to not merely overthrow Afghan Communism but, more importantly, to draw the Soviet Union into the conflict – to give them 'their Vietnam' as it was put by Zbigniew Brzezinski, the US national security advisor, and to ultimately hasten the disintegration of their empire. By the end of December 1979 the Soviets had taken the bait and the consequences are well-known history. The money was funded through Saudi Arabia, with Saudis matching the US contribution dollar for dollar but also providing the stream of recruits to the Mujahideen, including a man of high rank in Saudi society, soon to be their front line leader, Osama Bin Laden. 'Those were the prettiest days of our lives', he wrote, 'What I lived in those two years there, I could not have lived in a hundred years elsewhere' (cited in Unger, 2004, p. 106). And again, 'One day in Afghanistan counted for more than a thousand days praying in a mosque' (ibid., p. 106). Afghanistan hardened Bin Laden; at first he praised the Americans for helping 'us get rid of the seculist atheist Soviets' (ibid., p. 102), but later the penny must have dropped. For if such methods of unconventional warfare worked at getting rid of the Soviets, could they be used against the other wing of Western modernity, the United States? The Taliban armed by the West became the major centre for terrorism and began systematically to inspire, if you want, proxy terrorism in so many countries across the world.

Of course there are differences between terrorism and conventional warfare, much – although of course not all – terrorism is committed by those that are less powerful than those who conduct conventional warfare. But the similarities are much greater – at least from the perspective of the civilian population that such activities impact upon. That is, what is a world of difference from the point of view of the military and the élites which control them, is very similar from the standpoint of the civilian. There can be little doubt as to whose perspective one should rate the most highly.

Occidentalism

Ian Buruma and Avishai Margalit in their book, *Occidentalism: The West in the Eyes of its Enemies* (2004), point to how the Japanese Kamikaze pilots, the first suicide bombers in recent history, were not distant from Western culture and ideas. Far from it, a surprising number were from the humanities departments of top universities. Their letters reveal that they had read widely in German philosophy and French literature, quite a few were Marxists, while Nietzsche and the existentialists were of great interest. They were not distant from Western culture, but immersed in it. But it was this immersion that led to the rejection of the West as individualistic, decadent, corrupt, soft – all of the attributes of Occidentalism. So, as the West creates a discourse of Orientalism to depict the other, those othered create an Occidentalist discourse to reject that which denigrates and humiliates them. Thus, Buruma and Margalit describe the youth of the Third World:

> consumers at the lowest rungs of the new global economy: pirated DVDs showing Hollywood action films, cheap US-style leisure wear, and a twenty-four-hour din of American pop music as its local spin-offs. To idle youths living in these cultural wastelands, globalization, as the closest manifestation of the Western metropole, can be an endless seduction and constant humiliation. To the more highly educated ones, globalization has become a new word for imperialism. (2004, p. 36)

There is a seduction of a culture which at once attracts yet undermines all sense of one's own worth and identity, there is the denigration of being outside of the global realm of wealth and opportunity. Thus:

> The West in general, and America in particular, provokes envy and resentment more among those who consume its images, and its goods, than among those who can barely imagine what the West is like. The killers who brought the towers down were well-educated young men who had spent considerable time living in the West, training for their mission. Mohammed Atta received a university degree in architecture in Cairo before writing a thesis on modernism and tradition in city planning at the Technical University in Hamburg. Bin Laden himself was once a civil engineer. If nothing else, the Twin Towers exemplified the technological hubris of modern engines. Its destruction was plotted by one of their own. (2004, p. 15)

Indeed Osama Bin Laden is a member of a family who spent much time in the West, owning mansions, staying in the best hotels, investing widely, many members of which were playboys with expensive tastes in race-horses and aircraft. Hardly a person to whom the West was unknown. Indeed it was the knowledge of the West that spurred his loathing of it. As the English journalist, Nick Cohen, put it: 'The clash of civilisations is inside people as well as between them. Osama Bin Laden was as Westernized as Omar Sharif ... although Bin Laden probably wouldn't thank you for explaining this to him' (2003, p. 3). And for others living in the West, experiencing cultural denigration, prejudice and (unlike bin Laden) impoverishment, the experience of alienation must be even greater. If one thinks of the Moroccan group around the Madrid March 2004 bombing, or the IRA volunteers in the pubs of Kilburn in North London in the 1980s, or indeed the London bombers of July 2005, one can see how such alienation can emerge, as well as a level of support from fellow immigrants. Paul Berman makes a similar point, noting: 'The 9/11 terrorists most of them, likewise, turn out to have been people with claims to both the Arab past and the Western present' (2004, p. 18). Further, such an overlap of worlds followed by revulsion and *ressentiment* occurs at all levels of society.

The House of Bush and the House of Saud

Let me, as an interlude, present a glimpse into the overlap of worlds. On 11 September 2001 the top executives of the Carlyle Group – a giant private equity corporation firm with assets of over $16 billion dollars, and illustrious members such as George H.W. Bush, Frank Carluccia and John Major, got together in the Ritz Carlton Hotel in Washington DC for an investors' conference. It was customary that coffee and pastries were served at 7.30 am and for the presentations to start at 8.00 am. But the procedures were disrupted – as they were at meetings across the world – for at 8.46 am the first plane hit the World Trade Center. And by the time of the second collision the Carlyle Group's investors were glued to the hotel's television monitors. By all accounts, two men sitting in the same room, Baker – former presidential Chief of Staff and Secretary of State and of the Treasury – and Bin Laden got up and left the room, Bin Laden removing his name tag, and left quickly in their separate cars.

Baker and Bin Laden were close acquaintances and Bin Laden was not, of course, Osama Bin Laden but his brother, Shahig, who was representing the family firm, a collossus of a construction firm with massive US investments, including in the Carlyle Group with its close links to the Bush family. Over the next two days, as Craig Unger points out in his book *House of Bush, House of Saud* (2004), the most extraordinary event occurs. For 48 hours all commercial and private aviation was grounded across the United States. Yet an intensive evacuation plan took place to pick up Saudis from across the United States and fly them back to Saudi Arabia. All of this despite the fact that 15 of the 19 hijackers on 9/11 were Saudis. Imagine in contrast the difficulty of getting out of Britain if you were from a suspect nation or country of origin after the July 2005 tube bombings. All that can be said is that on 14 September the Saudis dispatched 9 million barrels of oil to the United States and the price dropped from $28 to $22 a barrell (Unger, 2004, p. 11); a post-9/11 oil crisis was averted.

The two contradictions: inside and outside the First World

Let us put the phenomena of Orientalism and Occidentalism in a more systematic sociological context. As was argued earlier, the forces of economic and cultural globalisation impact in very similar ways in both the First and

Third Worlds. They result in contradictions *within* the First World and *between* the First and Third Worlds.

In the case of the First World, increased levels of income inequality, coupled with job insecurity, breakdown of community and endemic marital instability, create a society where there is both widespread relative deprivation and sense of social injustice, coupled with ontological insecurity and crises of identity. If relative deprivation generates a diffuse feeling of anger, the crisis of identity focuses it. For a common solution to ontological insecurity is to insist on some essential and highly valorised characteristics of oneself (be it through nationalism, religion, ethnicity, or machismo) and to substantiate this by contrasting it with a dehumanised 'other' who lacks these qualities. As we have seen, in the case of the First World, this is evidenced as an othering of those in the lowest part of the social structure and where a widespread hostility and xenophobia. In the United States such a process can be seen in widespread religious fundamentalism, excessive patriotism and flag-waving (see Welch, 2000), punitive penal policies and the build up of a Gulag-sized prison population, highly racialised in its focus (see Wacquant, 2000), and support for foreign wars which seek to punish enemies and export American values. It is on this basis that the populist base for Orientalism is generated.

In the Third World the impact of cultural globalisation cannot be overestimated. The Western media, permeating every part of the globe, spread images of the good life, material comfort and abundance, together with a stress on meritocracy and equality of opportunity which is, of course, strikingly absent in reality. Whereas harsh – and increasing – economic differences (half of the world – nearly three billion people – live on less than $2 a day) can be concealed in a world which is hermetically separated, this is no longer true in a world of cultural globalisation. Merton, in his classic 1938 article 'Social Structure and Anomie', sought to explain the reason for the high crime rate in the wealthy United States in contrast to the low crime rate in Italy. His explanation, well-known to every sociology student, was that, in the United States, the universalistic, meritocratic cultural ideal of the American Dream contradicted with the actual structural limitations of success, and generated a situation of anomie which in turn led to crime. No such belief systems occurred in the Italy of that time, so that discontent, despite widespread grinding poverty, was less than in a much wealthier nation, such as the United States. Nowadays we may talk of a 'Global Merton', a ubiquitous situation of anomie where widespread aspirations have been generated by the forces of globalisation and where massive relative deprivation is engendered in the Third World giving rise to a discontent which is unlikely to be allayed. For how conceivably can one justify on a meritocratic basis such disparities of income which occur merely become of the arbitrary factor of place of birth? Indeed, massive movements of immigration spurred on by precisely such concerns, only serve to magnify this sense of unfairness – as it is precisely such populations which form a large, badly paid service class at the bottom of the class structure of the West. But it is not relative deprivation alone which foments discontent: the hubris of Western culture, its world dominance, challenges the traditional and the local, the political and economic power of the First World sidelines and denigrates the 'developing' nations. They are backward and insignificant, they have to be cajoled by the IMF, their markets have to be opened to Western goods and competition, they must be advised on everything from birth control to criminal justice. In an uncanny echo of the First World's attitude to its own poor, they are blamed for their poverty – they are poor because they lack the sensibilities and rationalities of the West. Such an Orientalist discourse denigrates on the level of identity and ontology: so that it is not simply injustice experienced on the levels of material goods and resources, it is a much more combustible combination of poverty and indignity.

The responses to the predicament of denigration can be manifold and exactly parallels the strategies of subordinate – and other racialised – groups within the First World. The stereotypical other can be accepted, assimilated, acted out. But the othering can be met by a counter-essentialisation, an elevation of the perceived virtues of the oppressed as a counterpoint to the denigrating stereotypes. And to achieve such a construction of a substantial and valued essence, precisely such a tit for tat othering occurs. Thus, in response to Orientalism, a discourse of Occidentalism occurs which defines itself over and against the supposed defects of Western culture and behaviour. Such a counterpart othering thus brings about familiar contrasts:

Economic success	Materialism
Individualism	Collectivism
Female empowerment	Female exploitation
Sexual freedom	Decadence
Rule of law	Hypocrisy

Such is the populist basis for Occidentalism, items which could well be part of a reasoned (and reasonable) critique become instead understood in terms of essences, of the positing of essential differences between the two worlds. And such differences are constructed on the basis of a parallel process of dehumanisation of the other. That is, in Orientalism, the East is in essence lacking in the human virtues of rationality, of controlling the impulse to violence, of orderly social behaviour, of dispassionate bureaucracies, whether of politics and business or a civil service relatively immune to corruption and self-serving behaviour. Whereas, in contrast, Occidentalism evokes the West as lacking in the most important of human virtues, honour, respect for tradition and community, sexual propiety and family values. Such essentialism alone, on either side, does not lead inevitably to violence but what it does is facilitate it. For, to the extent that dehumanisation allows the actor to render the other as outside, or on the periphery of humanity, it *permits* violence. None of this leads immediately to violence, but it sets up its precursor. It is when dehumanisation is linked to some perceived threat of actual harm, when the other is seen as the cause of the problem, that essentialisation gives place to denigration and outright violence is likely. And, of course, when war – whether conventional or terrorist – occurs, then a spiral of such demonisation occurs and each side experiences clear evidence of the inhumanity of the other. For once the battle is on, the furies of dehumanisation are constantly stirred into being and all stereotypes reinforced. It is war, of all human institutions, which both facilitates dehumanisation and, as Chris Hedges has so brilliantly analysed, served to provide the most seductively secure identities and gripping narratives. Hence, the title of his book, *War is a Force that Gives us Meaning* (2003).

Finally, in this discussion of the fundamental symmetry of conventional war and terrorism, let us detail the actors themselves. It is an irony that the combatants in such conflicts are strikingly similar in their social characteristics. Young men, the dispossessed, those at the bottom of the structure provide the recruits for both war and terrorism. In the First World, recruits are disproportionately from ethnic minorities, the lower working class – those who join because of lack of work and a desire for educational advancement.

Symmetry and differences

I have talked about the symmetry of violence both in terrorism and in what one might call anti-terrorism terrorism, which is how modern conventional warfare has been recast. But there are significant differences – or at least there are significant differences in the *imaginaries* that each opponent has of itself. For just as the West's imaginary of the East (Orientalism) differs from the East's imaginary of the West (Occidentalism) the process of othering, so the stereotypes of self – particularly in relation to violence – vary.

The recent Western image of warfare, particularly that of the United States, is that it is an instrument of modernity; it brings democracy instead of dictatorship, the rule of law rather than oppression, order rather than chaos, equality rather than ethnic rivalry and female subservience, the Free Market rather than corruption or state subsidy. Yet if we examine the discourses of terrorism and the counter-terrorism terrorism, that of the Orient and the Occident, there are clear differences in their declension of the rules of violence.

I have argued that, in order to do evil, to act with excessive violence towards other human beings, a discourse must be developed which allows for the moral release of the perpetrators from the normal human values which deeply eschew interpersonal violence. We have seen how the process of essentialisation of the other can give rise to a dehumanisation that permits violence. But violence itself occurs when such dehumanised others are seen as a source of harm to oneself: particularly agents of violence. In this fashion ' illicit' violence begets 'legitimate' violence. Furthermore, such a process of othering is mutual, each side generates images of dehumanisation and enacts violent acts which confirm the stereotypes of inhumanity. In a war situation, such a process spirals rapidly, mutually reinforcing the discourses of either side. And indeed the 'metaphor of war' *permits* violence.

The sanitisation of evil

The Western image of its own violence is a process of sanitisation. It is a surgical intervention to root out the sources of violence and – in contemporary neo-conservative parlance – to bring about a healthy modern society with all the benefits of democracy, the rule of law, and free markets. Violence is not excessive, it is minimal: the collateral is low, the very use of the word, of course, shields us from torment and suffering. The strikes are 'surgical', the passion of the killing absolutely minimal, it is a video screen with a cross target, distant both physically and mentally from the combat. The casualties on our side should be nil (surgeons don't die), the casualties on the other should be minimal (a few patients die). There are few bodies in sight: body bags are kept out of the glimpse of the media, images of coffins returning frowned upon, even listing the dead is seen as unpatriotic and distasteful. The returning dead and, even more curiously, the returning wounded are rendered invisible.

Overall this is a remarkably unemotional task, a job to be done: the very distance from the enemy (of which there is very little contact or knowledge) underscores this. There is a hint of what Bauman (1995) calls adiaphorization: the stripping of moral evaluation from human actions. Killing by the mobilisation of the most advanced technology the West can muster, utilising awesome weaponry that is designed with science and engineering at the very edge of human endeavour, is to be conducted then without passion and with an eye on precision. It is this distancing and neutralisation which permits acts of extreme violence; it is as if the very technical sophistication of the weaponry enables massive acts of violence while occluding the actual pain and torment of killing (see Shaw, 2003).

The beatification of evil

The discourse of terrorism is almost the reverse of sanitisation, whatever the similarity of the impact. For the suicide bomber, the act of killing is almost

Table 8.1   Violent Discourses: East and West

	East	West
Violence	Beatification	Sanitisation
Locus	Corporeal	Virtual
Enemy	Known	Unknown
Proximity	Immediacy	Distance
Motive	Humiliation	Humanitarian
Collateral deaths	Maximised	Minimised
Perpetrators	Many martyrs	Few heroes
Discourse	Joy of martyrdom	Unemotional, banal
Own casualties	Celebrated	concealed

intimate, the targets, whether in the bus, the café, the club or checkpoint are in immediate proximity. It is propelled by the visceral feeling of humiliation, it is enacted by the almost epitome of corporeality: the bomb, together with its shrapnel and detonators, is strapped onto the body. Both the suicide bomber and the assailants who face almost certain death, their motivation uppermost in their mind is not to avoid death but to embrace martyrdom. If one were to proffer the way that so many people will volunteer for this: martyrdom is, of course, the greatest reason, but martyrdom is also the ideology which facilitates such acts of grievous violence and harm.

The logic of the West

The material and political background to sanitised evil is considerable: the end of mass conscription in most Western countries means that substantial losses cannot be sustained and mass confrontation avoided at all costs. The return of too many body bags is seen as an electoral danger and, most importantly, the public has little stomach either for massive casualties, whether of our own troops, those of the enemy, or of innocent civilians. The moral changes in public tolerance of violence evident domestically within the wider society are extended to warfare. We are now lightyears away from the public willingness to accept massive casualties as in the First World War: even the initial tolerance for the slaughter of Vietnam seems of another era. Lastly, the technical fix: the availability of vastly enhanced delivery vehicles, coupled with sophisticated computer systems with the promise of pinpoint targeting and optimum surveillance, where the epitome of the future is the Predator missile, all hold out the possibility of the surgical attack and the sanitised slaughter (see Shaw, 2003).

The Western case for the use of violence is presented as an item of linear logic: it is fair, reasoned, it justifies the impalatable – the use of violence by the State – in a parallel fashion to how the liberal state justifies punishment against its citizens. But the case for war and its presentation is, of course, imaginary, in that this is how many people fondly imagine war today; but it is, of course, not what actually happens. Use of force frequently involves extreme and brutal collateral damage, the smart bombs don't work, the military don't sufficiently care, it is always exceedingly disproportionate to the harm exerted by the enemy, private vested interests (whether, for example, about oil or about minerals) and public interests (the protection of the countries' strategic interests) are thinly concealed. Furthermore, once the troops are on the ground, when they are actually forced to encounter the enemy, the war becomes messy, sanitisation virtually impossible, and concealment of both civilian deaths and troop losses impossible, and the brutal reality of war becomes transparent.

Paul Berman (2004) in his influential book, *Terrorism and Liberalism*, points out that there is no linear logic between the grievance of a group of people (which is often legitimate) whether because of resources denied or identity thwarted and its expression. The danger of liberalism, he argues, is that we are looking for a rationality of intention and, because of this, are blind to irrationality: to the distorted logic of the frustrated and the denigrated. The mistake he makes is to assume that the font of irrationality is the East with the West as vantage point of the rational. It is to give way to Orientalism; nothing more could underscore this than the events of Abu Grahib prison.

The photographs from Abu Grahib

Let's discuss the pictures from Abu Grahib. We are immediately struck by their overt nature, their sexuality, the enjoyment on the faces of the guards – the *lack* of furtiveness, the degradation in the corridors, not in the depths of the cell. These pictures are, of course, the very epitome of Occidentalism: the sexuality, the decadence, the immorality, the hypocrisy, the blatant sexuality of the woman involved, the degradation of the human body, a photographic satire on bourgeois individualism worthy of the Marquis de Sade. As Senator Dianne Feinstein remarked to *The New York Times* columnist, Maureen David: 'They're disgusting … If someone wanted to plan a clash of civilisations, this is how they'd do it. These pictures play into every stereotype of America that Arabs have; America as debauched, America as hypocrites' (2004, A25).

So, as they serve to confirm Occidentalism, they wantonly destroyed our Orientalist notions of ourselves, for how far from the dispassionate, clean pursuit of progress are these pictures taken in, of all places, Abu Grahib, Saddam's notorious torture prison. To some extent, then, paradoxically, the pictures are likely to have more effect in the West rather than the East. They are, of course, a searing commentary on modernity: for it took the most advanced technology in the world, the most sophisticated weaponry, the greatest scientific superiority, to achieve a stunning victory only to be followed by the long attrition of terrorism and the exposure of decadence and hypocrisy.

The photographs disturbed the West because they violated our conception of ourselves as rational, rule-following, law abiding, progressive, engaging in a war the purpose of which was to bring democracy, modernity and law and order, to bring reason to a dictatorial and arbitrary society. They violated our Orientalist sense of ourselves. To the Arab world, as Jonathan Raban has so stridently put it, the pictures are scarcely a surprise, they were rather confirmation: 'To most of the Arab editorial writers, and perhaps to most Arabs, the digital photos merely confirmed what they had been saying since long before the invasion of Iraq took place: America is on an Orientalist rampage in which Arabs are systematically denatured, dehumanized, stripped of all human complexity, reduced to naked babyhood' (2004, pp. 1–2). And, he adds, 'The pictures appear to be so single-minded in their intent, so artfully directed, so relentlessly Orientalist in their conception, that one looks instinctively for a choreographer – a senior intelligence officer perhaps, who keeps Edward Said on his bedside table, and ransacks the book every night for new ideas' (ibid., p. 5). Similarly, when the New York *Daily News* on 31 May 2004 greeted the slitting of hostages throats by terrorists in Saudi Arabia with the front page banner headline 'BARBARIC', this was an exclamation of shock but not of surprise. For this was precisely our Orientalist image of them.

It is not my intention here to analyse in-depth this incident. Only to point out that such regimens of degradation were scarcely limited to Abu Grahib, they existed in prisons in Afghanistan and at Guantanamo Bay, they occurred in the British as well as the American sectors of Iraq. It also has a resonance at home in the American prison system where such scandals are frequent and where, as in the war abroad, there is the paradox of the proclamation of the rule of law and the incidence of the most extreme lawlessness. As for culpability, there is no doubt a chain of command which instigated such humiliation, yet one must also note the level of enjoyment, of pleasure on the guards' part. This is certainly not a procedure which they are being forced into. The seductions of humiliation, particularly by those who themselves have been socially subordinate, has been noted before in wartime and genocidal situations as well as in violent crime (see Katz, 1988; Sothcott, 2003).

Love was all they had to set against them

I have examined two ways of dehumanisation: reciprocal perspectives which feed off each other but which facilitate violence against other human beings. Let us conclude with the poignant comments written by English novelist, Ian McEwan, just after 9/11. He recalls the last messages made by people in the Twin Towers or on the planes to their loved ones. In the words of his piece, 'Love was all they had to set against their murderers.' He writes:

If the hijackers had been able to imagine themselves into the thoughts and feelings of the passengers, they would have been unable to proceed. It is hard to be cruel once you permit yourself to enter the mind of your victim. Imagining what it is like to be someone other than yourself is at the core of our humanity. It is the essence of compassion, and it is the beginning of morality.

The hijackers used fanatical certainty, misplaced religious faith, and dehumanising hatred to purge themselves of the human instinct for empathy. Among their crimes was a failure of imagination. As for their victims in the plane and in the towers, in the terror they would not have felt at the time, but those snatched and anguished assertions of love were their defiance. (2001)

The London bombing and the banality of evil

Martine Wright, a woman going to work, aged 31, running towards the open doors of a tube train, hesitates for a moment, it is terribly crowded, slips through the closing doors, sits in the nearest seat, 8.49am, Thursday 7th July. Thirty seconds later her life is totally and utterly devastated. Three seats away Shahzad Tanweer, aged 22, pulls the cord which explodes his backpack. There is a moment of silence, then people are screaming in the dark: a half an hour later the paramedics arrive triaging the injured from those who cannot be saved. Martine Wright survives, she has lost both legs below the knee, suffered a fractured skull and severe lacerations to her arms. She was still, in October 2005, in rehab.

We often concentrate on the dead and forget the injured – over 700 in three packed trains and a London bus, often with life-changing wounds and psychological trauma which continually structures and reconstitutes their lives. This was the worst terrorist attack in Britain and the first suicide bombing. The enemy, moreover, was *within*; it was not an attack of external malefactors such as the 9/11 bombers or the volunteers of the IRA. These bombers had Northern accents, jobs, universities, family – seemingly solid roots within the country, the CCTV footage captures them wearing anoraks, baseball caps, one of them wearing a New York City tee shirt – I am certain without any trace of irony.

Hassib Hussain, aged 18, second-generation, from Holbeck Leeds, GNVQ in business studies, cricketing fanatic.
Shahzad Tanweer, aged 22, second-generation, from Beeston Leeds. Great sportsman, cricketer, studied sports sciences at the University of Leeds.

Germaine Lindsay, 19, arrived from Jamaica when he was young, a recent Muslim convert, worked as a carpet fitter, a 'loving husband and father': with a fifteen month old baby and a wife who was pregnant.

Mohammed Sidique Khan, 30, of Dewsbury, studied at Leeds University, a teaching assistant working with vulnerable children, a mentor in a primary school, left a fourteen year old daughter and a pregnant wife.

The *Daily Mail* of 13 July showed a picture of the bland streets of the Beeston area of Leeds, semi-detached houses and a church on the corner with the headline: '*These utterly British streets produced twisted young men who hated this country so much that they gave their lives to become* SUICIDE BOMBERS FROM SUBURBIA'. Such a puzzle is picked upon much more poignantly by Shami Chakrabarti, the director of Liberty, the British civil liberties organization:

> I've thought a lot about what Mohammad Sidique Khan said in the video he recorded before the bombings. It's particularly chilling to me as a British Asian. He was 30 years old. I'm 36. He's got a broad Yorkshire accent and I've got a London accent. But he's as British as I am – fish fingers, Blue Peter, the whole thing. (2005, p. 29)

She tries to imagine what she would say to him beforehand to dissuade him – imagines being in a living room with him arguing.

But it was Jonathan Freedland of The *Guardian* who best captured this paradox of normality and its implications for future security:

> That these men wanted to kill and die is bad enough. That they were, it seems, born and raised in this country is even worse. If they had been a foreign cell, like that responsible for the Madrid bombing, we could have comforted ourselves that this was an external phenomenon, an alien intrusion. The remedies would have been obvious: tighter border controls, more international cooperation.
>
> But there can be no such comfort if these killers were British citizens. We could shut out every last asylum seeker, expel every illegal immigrant, and it would make us no safer. This attack came from within. (13 July, 2005)

Behind all of this there is a more pressing question: one which is the key focus of the criminology of war and of genocide. Namely: how do normal people do evil things? On my daily commutes on the London Underground as I pass through the Kings Cross/Euston area and gaze around on those cramped trains at the men, women and children going to work and to school, the wantonness of such acts beggars belief. Such an outrage was captured by Ken Livingstone, Mayor of London, on the day of the bombings:

I want to say one thing specifically to the world today. This was not a terrorist attack against the mighty and the powerful. It was not aimed at Presidents or Prime Ministers. It was aimed at ordinary, working-class Londoners, black and white, Muslim and Christian, Hindu and Jew, young and old. It was an indiscriminate attempt to slaughter, irrespective of any considerations for age, for class, for religion, or whatever.

I will return to this problem of evil later, a problem which Hannah Arendt famously called 'the banality of evil', the banality of the people involved and their actions. But let us first examine the process which led up to this atrocity. It is a dynamic of social construction, of othering and counter-othering.

The dialectics of othering and the problem of evil

In the last chapter I examined the disturbances in the Northern cities of England in 2001, the most significant rioting in Britain since the 1980s. This was a result of widespread disaffection of a minority of Asian youth brought about by limited job opportunities, widespread racism, ethnic segregation and inept and prejudiced policing. Some 10 miles south of Bradford and four years later three of the bombers plotted a much more drastic and tragic solution to their problems. I want to argue that this process, which begins with disaffection in the streets and ends in a martyrdom, is not mindless nor particularly alien but is deeply embedded in the most conventional of norms and the most otherwise laudable of dispositions. I shall briefly detail three stages of this process: the generation of anger, the othering of the otherer, and the summoning up of violence.

The generation of anger and the frustrations of normality

As we have seen, the experience of second-generation immigrants places particular strains upon them and that this is particularly true among the Pakistani and Bangladeshi populations of the Northern towns. On the material level they are bombarded from the media, the schools, the agencies of government and civil society with the mantra of liberty, equality, fraternity, the key values of liberal democracy. Yet in the job market, in the factories and schools, on the street, in the face of a prejudiced police force and a hostile white working class all of these values are daily thwarted. They suffer both an experience of relative deprivation, materially, and a stigmatised identity. I have characterised this as a bulimic process – they assimilate the values of their host and are rejected by it. It is not an experience of being alien, it is a process of being alienated. Colin Webster (2003), in his broad ranging study of the Northern towns conducted in the wake of the riots, concurs with this analysis: the British Pakistanis and Bangladeshis, rather than being a repository of alternative values, suffer from a 'surfeit' of values: 'which are internalised as rage and desperation ... this is how relative deprivation is "felt"'. Webster importantly stresses the *variability* of cultural identities which evolve out of this – hybridisation, crossover, even a sense of shared values with an impoverished white working class who also face crises of relative deprivation and identity. But *one* of these adaptations is fundamentalism. Further note that this is not an identity directly derived from the religion of their parents, which tends to be traditional and neither radical nor conducive to violence. Indeed, a significant minority of activists are converts.

The othering of the otherer

I described earlier in the chapter how the act of othering, of bulimia and rejection, is reversed in a struggle to maintain dignity, respect and identity. The counterpart of the 'orientalism' described by Edward Said, the depiction of the 'other' as subnormal, exotic and irrational, is the 'occidentalism' ably depicted by Buruma and Margalit. This involves – in a clumsy phrase – the othering of the otherer: where those who are stigmatised reverse the tables, and change the rules of the game, in a tactic which attempts to rescue dignity and command respect. Here the values of the host society are reversed or found wanting. Thus the rule of law is deemed a sham, a hypocrisy, equality between the sexes, a sham concealing the the objectification of women – the turning of women into sexual commodities, while the enterprise of capitalism itself is an obsession with money, the pursuit of interest and unearned wealth.

Note that this assertion of difference is made easy by the evident contradictions in the First World, the injustices which are all too evident. As I have argued, there is no great need to import outside virtues to perceive the failings of Western reality as experienced by the poor in the slums of Burnley, the banlieues of Paris or the ghetto of East New York. And once the train of difference is set off, it is the most conventional of liberal values which speed it on its way and encourage it to achieve its distance. For mainstream multiculturalism evokes the notion of essential differences between ethnic groups, nationalities and religions. It champions difference and it encourages the discovery of one's 'roots', as a key to personal understanding. Its mindset ignores blurring, crossover, the merging and hybridisation of cultures. Indeed it is fearful of such processes because it mistakenly views this as a cloak for assimilation, for the ironing out of cultural differences and the domination of the majority culture.

Conventional multiculturalism is, therefore, only too ready to divide the world into black and white, Muslim and Christian, Protestant and Catholic, and to ignore the shared and cross-cutting interests of people. The categories of fixed and essential difference do not have to be invented by the would-be Occidentalist. They are there waiting to be elaborated on. This is not, of course, to suggest that multiculturalism causes ascerbic division and enmity – the energy and force comes from the experiences of exclusion and humiliation, that is, from the injustices of distribution and recognition outlined in the last section.

However, neither the anger of injustice nor the channelling of declared differences between the immigrant and the host are sufficient to explain the ability of normal people to engage in acts of wanton evil.

The summoning up of violence

The question: 'how do normal/decent people do evil things?' runs like a thread through recent writing in the criminology of war and genocide. It is a question that resonates through discussions of the Holocaust (see Goldhagen, 1997, Morrison, 2005), war crimes such as the Mai Lai massacre in Vietnam (Sothcott, n.d.), and of torture (Huggins et al., 2002).

Because it relates gross deviance to normality, it obviates questions of pathological personality and leads us into areas of how such behaviour connects up with and, even perhaps, exemplifies certain aspects of conventional values and morality. With this in mind the work of David Matza and Gresham Sykes is frequently evoked (see Sykes and Matza, 1957; Matza and Sykes, 1961; Matza, 1964, 1969). This work is characterised by an early recognition of post-modern irony: for example, how conventional values spur on delinquency (particularly Matza), how prisons produce criminality (particularly Sykes). Famous here are Matza and Sykes' notion of techniques of neutralisation and, a little less well known, the concept of subterranean values.

The techniques of neutralisation allow us to make excuses to dominant norms and to exempt ourselves from their dictates. 'Denial of responsibility', for example, allows a delinquent to propose that they could not have acted otherwise, that they were pushed by forces or pulled into situations beyond their control. 'Denial of the Victim' denies that they are the real victim, rather they are the offender and had it coming. 'Appeal to higher loyalty' puts the loyalty to his or her friends about the norms against delinquency. Stan Cohen makes good use of this concept in his book *States of Denial* (2002) where he discusses, among other things, how 'normal' Germans could bring themselves to be involved in the mass slaughter of Jews. That is, he takes a concept introduced to explain mundane delinquency and violence and ratchets it up to explain extreme violence.

With the concept of subterranean values Matza and Sykes go further. Techniques of neutralisation alone, they argue, allow us to explain how deviance is facilitated, how norms are reinterpreted and neutralised, but 'it leaves unanswered a serious question: what makes delinquency attractive in the first place? Even if it is granted that techniques of neutralisation or some similar evasions of social controls pave the way for overt delinquency, there remains the problem of values or ends underlying delinquency and the relationship of these values to those of the larger society' (Matza and Sykes, 1961, p. 713).

In this article they argue that although violence is prevalent in society, we are in a state of denial about it; for the irony is that what we most fiercely condemn we most wholeheartedly embrace:

> ... we would do well to question prevalent views about society's attitudes toward violence and aggression. It could be argued, for one thing, that the dominant society exhibits a widespread taste for violence, since fantasies of violence in books, magazines, movies, the television are everywhere at hand. The delinquent simply translates into behavior those values that the majority are usually too timid to express. Furthermore, disclaimers of violence are suspect not simply because fantasies of violence are widely consumed, but also because of the actual use of aggression and violence in war, race riots, industrial conflicts, and the treatment of delinquents themselves by police. There are numerous examples of the acceptance of aggression and violence on the part of the dominant social order. (ibid., p. 717)

I must admit that I am in something of a quandary here, for if the techniques of neutralisation would suggest the evasion of norms, subterranean values suggest that they do not need to be sidestepped. They exist because they are attractive: because excitement, short-term hedonism, and violence are attractive in their own right. Matza and Sykes attempt to solve this contradiction by suggesting that there is a time and place for the subterranean, that immediate gratification has a place in leisure and not in the workaday world, and that juvenile delinquents in a way get their timing wrong, they exhibit inappropriate behaviour at the wrong time, in the wrong place. This is not an altogether satisfactory resolution – I don't think that subterranean fully captures the centrality of these values, and if it works for pleasure it is not so simple for aggression.

It is often assumed that at its very basis our social values are against violence and that violence where it occurs is a product of extraneous influences in our society (the IRA, Islamists) or of aberrations produced within it (e.g. the 'gang'), or most popularly of a mass media which plays on our baser instincts and carries supposedly gratuitous depictions of violence. In this case the mass media, particularly the popular media, are seen to step out of line. In a study of the mass media and aggression carried out as part of a Hippocrates project, Jayne Mooney and I (2002) argued that such violence in the media, far from being gratuitous, is presented as part of a rubric of core values which we termed 'the paradigm of violence'. In this we argued that the problem of 'effects' research in mass media studies – in particular the reason for the uniformly inconclusive results over the last three decades (see Reiner, 1997) – is that it ignores the context in which violence is set. It concentrates quantitatively on how much violence there is in the mass media and what is its effect on behaviour, ignoring the narrative, the stories within which the violence is placed. First of all the paradigm sorts violence into two sorts: pro-social and anti-social. Pro-social violence is perceived as a response to anti-social violence – it is seen as normatively distinct, although in actuality it is behaviourally virtually indistinguishable. For example, as I argued earlier in the chapter, the legal or social scientific definitions of terrorism would be basically tautological if the phrase 'unlawful' is removed. What such a paradigm carries is not a condemnation of violence, but a series of techniques of neutralisation, a vocabulary of motives of when and where violence is justified. Violence is scarcely subterranean, it is overt and glorified. This narrative of violence stretches from video games to Hollywood, from the arcades to the multiplexes, it is in the violence of politicians, witness the 'axis of evil', and the 'crusade' against it, from the everyday news stories to the actual situation of near perpetual war we have been in over the last century. It carries with it the simple notion of 'the good guys' and 'the bad guys'. There is, as Christopher Hedges points out, a strange indifference about the fate of bad guys and an obsessive concern with our own:

While we venerate and mourn our dead we are curiously indifferent about those we kill. Thus killing is done in our name, killing that concerns us little, while those who kill our own are seen as having crawled out of the deepest recesses of the earth, lacking our own humanity and goodness. Our dead. Their dead. They are not the same. Our dead matters, theirs do not. Many Israelis defend the killing of Palestinian children whose only crime was to throw rocks at armored patrols, while many Palestinians applaud the murder of Israeli children by suicide bombers. (2003, p. 14)

Violence and the metaphor of war

Hedges, in *War is a Force Which Gives Us Meaning* (2003), painstakingly examines the attractions of war to him as a war correspondent. It is, he claims, a narrative of the highest order and it is a narrative which not only gives meaning but which thrills, fascinates and excites:

The enduring attraction of war is this: Even with its destruction and carnage it can give us what we long for in life. It can give us purpose, meaning, a reason for living. Only when we are in the midst of conflict does the shallowness and vapidness of much of our lives become apparent. Trivia dominates our conversations and increasingly our airwaves. And war is an enticing elixir. It gives us resolve, a cause. It allows us to be noble. And those who have the least meaning in their lives, the impoverished refugees in Gaza, the disenfranchised North African immigrants in France, even the legions of young who live in the splendid indolence and safety of the industrialized world, are all susceptible to war's appeal. (2003, pp. 3–4)

In a world where narratives are at a premium and where tedium and vacuousness beset us, 'the anodyne of war' is a most powerful drug. It is this seduction of war (and of genocide) which belies Hannah Arendt's famous notion of the banality of evil. Rather, I would stress, in line with the work of Jack Katz (1988), that it involves the very opposite – an attempted escape from banality. And note the irony, which I discussed earlier in this book, that it is precisely those sections of youth who experience, most pressingly, such disjunctions of narrative and the tedium of everyday life who are by no coincidence, the greatest consumers of mass media carrying the message of the paradigm of violence. And in turn, find themselves drawn to the militant rhetoric of fundamentalism while, in others, queue manfully outside the army recruiting posts sited in poor areas of the United States and Britain.

The appeal of this narrative of violence is well brought out in Evan Wright's book, *Generation Kill*, where the journalist goes into battle with the Second Platoon of the US Marines First Reconnaissance Battalion as they race in their Humvees, as the advance guard in the Invasion of Iraq, 2003.

At least one Marine in Colbert's Humvee seems ecstatic about being in a life-or-death gunfight. Nineteen-year-old Lance Corporal Harold James Trombley, who sits next to me in the left rear passenger seat, has been waiting all day for permission to fire his machine gun. But no chance. The villagers Colbert's team had encountered had all been friendly until we hit this town. Now Trombley is curled over his weapon, firing away. Every time he gets a possible kill, he yells, 'I got one, Sergeant!' sometimes he adds details: 'Hajji in the alley. Zipped him low. I seen his knee explode!'

Midway through the town, there's a lull in enemy gunfire. For an instant, the only sound is wind whistling through the Humvee. Colbert shouts to everyone in the vehicle: 'You good? You good?' Everyone's all right. He bursts into laughter: 'Holy shit!' he says, shaking his head. 'We were fucking lit up!' …

Trombley is beside himself. 'I was just thinking one thing when we drove into that ambush,' he enthuses. 'Grand Theft Auto: Vice City. I felt like I was living it when I seen the flames coming out of windows, the blown-up car in the street, guys crawling around shooting at us. It was fucking cool"'. (2004, pp. 4–5)

Let us pause for a moment and examine the potency of the metaphor of war. It provides a vocabulary of motives which transforms one's mindset and achieves a gestalt in behaviour: it is a rich and intense narrative, not so much techniques of neutralisation as rules of engagement. The metaphor of war allows murderous anger to morph into patriotism, brutality to be lionised, the unspeakable to be bemedalled, the despicable to be the act of martyrs. Its rhetoric magically transforms its participants; our sacrifices are their bloodlust, we defend, they provoke, their wantonness justifies the steel of our response. And it is a grammar of symmetry where both sides speak the same language, but somehow only rarely understand each other.

On 25 August 2005, as the peace activist Cindy Sheehan camped outside the President's Texas ranch attracting greater and greater public support, George W. Bush decided to stage a meeting with pro-war military families. In his speech he seemed to minimise Sheehan, whose son Casey was killed in Iraq the year before, specifically pointing to Idaho's Tammy Pruett, who has five sons and a husband all who have served in Iraq. The audience erupted into chants of 'U-S-A, U-S-A, U-S-A', when quoting Pruett, Bush said 'Tammy says this – and I want you to hear this: "I know if something happens to one of the boys, they would leave this world doing what they believe, what they think is right for our country"'.

The cloak of martyrdom, the metaphor of war can change people: it can turn the kid from Idaho into a Marine firing white phosphorus shells which cling to the skin, burn to the bone in 'shake and bake' attacks at the siege of Falluja, it can metamorphose an Irish lad living in Kilburn into a soldier, a 'volunteer', who is thus enabled to plant a random bomb in Victoria Station, it can transform young men from the North of England into warriors on a mission in the heart of London. Yeats talked of Padraig Pearse, one of the leaders of the Easter 1916 Rising as 'long looked upon as a man made dangerous by the Vertigo of Self-Sacrifice'. Whatever the righteousness of the cause, this is a narrative which engenders violence, and a certain element of recklessness – the willingness to sacrifice others and to sacrifice oneself for others. It has uncanny similarities both sides of the line of terror.

To return to the image of the train: it is fuelled by the anger over assimilation into Western ideals, coupled with rejection and humiliation, it travels along tracks directed by points clearly differentiating on the principles of Western multiculturalism, while the zeal with which the drivers speed towards collision is scripted by Hollywood, video games, and the daily news. If the badge on some of the trains is that of the star and crescent, so be it, but this determines more the direction of the train than the speed and thrill of collision.

I have argued in the last chapter how the social construction of the immigrant permits us to explain away homespun social problems as the result of aliens entering from without. The homespun terrorist, one who has grown up in this country, creates, as we have seen, particular problems: it does not facilitate such easy mental gymnastics. A fallback response, then, is to claim that second-generation immigrants are particularly prone to alien ideas, that fundamentalist Islam is the infection which spawned the terror. I have no doubt that there is much in the language of the Koran and in the discourse of the jihad to inspire and justify violence – as there is in Old Testament Christianity or Judaism for that matter. The question is not whether there is intrinsic aggression in these scriptures but what is the impulse and the basis to interpret them with such a fundamentalist spin. I am not arguing (as a British Home Secretary so foolishly maintained) that the Iraq War has no relationship to such terrorism nor the oppression of the Palestinian people. Rather that resort to violence is as American as apple pie, as British as the origins of the Empire. My point is that the impulse to commit violence is fuelled by Western values thwarted, the notion of fixed differences is enhanced by conventional multiculturalism, and the metaphor of war and all it permits is a core part of Western culture. This grammar is there to inspire the home-grown terrorist of whatever persuasion, whether religious or in situations where there is no trace of Islam in sight, witness Timothy McVeigh and the Oklahoma City bombing (see Hamm, 2004), as it is there to inspire the conventional warfare of phosphorus shell, cluster bomb and patriotic martyrdom.

Finally, let me add idealism to this cauldron of emotions. Idealism may be the last thing anyone wants to hear about when we countenance the vicious murders in the underground of London, the railways of Madrid, or the twin towers of New York. Yet if we do not understand the idealism behind these horrors we will never understand them. Idealism: the fight against the greatest military machine in the world, the monstrous enemy which invades countries without reason, humiliates nations, kills children in Palestine, backs the destruction of the Lebanon. An enemy that is rich, smug, self-satisfied and cynical. Disagree with all of this if you will, but a great many people around the world think likewise. And but unless you understand the world from this perspective, see it through their eyes, you will never understand terrorism.

I gaze at a photograph by Veronique de Vigueri in *The Guardian* (16 September, 2006). It is a picture entitled 'Brothers in Arms', of fighters in the Ghazni province of East Afghanistan who, as the caption says, are 'challenging George Bush's assertion that the war has been won'. They stand together, gangly boys with their AK7s and rocket launchers; one looks at the camera with a slight smile upon his face. You would have to be a fool to deny the solidarity, the comradeship, the unity of purpose and yes, the excitement of such groups. Believe you me it sticks like a craw in my throat to say this, but what this international gathering of young people fighting against injustice seems like is the International Brigades in Spain in the 1930s. But the liberal in me tells me that the fight against fascism was a good thing, a generous and a progressive cause, and that this fight is almost precisely the reverse of this: the creation of some form of fascism as a reaction to injustice. For the attacks on London, Madrid and New York were attacks on the innocent and attacks on diversity, and the dead are a roll call of men and women from many cultures who lived together; it was an assault on all that is positive about this modern world, in the name of bigotry and essentialism.

If there is one thing a critical criminology can tell us it is how the experience of injustice can lead to further injustice. Righteous anger does not with any necessity lead to righteousness, it can lead to further injustice and, as we have seen, the creation of demonisation and othering can permit the impermissible. Evil can arise out of the experience of humiliation and unfairness and evil can come out of motivations that are normal, conventional and mainstream. Further, the countering of such acts can very often take on the shape and form of retaliations that quite rightly are labelled atrocities and which simply generate further adherents to the cause. Unless we can grasp the nature of these ironies, we will never be able to understand terrorism, let alone combat it and bring it to its end.

ELSEWHERE: ON THE D TRAIN TO MANHATTAN

I am sitting on the subway crossing the Manhattan Bridge on the D train, the Express train from Brooklyn to Manhattan. You emerge out of the converted lofts of Dumbo, past the Watchtower building of the Jehovah's Witnesses, below you is a small park with a pebbled beach, on one side the iconic view of the Brooklyn Bridge and further on the gigantic commercial towers of downtown Manhattan. On your right side the East River turns lazily past Williamsburg and the Upper East Side glistens in the sun. It is one of the greatest sights in the world. But nobody on the subway is looking, no one is looking out of the windows: my nearest companion is asleep, people are folded into their newspapers, America Oggi, Novoye Russkoye Slovo, Sing Tao, Korea Times, El Nacional, as well as The Post and The Daily News. Someone (I guess) is listening to the Grateful Dead on their headphones, somebody else (inevitably) hip hop, polka, country and western, the greatest hits of the 1960s. An English-looking gentleman listens to last week's BBC news from a podcast. A young black man, eyes closed, is swaying to rap on his leaky headphones, mouthing the lyrics. Two kids hunched over their PSPs fighting some battle light years away in another galaxy at the edge of the universe. A Jewish woman mumbles the Torah, the book grasped tightly in her lap. Someone is into a heated conversation on his cellphone ('I told him don't give me that shit'). Two girls gently dance together to Reggaeton on a joined I-Pod. Everyone is elsewhere, another place, another time, another sentiment, in dream and in trance, another feeling: everyone is going to work but no one is at work apart from the grey-suited man with red suspenders, anxiously reading the Wall Street Journal. By now we are approaching China Town at a fifth floor level, the perspectives wobble and clash, the Empire State Building is in the distance, the Chrysler Building to the far right, immediately Chinese graffiti dance on worn out buildings. But I am the only one looking out of the window, three years in Brooklyn and still a tourist.

URBAN SONAMBULISM: ELSEWHERE IN A BROOKLYN DELI

I am in our local deli in Park Slope. Dwelling over which of the numerous varieties of milk to purchase (1%, skimmed, full, soya, organic, etc.) when a woman walks into the store talking measuredly to her cellphone. She elbows me aside, though elbows is probably the wrong word because she doesn't really notice me. She moves around the shop collecting items while talking continuously into the 'phone and weaving between other customers to all intents and purposes as if she were a player in a video game and we and the shop were a virtual reality. She very seriously – and audibly – is planning the schedule for her week's work. She reaches the desk, placing the items on the counter. The shopkeeper says 'Hi', she doesn't look up from the 'phone or stop in her conversation, he says 'ten dollars fifty', she silently pulls some money from her pocket, the shopkeeper hands her the change saying 'thank you', she doesn't respond but continues steadfastly her deliberations on the 'phone. She is out the door, still talking, elsewhere; I raise my eyebrows at the shopkeeper. He smiles ruefully, 'I try to be human', he says.

9

THE EXCLUSIVE COMMUNITY

There is commotion around the need of community mainly because it is less and less clear whether the realities which the portraits of 'community' claim to represent are much in evidence, and if such realities can be found, will their life-expectancy allow them to be treated with the kind of respect which realities command. The valiant defence of community ... would hardly have happened had it not been for the fact that the harness by which collectivities tie their members to a joint history, custom, language or schooling is getting more threadbare by the year. In the liquid stage of modernity, only zipped harnesses are supplied, and their selling point is the facility with which they can be put on in the morning and taken off in the evening (or vice versa). Communities come in many colours and sizes, but if plotted on the Weberian axis stretching from 'light cloak' to 'iron cage', they all come remarkably close to the first pole.

(Zygmunt Bauman, *Liquid Modernity*, 2000a, p. 169)

... we have been living – we are living – through a gigantic 'cultural revolution' an extraordinary dissolution of traditional norms, textures and values, which left so many inhabitants of the developed world orphaned and bereft. ... Never was the word 'community' used more indiscriminately and emptily than in the decades when communities in the sociological sense become hard to find in real life. Men and women look for groups to which they can belong, certainly and forever, in a world in which all else is moving and shifting, in which nothing else is certain.

(Eric Hobsbawm, *The Age of Extremes*, 1994, p. 40)

One transfixing image of late modernity is that of social dislocation, of broken narratives and unhinged structures: of a fragmented world where space and culture no longer coincide, an amalgamation where each point of space links elsewhere to some other place or time or figment of the individual imagination. The woman on the cell phone in the crowded subway talking elsewhere, oblivious to the bustling world around her. People being closer and closer in the city, yet seemingly further and further apart in reality. A wasteland of anomie, the disconnected, the uninterested: of free floating atoms unaware and unconcerned about each other. How, conceivably, can social cohesion and a personal sense of coherence occur in such a fissile world of fragmentation and division?

Richard Sennett in two books, *The Conscience of the Eye* (1991) and *The Corrosion of Character* (1998), poses such questions. In the first book he uses the haunting phrase 'the maintenance of order among lightly engaged strangers'. How can an immense congregation of city dwellers who have little in common, and no small level of distaste for each other, hold together? In the second book he moves from the social to the personal, asking:

How can long-term purposes be pursued in a short-term society? How can durable social relations be sustained? How can a human being develop a narrative of identity and life history in a society composed of episodes and fragments? The conditions of the new economy feed instead on experience which drifts in time, from place to place, from job to job. (1998, pp. 26–7)

Both on the level of social cohesion and the closely related level of personal narrative, the late modern world offers precious little security or palliatives to vertigo.

The organic community

Before I examine the paradox of the turn to community noted by both Bauman and Hobsbawm, let us outline the attributes of the organic community of the past, albeit in a rather ideal typical fashion. The community of the post-war period was characterised by a sense of permanence and solidity. Placed there by the needs of capital around large-scale manufacturing industry or labour fixed to land for centuries it involved the following characteristics:

- Intergenerationality
- An embeddedness of the individual in locality
- Intense face-to-face interaction
- Much direct information with regards to each other
- High level of informal social control
- Provision of a localised sense of identity
- An identity of local space and local culture.

The obverse of the organic community is posited as an anomic community, the locality without norms, and the inevitable consequence of this is seen as the proliferation of crime and anti-social behaviour. It is the 'lightly engaged' society of strangers where individualism and self-seeking takes priority over collectivity and shared values. As we shall see, I have serious reservations about this formulation: at the very least it underestimates *both* the malign and benign effects of the shift to the late modern. But let us, for the moment, reflect on the process by which community is transformed. Sennett notes that:

> One of the unintended consequences of modern capitalism is that it has strengthened the value of place, aroused a longing for community. All the emotional conditions we have explored in the workplace animate that desire: the uncertainties of flexibility; the absence of deeply rooted trust and commitment; the superficiality of teamwork; most of all, the spectre of failing to make something of oneself in the world, to 'get a life' through one's work. All these conditions impel people to look for some other scene of attachment and depth.
>
> Today, in the new regime of time, that usage 'we' has become an act of self-protection. The desire for community is defensive, often expressed as rejection of immigrants or other outsiders – the most important communal architecture being the walls against a hostile economic order. To be sure, it is almost a universal law that 'we' can be used as a defense against confusion and dislocation. Current politics based on this desire for refuge takes aim more at the weak, those who travel the circuits of the global labor market, rather than at the strong, those institutions which set poor workers in motion or make use of their relative deprivation. (1998, p.138)

The decline of work as a source of expressivity and of narrative leads to a turn to community to provide identity and continuity. Yet as Hobsbawm has argued, it is precisely the self-same late modern capitalism which has destroyed community and rendered destitute the bank of social trust that underwrote it. The local community becomes increasingly more invoked as a place of identity and moves to become a major part of the rhetoric of political mobilisation just at the time that it is transforming and alienating. For the organic community is in decline, affected by both the globalisation of the economy and of culture. Manufacturing industries shrink and in many instances disappear, leaving areas bereft of work, service industries proliferate, often with small sizes, commuting increases to and from work, local cultures become less self-contained, much more penetrated by the global. They become, in Giddens' graphic phrase, 'phantasmagoric', constituted by the ghostly presence of distant influences (1990). The paradox, then, the self-same capitalism which fuels the turn to community undermines the very organic community in which people seek meaning and solace. This, as we have seen, is the political paradox that Thomas Frank uncovered with regards to the dynamics of the last American Presidential Election. Rural and small-town Americans in search of the traditional values of small-town America voted in precisely the party of billionaires whose policies undermined local communities and whose inegalitarianism mocked meritocracy.

But there is more to it than this. First of all, the search for community does not end here: people do not remain passive in their quest for meaning. Secondly, as I have argued throughout book, the passions undercutting the search for identity are more intense and indignant than a mere confrontation with anomie, a disappointed encounter with normlessness, would suggest. Lastly, the notion of society as anomic and an agglomeration of isolated individuals fundamentally misconstrues the nature of the late modern community.

Earlier I discussed how one remedy for personal feelings of ontological security is a resort to essentialisation – to believe that one's identity is based on a fixed essence. The resort to identification with community or indeed nation is a powerful fixative in such a project. The dynamic of this process of reinforcing identity is the negation of the other either by characterising them as wicked/evil – the inversion of oneself, as in conservative othering or as less than oneself, lacking in civilisation and the correct norms, as with liberal othering. The whole conception of community, of 'we', as Sennett puts it, 'becomes an act of rejecting "them".' Community becomes defined by its opposite – indeed the very idea of an 'inclusive community', Bauman notes, would be a contradiction in terms and, later on in *Liquid Modernity*, he is even more bitter, talking of how 'the inner harmony of the communal world shines and glitters against the background of the obscure and tangled jungle which starts the other side of the turnpike' (2000, p. 172).

The building of community, its invention, becomes that of a narrative which celebrates and embraces one side and vilifies and excludes the other. Such stories of difference can be tragic in their consequence if banal in their conception. Let me first take two very dramatic examples, one from abroad in the Balkans, the other from nearer to home. Michael Ignatieff tells of sitting in an abandoned farmhouse in March 1993, in a village called Mirkovci in East Croatia, which has been cut in two by the Serb–Croat War. It is four in the morning and he is at the command post of the Serbs; the Croatians are about 250 yards away. Every now and then there is a burst of small arms fire and the odd bazooka round. These Serbs and Croats went to the same school, went out with the same girls, lived happily together. The rate of ethnic intermarriage was as high as 30% and nearly a quarter of the population before the war claimed their nationality as Yugoslav – not Croat, Serb or Muslim. Ignatieff cannot believe that there is a fundamental difference between them stretching back through history:

Theorists like Samuel Huntington would lead me to believe that there is a fault line running through the back gardens of Mirkovci, with the Croats in the bunker representing the civilization of the Catholic Roman West and the Serbs nearby representing Byzantium, Orthodoxy, and the Cyrillic East. Certainly this is how the more self-inflated ideologues on either side see the conflict. But at worm's-eye level, here in Mirkovci, I don't see civilizational fault lines, geological templates that have split apart. These metaphors take for granted what needs to be explained: how neighbors once ignorant of the very idea that they belong to opposed civilizations begin to think – and hate – in these terms; how they vilify and demonize people they once called friends; how, in short, the seeds of mutual paranoia are sown, grain by grain, on the soil of a common life.

On the bunk next to me, leaning against the wall, wearing combat fatigues, is a compact and dapper middle-aged man with bright, wily eyes and a thick, stylish mustache. With a certain false naiveté, I venture the thought that I can't tell Serbs and Croats apart. 'What makes you think you're so different?'

He looks scornful and takes a cigarette pack out of his khaki jacket. 'See this? These are Serbian cigarettes. Over there," he says, gesturing out the window," they smoke Croatian cigarettes.'

'But they're both cigarettes, right?'

'Foreigners don't understand anything.' He shrugs and resumes cleaning his Zastovo machine pistol.

But the question I've asked bothers him, so a couple of minutes later he tosses the weapon on the bunk between us and says, 'Look; here's how it is. Those Croats, they think they're better than us. They want to be the gentlemen. Think they're fancy Europeans. I'll tell you something. We're all just Balkan shit.' (1999, pp. 35–6)

Ignatieff delights in this exchange: for at one point the Serb claims that the difference is obvious, then cannot find much difference other than the Croats think they are different *and* better, and lastly consigns both Serbs and Croats to the Balkans, that time immemorial Other of Europe.

Othering in the Ardoyne: at holy cross school

The policewomen wear black Balaclava hats covering their heads and faces: their eyes looking through slits, their dark militaristic uniforms sinister, sadomasochistic like fetish dolls. Little girls, their hands clasped tightly in their mothers', hurry between the rows of police. In the background the full armoury of the British Army looking strangely absurd in a working-class street. There is cursing, swearing, heckling all the way (last week they threw plastic bags full of urine); the girls look at the ground, the mothers hurry on. Most disturbing of all is the hecklers shouting at the girls, working-class women – mums themselves, no doubt, whose greatest treasure is their children, girls just like this. Last week, I am told, a Bishop from the south of England came over to join the march, he broke down in tears before the end. 'Kill the nits before they grow into lice!' Unbelievable ... Unbelievable, it is like the films of the civil rights marches but without any differences of skin colour. I can't tell the accents apart, neither can they, I dare say, they have to ask what school you went to – whether you're Séan or John. It is like a savage satire on prejudice.

Later that day I talk to a community worker who lives on what is drolly called the Peace Line. His house backing onto the Protestant area of North Belfast. Identical houses, small back yards facing small back yards; the housing on each side adequate, a good public provision, tidy and well cared for. Last week someone threw

THE EXCLUSIVE COMMUNITY

a pipe bomb into his back yard. It didn't go off but he is fearful for his little girl and doesn't let her play outside any more. He knows the old lady in the house behind his on the other side of the line. They get on alright – last week he helped her look for her cat.

That night I sit at the bar with a Guinness in my hand in the little pub-come-hotel where I am staying near Queens University – far away from the Ardoyne. A secular area, I think, away from the troubles. The kindly faced Irishman behind the bar tells rambling cat and dog stories. He asks me to sign the visitor's book. 'W.S.' he asks, 'what does that stand for?': 'William Stewart Young' I say (Jock is my nickname). He smiles. Later he begins to regale me with stories of Catholics with enormous families living on welfare. He rants on about his own parodied version of the underclass. It is as if he had totally changed. I suddenly realise that he has classified me as a Prod (after all, what could be more Protestant than Billy Stewart) – a fellow member of his tribe. Here I am a lifelong card-carrying atheist being classified by a bigot as a co-religionist whether I like it or not. In a society of binaries you have to be on one side or the other.

The turn to the dark side

'Thus it is that no group ever sets itself up as the One without at once setting up the Other over against itself. If three travellers chance to occupy the same compartment, that is enough to make vaguely hostile 'others' out of all the rest of the passengers on the train. In small-town eyes all persons not belonging to the village are 'strangers' and suspect; to the native of a country all who inhabit other countries are 'foreigners'; Jews are 'different' for the anti-Semite, Negroes are 'inferior' for American racists, aborigines are 'natives' for colonists, proletarians are the 'lower class' for the privileged.

(Simone de Beauvoir, *The Second Sex*, 1953, p. 16)

I have taken, of course, extreme examples, the horrors of the Serb–Croat War, the idiocies of communal hatreds in Belfast as well as, elsewhere in this book, the pathways to terrorism and the inter-ethnic riots of the Northern English towns. The day-to-day interactions in the city are not, of course, at all usually like that. But nor are they the relationships of 'slightly engaged strangers'. The anomic subway carriage, the urban street of disconnected strangers, are permeated by relationships of class, race, gender and age – often hidden, wishfully repressed, yet thinly concealed. The decisions of urban life, say the choice of school or neighbourhood, is fraught with tensions: the thin patina of rational choice all so frequently overlays the undersurge of avoidance. They are mediated by narratives of inclusion and exclusion. All sorts of tensions haunt the everyday world: erupting with regularity – the violence of race, of gender, of class and of youth, the slow riot of crime and violence, of insult and disrespect, dog the official visions of calm and consensus. Georg Simmel, in his famous article 'The Metropolis and Mental Life' depicts the reserve and the distance of the urban dweller, but then notes: 'Indeed, if I do not deceive myself, the inner aspect of this outer reserve is not only indifference but more often than we are aware, it is a slight aversion, a mutual strangeness and repulsion which will break into hatred and right at the moment of a closer contact, however caused.' (1950, p. 275). I have tried to ground this repulsion, this uneasiness in the city in wider social processes; it is not so arbitrary as Simmel makes out nor as inevitable as de Beauvoir maintains yet, as I will argue shortly, it is only one side of things – only a fragment of the contradiction. I want to argue that this paradox of a search for identity in community when organic community is failing and whose failure to provide tradition and embeddedness is a core reason for the search for identity, is not nearly as cataclysmic as either Sennett or Hobsbawm would have it. In part this is because they cannot envisage the notions of association and trust outside of the image of the face-to-face, organic community. A key component of this is the emergence of virtual realities, of mediated relationships as a major source of personal narrative and social experience.

But first of all let us look a little critically at the idealisation of organic communities.

The fallacy of privileging community

Iris Marian Young has been one of the most ardent advocates of urban life as an ideal and, at the same time, effective critic of the privileging of the organic community:

> theorists of community privilege face-to-face relations because they conceive them as *immediate*. Immediacy is better than mediation because immediate relations have the purity and security longed for in the Rousseauist dream: we are transparent to one another, purely copresent in the same time and space, close enough to touch, and nothing comes between us to obstruct our vision of one another.
>
> This ideal of the immediate copresence of subjects, however, is a metaphysical illusion. Even a face-to-face relation between two people is mediated by voice and gesture, spacing and temporality. As soon as a third person enters the interaction the possibility arises of the relation between the first two being mediated through the third, and so on. The mediation of relations among persons by the speech and actions of other persons is a fundamental condition of sociality. The richness, creativity, diversity, and potential of a society expand with growth in the scope and means of its media, linking persons across time and distance. (1990, p. 233)

She has no doubt about the oppressive nature of many relationships in modern urban societies and the real dangers of the city nor that the closest relationships are those of immediate intimates. But the city in its anonymity allows deviance, freedom to develop (of which more later), its difference offers a frisson of excitement and entertainment, its access to such a huge bulk of people via the mediation of telephone and mass transit allows for the creation of vibrant new communities of difference. Frank Webster puts this well:

We have emerged from a world of neighbours and entered what has increasingly become one of strangers. Here we have the old theme in social science of a shift from *community* (crudely, the familiar, interpersonal and village-centred life of pre-industrialism) to *associations* which involve the mixing of people unknown to one another save in specific ways such as bus conductor, shop assistant, and newsvendor (crudely, the urban-oriented way of life of the modern). Ever since at least Simmel we have appreciated how disorienting and also often liberating the transfer from closed community to a world of strangers can be. The city may fragment and depersonalise, but in doing so it can also release one from the strictures of village life. With the shift towards town life comes about a decline in personal observation by neighbours and, accompanying this, a weakening of the power of community controls that are exercised on an interpersonal basis. Entering urban-industrial life from a country existence one is freed from the intrusions of local gossip, of face-to-face interactions, from close scrutiny of one's everyday behaviour by neighbours. ... By the same token, in the urban realm one can readily choose freedom, to be as private as one likes, to mix with others on one's own terms, to indulge in the exotic without fear of reprimand, to be anonymous ... (1995, pp. 56–7)

The breakdown of the organic community, the deterritorialisation of the local, is, on the face of it, an immediate gain in terms of personal freedom. Freed from the constraints of control of the organic community people become more free to change. Narrow chauvinisms, conceptions of masculinity rooted to industrial plant and local pub, respectabilities which were once policed by gossip and sanctioning all crumble.

It is conventional, particularly in liberal political philosophy, to think of that which is public as good and that which is private as concealed and possibly reprehensive. But such liberalism which sees freedom as bringing private problems into the light of public debate, however commendable, forgets the sociology of resistance and subterfuge (see Fraser, 1997). For the public world, whether it is the local community or the wider polity, consists for the powerless of distinctly unequal partners and fellow citizens who can be potentially both censorious and coercive. Youth culture, for example, would be moribund and conformist, if it did not learn to manoeuvre the restrictions of family by the device of deviance and half truth. Likewise from the black diaspora (see Gilroy, 1993) to the gay community (see Plummer, 1995) subcultures develop in the freedom of the urban landscape and spread into a virtual community of mass media and cultural artefact. The privacy, therefore provided by the late modern city permits the exercise of freedom – it is surely more possible, here, to develop genuine identity and sense of self than in the stifling atmosphere of the organic community?

Enter virtual reality: elsewhere in the east end

It is nearing Christmas, I am at a dinner party late evening in East London, in Dalston E8. Everyone is talking about issues of the day: reality TV, the war; an elegant 1860s Victorian house in this gentrified enclave deep in working-class Hackney. I make an excuse, go out to get some fresh air. Wander towards London Fields and notice that I am a few hundred yards from the mythical setting of the soap opera EastEnders with its millions of viewers a night. It is not actually filmed here, of course, but miles away in Elstree, Hertfordshire, but this is its spatial point of inspiration. I notice a pub on the corner, the temptation is irresistible: step in and sample a real slice of Cockney life.

There are about 12 or 13 people in the saloon, it is quiet, traditional, unchanged completely unlike the dim lights and neon of the city bars two miles down the road in Hoxton. The barman, Australian I think by his accent, serves me a pint: he is neither friendly nor unfriendly, halfway through his shift. I turn to look across the bar and see a wonderful coincidence: EastEnders is on the television, the console just above the heads of the seated viewers. Nobody is talking to each other except for two bar flies in the front: eyes are on the television, people are seated separately, a couple sit together silently watching the screen.

After the episode they began talking, I was struck by the fact that people seemed to know more about the characters of EastEnders than they did about their neighbours. Indeed, they knew more about the lives of the actual actors for that matter. It was not that they did not know each other, but rather this knowledge was shared between them and it was, in a way, more intense. I began to think about being bemused at the extent of the public grief at the funeral of Lady Di ten years previously and thinking how they probably cried more over her than, say, the decease of their Aunt Lilly. This was, I now realised, because they knew more – or at least thought they knew more – about Lady Di than they did about their Aunt Lilly.

How does one interpret this? Some dystopians, such as Jeremy Seabrook (1984) in his *Idea of Neighbourhood* (and in this case he talks about the soap opera *Coronation Street*) see it as a frozen unreality which gives us continuity, a shadow community which generates reassurance for a substance now departed and with the working class now cast as atomised spectators. Others more optimistically (not surprisingly), like Mal Young (Head of Drama Services for the BBC) in his 1999 Hugh Weldon Memorial Lecture, claims:

As real life communities, and the traditional family group has deconstructed, so our reliance on the virtual communities of soap has become more important in our lives. The TV audience may be going through massive changes but the soaps are the sole remaining shared experience.

Now I do not think that this is true and indeed, when Anthony Giddens writes that 'in the sense of an embedded affinity to place community has indeed largely been destroyed' (1991, p. 250), he is exaggerating a trend which may be true of some places and some people – at least for part of their lifetime – but it is not a generalisation that can hold its ground. Indeed let me talk from personal experience: I was happily writing about the death of community at least in terms of postcode and contemplating the fact that my circle of friends lived across London or indeed across the world when our son Joseph, then 5, entered primary school. In the subsequent months I found that I could no longer walk down the street without encountering numerous fellow parents and sharing their anxieties with regards to local schools and community. Three years later we moved to Brooklyn and I was surprised to find that all my generalisations about anomie and living in large cities were based on my experience of London. Community may be dead if one thinks of Lowry's Salford, with matchstick workers clustering around factory and neighbourhood, but community and identification with neighbourhood is far from dead, albeit patchy and attenuated.

Stars, celebrities: guiding narratives for a shifting world

Let us pause for a minute to examine the role of these virtual reference groups. The soap operas are the most intimate: they provide narratives for a late modern world. They are multicultural, and multilayered: here is the single mother, the small businessman, the man growing old, the villain, the lad gone wrong, the couple living on the edge – they deliver a host of narratives which are followed by millions. They have the continuity of a nineteenth-century serialised novel – say of Charles Dickens or Thomas Hardy – but the audience is much less an observer, the story much less certain, the characters less rounded. Yet they are easy to enter into, to identify with. In a world of tenuous identities, fictional mundane narratives as tentative and hesitantly written as reality have a great attraction. But the soaps also make stars, and contribute to the myriad of sources that celebrity springs from: sport, music, television presenters, the movies, the world of fashion and at times even weather presenters. There is something innovative about celebrity. The role of these new stars is not merely to shine, they do not simply glisten, they are there to guide. They are not just dreams of aspiration, but sources of narrative. As such they become important points of orientation. Of course, the reference groups of next door neighbour, colleague at work, fellow-parent at school do not disappear, but such reference points are now, as I have suggested, more chaotic: they no longer present themselves as if in serried ranks arrayed for comparison. They have become more horizontal, more jumbled. They have become supplemented with the new reference group of celebrity which has, as I touched upon in Chapter 3, several defining features. It is a focal point of intense interest where the life narrative is followed as a point of reference rather than an object of adulation. And, just as the underclass, as I have documented, provides a guiding narrative from below, a negative orientation point, the celebrity provides one from above: a point of fantasy and identification. The celebrity epitomises the new dream of expressivity, a job which carries with it personal development and realisation, where wealth is a platform for individual take off and future projects rather than a successful end in itself. It has a universal purchase, celebrity cuts across audiences of class and indeed very frequently the boundaries of the nation state. It is remarkably democratic, not just in the backgrounds of those called to celebrity but in the talents which brought them there. Some are immensely gifted, some are famous for being famous, some are just like us but had a lucky break: the kid with the drum kit in the right place, the catchy tune that struck in everyone's mind, the actor who stumbled into the movies. Everyone should have 15 minutes of fame, said Warhol, famously, in his manifesto for an expressive democracy. They are our delegates (by virtue of their class, gender, age and race) *our* representatives in the spotlight. They are democratic in their relationship with their fans and their fans with them. Laurence Friedman re-tells the tale about Mae West. She was being interviewed in a restaurant and a man came up to interrupt and spoke to her very familiarly. When he left, the interviewer asked who he was and she told him she had simply no idea. 'He sounded as if he knew you', the interviewer persisted. 'They all do dear', she responded (1999, p. 31). Their narrative is open to us, followed by us, parallel to ours: the same but, of course, very different. Finally and, needless to say, the birth of *Big Brother* and reality TV is a logical conclusion of such a notion of the democratic celebrity.

The Cronus effect and broken narratives

If images of the underclass represent narratives of individual failure and failed communities, those of celebrity carry with them tales of dreams realised, individuals fulfilled, ideal communities, beautiful lifestyles. *Or at least they should* ... A while back (1981) I coined the phrase 'the nemesis effect' for the way in which the media portray deviants as inevitably getting their come-uppance, that their dissolute lives are seen as inevitably leading to misery. A little later I was toying with the parallel phenomenon of how

185

the media stalks and character-assassinates celebrities. Thus precisely the people they put on a pedestal as beacons for us all are very frequently portrayed as blowing it all, of achieving their own nemesis. I called this tentatively the Cronus effect. That is, we destroy those that we give birth to. I noted at the time that this was a recent phenomenon. It didn't happen in the past with J.F. Kennedy, despite his methyl amphetamine and his whores, it didn't happen with Elvis despite his gargantuan eating and his pharmacopoeic appetite for drugs, it did with Clinton despite the comparative minorness of his sexual peccadillo and it happens every day to Kate Moss. Every move they make is watched, from the slightest sign of flab on the beach, the illicit smooch in the club, the line of cocaine in the toilet. No wonder the stars wear dark glasses. But I was not sure of the reasons for this narrative of decline so strangely paralleling that of the underclass and the deviant at the bottom of the pile. But now it seems to be much clearer.

The paradox of adulation and *schadenfreude*, a perverse desire for emulation yet delight in the fall of the object of desire needs no recourse to some speculative psychology say of thanatos and Narcissus. Rather it lies in the structural position that celebrity finds itself in. For late modernity has upped the *ante* of surveillance and obsession. Think for one moment of the problems of walking down the street, entering the restaurant – all eyes upon you, never being incognito – worse being a walking script, a narrative for others which is detached from you yet which others feel they know intimately. Think of the problem of making friends. Think of wealth beyond scarcity: the homes in London, New York, the South of France. Imagine the card that Elton John sent to John Lennon on Lennon's 40th birthday:

> Imagine six apartments,
> it isn't hard to do.
> One is full of fur coats,
> the other's full of shoes

Durkheim, in *Suicide* (1970 [1887]), famously talks of the sickness of infinity, the remorseless anomie at the top of society, 'and the search for nameless sensations'. It is no wonder that hard drugs such as heroin which cocoon and insulate from the outside world become so attractive. Just think of the paradox of Bob Dylan, a master of personal invention and reinvention, a man who started off in rock and roll, playing Fats Domino and Buddy Holly, reinvents himself as a latter-day Woody Guthrie and then metamorphoses into an underground hero, shades of Jack Kerovac and Allen Ginsberg. Think of the great betrayal, Dylan being taken up in the 1960s by so many round the globe as a stellar narrative, an artist of constancy, and emblem of all that is progressive and forthright, going electric and rescinding on stage during the 1966 tour. The linear songs of struggle and progress becoming replaced by the elliptical and the disjointed: from *Only a Pawn in their Game* to *Visions of Joanna*, the stout certainty and direction of the acoustic guitar by the electric screech of the Yamaha. Then at the Manchester concert, the shout of 'Judas' from the audience so graphically depicted in C. P. Lee's *Like the Night* (1998): the howl of personal betrayal at a narrative broken. Indeed in *Chronicles* (2004) Dylan describes his anguish at being cast in the role of leader, of representing the zeitgeist: for rather like something out of *The Life of Brian*, the counter-culture pursued him climbing over his roof in Woodstock, demonstrators parading up and down outside his house in New York City asking 'the conscience of a generation' to lead them somewhere. His attempt to break the narrative that he had become, borders on the hilarious: he records an LP of extremely bland tunes entitling it *Self-Portrait*, he visits Israel and pretends to be a Zionist, he perpetually circles the globe on tour, Moby Bob, destroying his legend, a narrative breaker: generating more devotion, anxiety and scorn than any singer of his age ...

The extraordinary rise of celebrity is a product of the search for narrative: it is propelled by the ideal of expressivity and self-development, the First World Dream, it is fuelled by the insecurities of work, community, family. And the paradox is that celebrity, like many of the other strategies in the portfolio of guiding narratives, is a thing of fragility and brittleness.

The deterritorialisation of community and the rise of the virtual

Numerous cultural commentators have noted the fashion in which the late modern community has lost its mooring in the locale – in the coincidence of the social and the spatial. Thus Mike Tomlinson (1999) talks of its 'deterritorialisation', while John Thompson (1995) refers to the notion of 'despatialised commonality' and, perhaps a little more elegantly – as we shall see – Joshua Meyrowitz (1989) talks of 'the Generalised Elsewhere' and 'the erosion of space'. Important here is the way in which people through the various media can share experiences and identity despite the separation of physical distance. This is not to deny locality, people, after all, must live somewhere, but it is to point to the diminution and transformation of the local community and the rise of the virtual community.

John Thompson usefully classifies social interaction into three sorts:

1. Face-to-face interaction: the dialogical basis of the traditional community.
2. Mediated Interaction: which is two-way and dialogical like face-to-face interaction but occurs over space and time by telephone and e-mail.
3. Mediated Quasi-Interaction: the conventional mass media which is monological, yet where there is audience selection, interpretation and interaction. (Thompson, 1995, p. 85)

What is new is the rapid and perhaps revolutionary developments in the late twentieth and early twenty-first century of the second two. Let us note that mobile telephone companies are presently the fastest growing firms and that email communication has, in a short space of time, become part of everyday life. But even before this: the old fashioned landline telephone has had a major impact on people's lives. Thus Barry Wellman and other social network analysts have long pointed to the way in which social technology has liberated people from dependence on spatial locality. Thus, he argues that it makes more sense to perceive of *personal* communities and networks rather than communities of neighbourhood (Wellman, 1982). Indeed as Meyrowitz wryly comments: 'access to nonlocal people is now, via the telephone, often faster and simpler than access to physical neighbors.' (1989, p. 331). It is now very easy for *anywhere* to be *elsewhere*. At its most banal you never need be alone for lunch, on a more profound level you are no longer dominated by the culture of the locale physically around you, you continuously link back to people like you, whether they are or not physically located in one place. It allows people to connect up horizontally in a disembedded world, it is an aid to a new and closer embeddedness, a Spiderman's web of support in urban structures which now seem flimsy and phantasmagorical.

Elsewhere in an elevator, John Jay College, October 2004

I am in an elevator in college, a student stands beside me with heavy headphones: a tiny, tinny, crackly sound of rap is all that can be heard. He stands, incongruously with a bandana and low slung baggy hip hop jeans, a cell-phone in his hand peering mesmerically at the text; wherever he is, he is not here, in fact his social bearings are fixed as anywhere but here. He is elsewhere back in the hood, back in the burbs – all of the places that the college represents an exit from. He punches automatically the lift buttons, there is no response: he is in an up elevator and wants to go down. He comes to ... looks around, for the first time he takes cognizance of the other two people in the lift: relaxes, readjusts his phones. My companion is a black man, extremely tall, a basketball instructor – looks at me in anguish and amusement, shrugs his shoulders and gets out at the sixth floor.

The rise of multi-media and the uninvited guest

Furthermore within the more traditional mass media the rise of multi-media and the vast expansion of choice in radio and television allows the development of niche audiences and subcultures (see McRobbie and Thornton, 1995). Indeed the mass media takes up a surprisingly larger and larger proportion of people's lives. Such avid consumption should not be viewed so alarmingly, however, for as David Morley (1986) showed in his studies of television audiences: the television provides topics of conversation for those who, often very intermittently, watch it. The serried family ranks, mum, dad, two children and the dog, dutifully (and quietly) watching television in the post-war period has been replaced by the visual flaneuer, the bricollager and the disrespectful. The audience now has conversation which sometimes includes the television, the audience is not simply subject to a monologue from the box.

Similarly Taylor and Mullan (1986) in their witty study of television viewing, *Uninvited Guests*, deny any passivity in viewing patterns noting that it may have been true in the past that television was watched with reverence and respect, that it entranced the audience. But with multiple channels and pre-recorded tapes this is hardly true today. Moreover, people used the television to make sense of their lives. Thus the characters on soap operas such as *Coronation Street* and *Brookside* were talked about as real people, their triumphs and vicissitudes related to the everyday life of the viewers. To this extent despite the title, they are *invited guests*: they are talked about as real but they can be shown the door and turned off at will.

So, on one side the local is penetrated by the global in terms of distant events, consumer choices, values (such as those emphasising lifestyle choice, feminism, meritocracy, etc.), on the other, virtual communities develop on the back of the local which incorporate images, reference groups, favoured characters and celebrities from a global repertoire and which involve both mass media and mediated interaction. Indeed as Ulrich Beck puts it:

> the persons we experience as significant others are no longer restricted to those we know from direct encounters within a local community. Some persons, or perhaps even media-constructed and reproducible homunculi, serve people as mirrors of themselves. (2000, p. 156)

From generalised other to generalised elsewhere

> From a neuroscience perspective we are all divided and discontinuous. The mental processes underlying our sense of self – feelings, thoughts, memories – are scattered through different zones of the brain. There is no special point of convergence. No cockpit of the soul. No soul-pilot. They come together in a work of fiction. A human being is a story-telling machine. The self is a story.
>
> (Paul Broks, 2003, p. 41)

Thus Paul Broks, in his brilliant and disturbing study of human consciousness *Into the Silent Land*, describes his search for a site of the soul, for a physiological locale to base the self. But he cannot find one: instead he unwittingly moves towards the position of a humanistic sociology. That the self is a storyteller, that the most profoundly human activity is creating stories about oneself. The sociologist, John Thompson, influenced greatly by hermeneutics and symbolic interactionism, arrives at a similar position:

To recount to ourselves or others who we are is to retell the narratives – which are continuously modified in the process of retelling – of how we got to where we are and of where we are going from here. We are all the unofficial biographers of ourselves, for it is only by constructing a story, however loosely strung together, that we are able to form a sense of who we are and of what our future may be. (1995, p. 210)

But he then points to the fact that in a world of highly mediated communication the whole foundation of the self becomes totally changed:

If we adopt this general approach to the nature of the self, then we can see that the development of communication media has had a profound impact on the process of self-formation. Prior to the development of the media, the symbolic materials employed by most individuals for the purposes of self-formation were acquired in contexts of face-to-face interaction …

    These various conditions are altered fundamentally by the development of communication media. The process of self-formation becomes increasingly dependent on access to mediated forms of communication – both printed and, subsequently, electronically mediated forms. Local knowledge is supplemented by, and increasingly displaced by, new forms of non-local knowledge which are fixed in a material substratum, reproduced technically and transmitted via the media. (ibid., p. 211)

The notion of who you are becomes constructed on a much wider stage in late modernity. To understand this one must look at the late modern self and its reference points. Joshua Meyrowitz (1989), in a seminal article, develops the work of Charles Cooley and George Herbert Mead on the generalised other. The self according to the symbolic interactionist tradition, is given reality by its reflections in the significant others around us. Cooley calls this the looking glass self, Mead calls it 'the generalized other' – we see ourselves through our perceptions of others' perceptions of us. Now the relative decline in community and rise in the media has:

extended the generalized other so that those who we perceive as significant others are no longer only the people we experience in face-to-face interaction within the community. People from other communities and localities also serve as self-mirrors. The 'mediated generalized other' weakens (but surely does not eliminate) our dependence on locality and on people in it for a sense of self. (1989, p. 327)

Let me expand this a little further, for the series of other reference points against which we judge ourselves fairly or unfairly treated in comparison with others, widens out, as does our knowledge of what is fairness and unfairness and its distribution. Reference groups are much less attached to locality in late modernity, for instance, as Bottoms and Wiles (1997, p. 351) point out, the culture of Australia or the west coast of America can be as 'real' to British youth as anything else. Similarly Donna Gaines, in her wonderful book *Teenage Wasteland* (1998), focusing on youth in Bergenfield New Jersey, has kids who are simultaneously into Led Zeplin, Lynyrd Skynard, Slayer and The Dead. They are in Britain and America, retro and today.

I want to develop this concept of elsewhere in the context of our new multimediated world by first of all differentiating between horizontal and vertical media. The horizontal media – such as email and the mobile 'phone – allow the individual to link back to their friends, family and community wherever he or she is. They allow us to traverse the city yet to be elsewhere back in our community. In a real sense these examples of mediated interaction, to use John Thompson's term, *compensate* for the dislocation of the organic community, the erosion of culture and space. They continue to provide the traditional generalised other – and at times even more intensely than the locally focused community – after all, what, for example, could be more controlling than the mobile 'phone? You can never easily get away – you are always in earshot – and presumably with technological advance being what it is will soon always be in eyeshot.

By vertical media I refer to those media such as television, radio, the press and more recently, the internet, which carry both factual and fictional stories and which are much more monological. Here a generalised elsewhere occurs which provides a whole series of guiding narratives and orientation points outside of one's own directly known community. I have already talked of the guiding narratives of celebrity and of underclass, of reference groups and comparison points. But most importantly these stories carry with them vocabularies of motive (see C. Wright Mills, 1940), unending techniques of neutralisation which provide reasons for and justifications for action, whether social or anti-social, charitable or predatory.

All of these reference points can, of course, shore up any particular community, but it can also do this by creating social divisiveness and misperception between communities. For, as we have seen, many of these narratives are ones of othering, allocating virtues and vices, making sharp lines of delineation and essentialising differences. But, as we shall see, there is also a progressive side to the vertical media for, whether by net-surfing or channel hopping, they have the potential of exposing the individual to a pluralism of views. This elsewhere has a *porosity* whereas the horizontal elsewhere of mobile 'phone and email serves rather to maintain the boundaries of ingroup, the continuities of community.

How does this relate to order and disorder? What has happened is that people's notion of their self (and hence their sense of shame, of losing self-respect when certain norms are transgressed), the actual norms themselves – the informal mores which structure behaviour, the feelings of discontent which provide the wellsprings of criminality and transgression and the vocabularies of motive and justifying circumstances, all to a greater extent than ever before, are a product of discourses which are of a global rather than a local nature. Relative deprivation, for example, is global in its comparison points: aspirations jump frontiers. For example, discourses about crime (including notions of fear, risk and danger) are a free floating commodity of a world media, the informal mores of everyday life (including the introduction of new and more or less stringent definitions of deviance) are constituted within public cultures which are global in their reach.

From community to public sphere

Having discarded the notion of a series of organic communities either actually in existence or, as in the communitarian dream, to be greatly regenerated and refurbished, as nostalgic and impractical, can we, instead, substitute a series of virtual communities with some territorial basis – a multiculturalism of a late modern sort? Thus we have the gay community, the Sikh community, the Irish community, the black community, women, etc. Such a formulation is a currency of contemporary politics and the media: events are publicly examined and debated by turning to representatives of various 'communities'. There can be no doubt that such a formulation has some foundation. A whole series of what Nancy Fraser calls 'subaltern public spheres' occur where genuine debates occur and which can by careful argument and presentation influence the debate within the more general public sphere. A key example which Fraser gives, is that of second wave feminism which as a new social movement has elaborated extensive networks, journals, activist groups and discussion centres. Furthermore, such activism has produced wide debate in the wider public sphere over a whole series of issues concerned with crimes against women: sexual harassment, rape, domestic violence etc., many of which has resulted in changes in public attitudes and a broad raft of legislation. But it would be wrong to see such sections of the population as late modern equivalents of the organic community.

Nancy Fraser in her essay 'Sex, Lies and the Public Sphere' discusses the 1991 struggle over the confirmation of Clarence Thomas as an associate justice of the US Supreme Court who was passed to be only the second African–American on the Court in US history. Thomas was accused of sexual harassment by Anita Hill, a black female law professor who had served as Thomas' assistant at the Equal Employment Commission in the 1980s.

Fraser takes us through a fascinating account of the arguments surrounding this struggle: for discourses of gender, race and class each entered the public arena as the debate developed. What became clear was that there was no clear line from women, from blacks, from the middle or working class white males. It was not that self-conscious 'communities' of a sort existed, particularly in this context of American multiculturalism, but that each divided and crossed in their alliances. A result was what Nancy Fraser called 'the fracturing of the myth of homogeneous "communities"', (1997, p. 117). As a result, she continues, it would be better to consider:

> replacing the homogenizing ideological category of 'community' with the potentially more critical category of 'public' in the sense of a discursive arena for staging conflicts … In these respects, the concept of a public differs from that of a community. 'Community' suggests a bounded and fairly homogeneous group, and it often connotes consensus. 'Public', in contrast, emphasizes discursive interaction that is in principle unbounded and open-ended, and this in turn implies a plurality of perspectives. Thus, the idea of a public, better than that of a community, can accommodate internal differences, antagonisms, and debates. (ibid., p.118 and p. 97, n.33)

Indeed we can go further than this, for the notion of distinct communities pivoted on one dimension of ethnicity, religion, gender, age, class or sexual orientation assumes some sort of miraculous uni-vocal cohesion around one human attribute of many. It is unlikely in any society, let alone those of late modernity, despite the fact that the mass media frequently makes recourse to such fictions and community 'representatives' hasten to lay claim to be their spokespersons. Take, for example, the frequent mission of the British press, seeking to discover the opinions of the Muslim community. What could this be? If it means Muslim background it includes those who go daily to a mosque and those who would not be seen near one. It includes Saudis and Turks and at least 20 other nationalities. It includes old people and young people, men and women, the very poor and members of the bourgeoisie. It is a glimmer in the eye of would-be spokespersons, it is a cardboard piece played decisively in the opinion columns by the media commentators. But if there is a Muslim community then surely there is a Christian community? But no, we know this is a nonsense unless we mean members of a particular church and, even here, witness the Anglicans, where there are deep, one might say *fundamental* divisions. As a creature of opinion polls it will give us tendencies and shadowy figures of use up to a point, but these are things constructed out of random surveys of atomised individuals – the very opposite of community.

It is, of course, slightly astonishing that such a distinguished political philosopher should be surprised at finding heterogeneity of opinion. A clue to this is that Fraser's notion of community links to her concept of identity politics. As a political philosopher she is quite understandably concerned with political formations rather than the more sociological notion of community incorporating actual socially interacting individuals. And here, as we have seen in Chapter 4, she is happier with well organised political identities rather than those which are below the radar of the educated public. Even here, of course, as with second wave feminism, the discovery of dissent from a given line and of a vast heterogeneity of opinion outside of the world of middle class, educated, white women was a great trauma, greatly transforming and developing debate (see Barrett, 1988).

Let us then stick with the notion of community as involving at least a base of socially interacting individuals, however varied and vertical may be their reference points, and let us take on board from Fraser, that heterogeneity of opinion is the expected norm rather than any high degree of unity or cohesion of position. Indeed it is precisely the attempt to achieve such an illusory unity that fundamentalist spokespersons and community 'leaders' attempt to mobilise the rhetoric of othering whether it is around issues of race, gender, nationality or religion.

The community in late modern times

Organic communication, where communities communicate within themselves and then outwards, sending messages about their conflicts, oppressions and material conditions of existence, is breaking down. 'Community walls' now zigzag wildly around the urban mass. Immediate next-door neighbours may know nothing about each other's work, workplaces or wider kinships. Often they share only their postcodes. Organic communities and organic communications are slowly disappearing.

(Paul Willis, 1990, p. 141)

Now, physically bounded spaces are less significant as information is able to flow through walls and rush across great distances. As a result, *where* one is has less and less to do with what one knows or experiences. Electronic media have altered the significance of time and space for social interaction.

(Joshua Meyrowitz, 1985, p. viii)

We start then from noting how the notion of 'community' has changed remarkably in late modernity but, further to this, that what has taken its place is not simply a series of discrete multicultural communities with both local and virtual dimensions, but entities which both criss-cross and are contested. The community loosens its mooring in the locality and the various public discourses no longer have any one to one relationship to a specific section of the population.

For the single entity has long gone and any notion of fixity has disappeared – there is no reified community out there to mobilise or repair, no fixed thing in need of incorporation. Nor can this situation be solved by adopting the conventional language of multiculturalism and communitarianism. Namely, that there is now a series of communities to reinvigorate and galvanise. That is to replace the fallacy of a single fixed entity with the chimera of the multiple community. None of this fully captures the fluidity and plurality of late modernity.

Let us delineate the basic features of the late modern community:

1 *Difference* It is pluralistic not just in terms of ethnicity but in terms of age, gender and class.
2 *Fragmentation, crosscutting and hybridisation*: Such a pluralism by combination of ethnicity, age, gender and class offers to create on the one hand fragmentation, on the other crosscutting alliances, e.g. gender across ethnicity and class. Furthermore such subcultures bricollage from one another creating hybrids of crossover and reinterpretation.
3 *Intensity* It is pluralistic in terms of intensity. The same locale can contain high intensity, disorganised and atomised groups. For example, single mothers around the school can create intense coherent subcultures at the same time as unemployed men can be atomistic and withdrawn.
4 *Transience* Such subcultures change over time in composition, intensity and coherence. Individual biographies are experienced as shifts backwards and forwards from a sense of embeddedness to disembeddedness.
5 *Mediated* It is highly mediated, the global penetrates the local, creating a series of virtual communities some of which are territorialised and rooted in the locale some which are considerably deterritorialised.
6 *Actuarial*: Relationships are wary and calculative because of low information about a large proportion of the 'community'.
7 *Internecine conflict* There is a heterogeneity of opinion. Wealth and status is perceived as distributed in a chaotic fashion with no clear rationale or fairness. Relative deprivation both materially and in terms of status is widespread.
8 *Reinvention* The history of the 'community/ies' is constantly reinvented and the boundaries redrawn and redrafted.

Thus gradually our concept of community becomes less territorialised, less tethered to locality, for the social and the spatial, once soldered tightly together, begin to drift apart. Each step less moored to any specific place. We must take on board that many of the new communities have not only a considerable non-territorial basis in terms of telephone and internet friendships but have large components where the individuals concerned have never (nor probably will ever) meet each other, have significant reference points, which cannot be underestimated, which are fictional (e.g. soap opera) or artistic (particularly musical), and can actively create coherence and identity in their lives by reference to favourite news channels, newspapers and, indeed, newscasters. Further we begin to realise that the values of such 'communities' are rarely transmitted in a quasi-passive, traditional sense, as were those of the organic community, but are the subject of constant contest and reinvention.

CONCLUSION: ROADS TO ELSEWHERE

Late modernity is a society of the elsewhere, a society where culture and space separate, where anxiety, hope and aspiration have reference points global in their reach, where virtual realities mediate an already complex quilt of cultures and experiences in the everyday urban reality. It is the plural cybersphere and the plural city. It is the elsewhere of the migrant, the dream of a new future, a transnational identity which exists in both the before and the after; it is the elsewhere of the Third World looking at the implosive images of the First, it is the elsewhere of the poor in the First World daily witnessing and servicing a comfort outside of their reach. It is the elsewhere of the well-off in the First World, the 'contented' majority, who are propelled ever elsewhere by the incessant discontent of late modernity, the dream of personal development, self-realisation, a constantly receding tantalus never ever there, never quite reached.

Some notions of elsewhere proffer vignettes of success, fulfilment, celebrity, others provide maps of the fallen: the underclass, the lumpenproletariat of dysfunction, the junkie, alcoholic, the anti-social world of youthful yobs and teenage mothers. Elsewhere is a providence of vertigo as well as an image of security. And with such notions of elsewhere are routes out: narratives of deliverance.

The significance of the symbolic level has changed remarkably with the transition to late modernity. First of all a more individualistic society generates greater and greater demands for self-actualisation and recognition. Secondly, the increased sense of disembeddedness makes, at the same time, a sense of secure identity more and more precarious. Thirdly, a potent solution to this ontological uncertainty is that of essentialism. Fourthly such a fake sense of solidity is more easily achieved by regaling others as inferior, and lastly such a dehumanisation of others can be a potent facilitator of violence whether of the humiliated outsider or the punitive and righteous insider. Othering is a strange process, for it has a triple structure: the self is defined by the other, the group who are othered are liable to counter-other, to create a contrary fundamentalism, but more profoundly the self *itself* is hardened in a process of self-othering. The denigrated others are cast into an elsewhere of demonisation or of rank inferiority, the desired self is allocated to a fantasy elsewhere of fundamental superiority, whether of national, religion, class or gender. The net result is bad faith, a movement away from human spontaneity, reflexivity and action. It is, therefore, crucial that we attend to the problems of identity, arguing for policies which ensure a sense of self-worth and actualisation yet which do not rest upon the fake premises of essentialism where others are systematically denigrated and then abused. We must seek to construct, therefore, narratives of personal development and narratives of order which do not depend on rigidity, exclusion and foreclosure.

Affirmative and transformative inclusion

As we have seen, Nancy Fraser in *Justice Interruptus* (1997) develops an extremely useful typology of the politics of reform based on the two dimensions of redistribution and recognition. Reform, she argues, must recognise the necessity of changes in both these areas assuaging both the failings of distributive justice and misrecognition and devaluation. But to this dichotomy she adds a further distinction: between the politics of affirmation and the politics of transformation. Affirmative politics merely involves the surface transfer of resources without changing the basic underlying divisions whereas transformative politics seek to eliminate the basic underlying structures of injustice. Thus in the area of redistribution affirmative remedies involve, for example, coercing the underclass into the labour market at extremely low wages. Their underclass position is merely reproduced this time within the lower reaches of the market place. This movement of people from one category of exclusion to another is experienced, as I have argued above, not as inclusion but as exclusion. Relative deprivation would, of course, not be solved by such 'inclusionary' politics and the sources of discontent which are liable to generate high rates of crime and disorder would be unabated. Transformative redistribution, on the other hand, would involve such measures as retraining, so that jobs could be gained and then rewarded on a meritocratic basis – thus putting a genuine element of equality into equal opportunity policies; the recognition of non-paid work (e.g. child rearing, caring for ageing parents) as of vital importance for social reproduction; the creation of viable childcare infrastructures for women with children; and the enforcement of a minimum wage on a level which allows the individual an existence which is neither demeaning nor severely straitening in circumstance. Above all it would not fetishise paid work – it would not view such work as the vital prerequisite for full citizenship, for acceptance and inclusion in society.

An affirmative politics of recognition does not question the various essentialisms of difference. That is, in the case of conventional multiculturalism, what is stressed is the need for the positive recognition of various groups on equal terms, for example: Irish, African–Caribbean, gays, women, etc. In contrast, transformative politics seek to break down and destabilise the categories by questioning the very notion of fixed identity and essence. Thus the invented notion of tradition is challenged, the overlapping, interwoven nature of what are supposedly separate cultures stressed, and the ambiguity and blurred nature of boundaries emphasised. Diversity is encouraged and, where non-oppressive, celebrated, but difference is seen as a phenomenon of cultures in flux not essences which are fixed.

The politics of redistribution

Jonathan Freedland, The *Guardian* columnist writing in 2005, describes two bankers strutting into the Umbaba, a fashionable London bar, and asking the bartender to fix them the most expensive cocktail he could devise. He blended Richard Hennessy cognac at £2,000 a bottle, Dom Perignon champagne, added lychees and lemongrass and topped it with an aphrodisiac – an extract of yohimbe bark. This new drink, Magie Noir, cost £333 per glass and the final bill that night was £15,000. 'Why does this matter?', Freedland asked, isn't it terribly old fashioned to talk of inequality in this day and age? Who cares if 'starter homes' are advertised by London estate agents at £2.25 million and, if 1% of the British population earn 13% of the income. Hasn't the Prime Minister himself said it was irrelevant in these new times how much an individual earned – you could never be too rich? Surely this is the politics of envy, for do not the rich spend money, create wealth, employ many, the wealth spill down? Freedland begs to differ: he dares to be unfashionable: 'It may be beyond passé', he writes, 'but we'll have to do something about the rich'. Gross inequalities are an anathema in our society: the existence cheek by jowl of the very rich and the desperately poor is a vicious immorality. But as we have seen, the canker goes further than this. For the whole of the class structure is riven by great inequalities, it is not merely a tiny number of the extremely wealthy over against the rest. The lives and opportunities of the contented classes, the upper middle class, are light years away from that of the working poor and the fitfully employed at the bottom of society. The injustices of the sphere of distribution, the violation of the meritocratic principles which supposedly bind together our liberal democracies have reverberations which will not simply go away. From the banlieues of Paris to the streets of

Hackney, from the ghettos of Philadelphia and East New York, unrest and *ressentiment* is generated by the very institutions which promise stability: education, the mass media, the consumer marketplace. And when these injustices are amplified by the misrecognition of racism, by the humiliation of unjust and unfair policing, and by the whole classist stereotype that has built up around the underclass, then the humiliation of poverty is all the more exacerbated. It is no good, the great and the wise, the rich and the contented middle classes, being surprised by social disturbance, thinking that they are a once-off, or to believe that periods of calm herald a conflict-free era, for the tectonic plates of society conceal enormous pressures under the show of their seeming immobility.

On a wider level I have talked of a Global Merton, of the way in which economic and cultural globalisation has brought us closer together, where the arbitrariness of wealth, comfort, indeed of lifespan itself becomes all the more apparent. Imagine just for one moment a graduate working at a call centre in Delhi listening to the outsourced complaints of the privileged customers of the West. Imagine in a world of transnational identities: the Mexican in Los Angeles sending money home to Acapulco, visiting regularly friends and family, going backwards and forwards, the Jamaican crossing the Black Atlantic hither and thither between London and Kingston, an immigration no longer once and for all but with regular mobility, an identity no longer transfixed in one space but making regular comparisons of fairness and justice across the world. Imagine not just the outsourcing of work from the First World at lower rates, but the insourcing of immigrants to do all the jobs that 'our people no longer want to do', at much lower rates. Imagine the telephone lines buzzing and the contrasts being made.

And here I would differ with Jonathan Freedland, for he makes the comparison between the extravagantly rich and the rest of us, a comfortable contrast wherein the contented middle classes, the ranks of *Guardian* readers, are placed together with those at the lower part of the social structure. But as I have pointed out, the contentment of the upper middle classes is very much dependent on the lower wages and poverty of the considerable ranks of people – many but not all of them immigrants – who provide the services from childcare to shelf-filling which cushion and cosset their lives. The solipsis of the middle class is a major factor of life in late modernity. Thus, although we should, of course, be unfashionable and agree wholeheartedly with Jonathan Freedland that 'we'll have to do something about the rich', let us remind ourselves also of the economic circuits that bind much of the middle class into the system. Yet this having been said, the contradictoriness generated by the new economy create both the exacerbations of division and the possibility of solidarity.

Towards a new politics of inclusion

> The central fault line in modern post-industrial society is that between the winners and the losers in the global marketplace. The lion's share of the extraordinary productivity gains associated with the current capitalist renaissance has gone to the owners of capital, to a new techno-managerial elite and to a handful of stars in the increasingly global entertainment industries ... Confronting them are the losers: the anxious middle classes, threatened by proletarianisation; the increasingly casualised working class; and the burgeoning underclass. That fault line runs through the new Labour coalition. No project for social inclusion will work unless it captures some of the winners' gains and redirects them to the losers. The notion ... that the workfare state can turn the trick all by itself, that a mixture of training, education and moral suasion can transform the entire society into winners, and that this can be done at nil cost to those who have already won, is an illusion ... the losers' interests are bound to differ from those of the winners, and it is self-deception to pretend otherwise.
>
> (David Marquand, 1998, p. 85)

We live increasingly in a consensus of broken narratives: jobs lost, relationships ended, neighbourhoods left and localities transformed beyond recognition. The contrast in the post-war Golden Age between the mass of workers in steady jobs and the tiny minority of unemployed has gone as has the division between stable families and a minority of broken homes, all-embracing organic communities and the few nooks and crannies of anomie and disintegration. As we have seen, the discourse about social exclusion has nostalgically sought to resurrect this Golden Age, it has attempted to construct solidarity in terms which few in our society – let alone the poor – could seek to emulate. What, ironically, the mass of us have in common is exactly what this discourse disparages. Yet there is a considerable measure of potential solidarity on such issues – especially looking across the fissure which David Marquand so clearly demarcates: between the minority who have profited so well out of late modernity both in terms of income and recognition, and the vast majority outside of this privileged orbit. Similarly we live now in an increasingly diverse society both in terms of cultures of origin and those lifestyles which we have chosen to develop. Whereas the Golden Age saw inclusion as meaning assimilation into a massive, homogeneous culture, today inclusion means the recognition of our mutual diversity. Here again this shared diversity is something which can unite us. It is difficult to talk of 'them' and 'us' where there are numerous 'thems' and various 'us's'. The emergence of cities where people of great diversity live in close proximity is, however unintended, one of the great achievements of late modernity. It is this frisson of diversity which, as Iris Young (1990) reminds us, makes for the great excitement of the city and its attraction for so many.

But such politics which seek to transform the distribution of reward and celebrate diversity is counterposed against that which involves the internecine resentment of the fairly well-off against the poor and where uncertainties of identity are shored up by stigmatising and 'othering' vulnerable groups within the population. The discourse of social exclusion as presently constituted feeds into this latter regressive process. What we need is a reconceptualisation of inclusion to embrace a politics which enhances social justice and welcomes diversity.

The politics of deconstruction

Othering generates a hiatus between those in the upper and middle classes of the First World and those beneath them both within the First World and stretching beyond to the Third. Yet in fact, as we have seen, there are powerful economic circuits which connect the supposed underclass to the main body of society and which, through outsourcing and insourcing, migration backwards and forwards across the globe, generate both hybridisation and a transnational consciousness. Further, a parallel process of othering occurs between the 'normal majority' and other deviant groups, for example drug users, sexual deviants, and other outsiders often with class and racial undertones. Affirmative policies, as we have seen, even of the most liberal nature, simply maintain this hiatus. Indeed affirmative policies are a key manifestation of liberal othering. Transformative policies both in terms of distributive justice and social recognition seek to bridge this hiatus, to point to the similarities of situation and the interconnectedness of the human predicament.

Part of the experience of othering is the generation of solipsis: not only are the other distanced from ourselves but they are disavowed in terms of culture and values. The well-off of the First World exist in a phantasmagoric world: their superiority and separateness built upon illusion. This is not the place to discuss the irony of countries who manufacture less and less of the very commodities by which they seek to distinguish themselves from poorer nations (and in the case of the United States considerable financial indebtedness) yet who maintain an attitude of superiority, separateness and aloofness. Meanwhile, within the First World itself, the working poor have become rendered almost invisible to the very people who are dependent upon them for their services and the maintenance of a comfortable standard of living. Material comfort sits easily upon a cushion of solipsis. This detachment extends not only towards the poor but towards the wide swathe of deviant others that are available to us. For example, I have touched on elsewhere how such a hiatus occurs in images of drug use and what a transformative approach to drug use would look like (Young, 1999). Let us note how the conservative approach evokes a demonisation either of the addict or of the drugs – or both – whereas the liberal approach, that of medicalisation, involves an othering which utilises the metaphor of sickness to suggest a weakness, a lack of health. Both approaches involve a solipsis which denies the hefty amount of legal drug use that occurs in our society – from alcohol to ritalin, prozac and steroids. We sip our gin and tonics and pop valium at times of stress while they, God help them, take drugs.

Othering and community

The creation of a notion of 'us', of 'we', is associated and bolstered, as we have seen, by the generation of a notion of 'them', of a world of difference which gives meaning to ourselves. Conservative othering evokes images of evil, of rationalities which pursue unspeakable ends with unpardonable means. Liberal othering, on the other hand, speaks not of alternative despised rationalities but of a single, unquestioned rationality facing up to universes of irrationality; further it ties such irrationalities to the notion of deviations generated by poor material circumstances, lack of moral education, of recourse to the values of civilisation. Indeed individuals (say drug 'addicts' or 'alcoholics') are seen as suffering from a sick role, a product of a lack of self-understanding, of insight – all the virtues which the rational, normal person is seen to possess.

At the very heart of the sociological perspective is the socially grounded nature of human norms and behaviour. The sociological gaze is not, or should not be absolutist: for norms and standards vary with social situation. Liberal othering gets around this by suggesting that our middle class, First World norms are grounded in our superior material conditions, other groups lower in our class structure or those in poorer Third World societies would be like us if their material conditions caught up. Looking down the social structure or across to the Third World they see inevitably their past. They would be *just like us* if things were only better for them, if progress was made towards us. It is a seductive, appealing idea – it contains within it a hint of benevolence (we should help them be like us), a seeming lack of moral condemnation (it is, after all, not their fault) but, above all, the possibility of objectivity for we have a firm position from which to look across the gulf that divides us.

There are several problems with this. The first is that we live in a plural society – there is palpably no agreement about desired goals, preferred means, or indeed what is rationality. Even – or perhaps especially – the white middle class disagrees vociferously amongst itself about appropriate norms. Moreover, norms shift: what is *de riguer* today becomes rapidly dated and has palpably done so in our lifetime. You do not need to conduct an ethnography of the inner city to find difference: it is there in front of you, staring you in your face. Of course, religious fundamentalists; popes, mullahs, priests, etc. realise this only too well: they try desperately to halt the movement (the 'lowering') of standards, to draw certainty from their own particular tablets of stone.

As we have seen in our examination of teenage pregnancy: rational child-bearing becomes associated with the values of the upper middle classes – values which have in fact only emerged in recent years. Teenage pregnancy is cast as an irrationality, the values placed upon career, work, family, max-imising income, is assumed to be fixed. Liberalism presents itself as the rational, the obvious, the best that is possible and the inevitable future: it hijacks reason for itself. But all of these values have changed and will change again in the future. Similarly, if we take an ethnography like Elliott Liebow's *Tally's Corner* (2003 [1967]), the classic study of black men 'disengaged from society'. For Liebow the values of these men are seen as acts of self-deception, manly virtues, which could be transformed by a good dose of work, a breaking of the hiatus between them and society, a reintegration with reality. Their values of hedonism, pleasure, leisure and enjoyment are only recognised in the field notes at the end of the book, their feelings of rebellion and the need for political change are correctly and forthrightly talked about, but only in the last chapter which seems to have no connec-tion with the quiescence depicted in the bulk of the story (see Young, forth-coming). As I have noted, the lens of liberal othering focuses in on misery. It seems incapable of detecting fun and resistance. Rather, we see our role as helping them to change their behaviour then in order to make them happy, whether they are working class teenage girls or black men jiving on street corners, while our own happiness is strangely obvious, unrealistically secure.

Lastly I have noted how cultures change fast, how what are rational ends for one generation can become irrational desires, the vehicles of self-oppression, for another. Thus generations of kids have sat in the suburbs, despised the Malls, despaired at small-town chat, yearned for the city. They grew up revers-ing the logic of desiderata of their parents, they reversed their socialisation, they rejected, nay scorned, sometimes loathed what their parents saw as suc-cess – the signs that said they had arrived. They turned the road map around and headed for where many of their parents had gladly departed.

The banishment of unreason

Having circumscribed reason to a very stunted version of means and ends, a mixture of micro-economics and what the middle class actually do, neo-liberalism then proceeds to banish unreason from its theoretical compass. For there is no place in such an economistic model for the repressed desire, the malevolence of power, the anarchistic anger of humiliation, or the rigid conformity conjured in the midst of vertigo out of the fear of falling.

Whereas 50 years ago talk of the repression of motives, of displacement and hidden desire, would be commonplace, nowadays none of this is allowed to disturb the petty rationalism of neo-liberalism. Today the world is transparent, we can no longer hint at the real motives of transgression or most pertinently, the true motives of those who seek to ratchet up systems of control and punishment. Maliciousness, the pent up energies of humiliation, the transgressive qualities of violence all are concealed. Let us remind ourselves, for a moment, of the smiling faces of the jailors at Abu Grahib or the self-satisfied pride of the 'martyrs' videotaped before going out to bomb and commit suicide.

Not only, then, is rationality made one-dimensional and absolutist, but irrationality is ignored and denied. Throughout this book I have stressed the prevalence of irrationality in our society, whether it is in the shape of vindictiveness, moral panic, or transgressive violence, and the mechanisms which give rise to it. Conflicts between groups are widespread but such conflicts are also *within* the individual. Social conflict is propelled by the psychodynamics of hatred. In contrast to this the world of high modernity in the post-war period up to the mid-1970s seems more straightforward – values are more 'pure' and consistent, conflicts are more external and between groups, there is less tension and tumult within the individual. Nor is this the plastic world postulated by post-modernists, where the self is decentred, a function of myriad narratives, and where the actor playfully changes roles and guises. Rather it is a world of broken narratives; incoherent, contradictory and frustrating, where the individual struggles to maintain a centre, to compose his or her narrative. Contrary to post-modernist ideas, the achievement of a sense of self-development, a coherent progressive personal narrative, is an ideal. The condition of late modernity is not a comfortable distraction, but on the contrary a situation where narrative is plagued with doubts, insecurities and a sense of vertigo. Let us look at the mechanisms: first of all there is availability of a myriad scripts, a widened contact with a plurality of social worlds and conventions because of immigration and tourism and the mass media. Secondly, and very importantly, the chaos of reward generates feelings of an inchoate unfairness, where success is likely to be seen as transient and inadequately rewarded while failure is readily individualised and experienced as self-blame or the fault of those in one's immediate circle, whether family or friends. Such a moment of self-doubt is brought about not only by the ascendant values of a more individualistic society, but is undergirded by a whole series of agencies from government employment bureaux, through private therapeutic and self-help groups, to the tittle-tattle of advice columns and guides to better living in the popular press and daytime television.

The chaos of reward is amplified by the chaos of identity in part because of the interwoven links between class and status, but largely by the situation of disembeddedness and, as we have seen, the way in which conflicts of class are translated into those of status and involve the systematic denigration of groups lower in the social structure. Psychodynamically, *ressentiment*, whether of the moral indignation of the middle classes or the feelings of humiliation of the poor, are assuaged by attempts to essentialise identity, to achieve ontological fixity and closure. And the context of such othering, whether that of those low in the social structure towards celebrity, or those in the middle classes towards the poor, is suffused with thinly concealed envy and contradiction. Thus, as we have seen, although celebrities act out the fantasies of the many, they somehow never seem to live up to their privilege. They are, from Elvis to Princess Diana, from President Clinton to O.J. Simpson, from Pete Docherty to Kate Moss, incorrigibly flawed heroes. Miraculously the underclass are perceived to live likewise in a world outside of the sacrifices and pressures of everyday existence. Because of their perceived fecklessness in terms of sexuality, drugs and irresponsibility, they are the locus of anti-social behaviour, the focus of newspaper editorial and government piety. That their perceived transgressions are daily visible in the media, while their actual existence is largely invisible and overlooked – represents a sure sign of the projections and conjectures of the wider population. In all these ways the placid world of high modernity and the plastic world promised by post-modernity becomes superseded by the tempestuous self of late modernity.

Rationality, the new media and the public sphere

As we have seen, there has been a massive expansion both of the mass media and in mediated interaction. The proliferation of mass media channels, the mass use of videos and video outlets in every shopping area have introduced an element of choice into these monologic media whereas audience reflexivity has created a substantial base for what Thompson (1995) calls mediated quasi-interaction. All in all this is coincident with an extensive virtual reality. Taken together the expansion of television, radio and the written word has generated the widest choice of fictional and non-fictional reference points in history. All of this, as part of the process of cultural globalisation, has served to separate culture from space, to break the tight mooring between particular social roles and vocabularies of motives and spatial and social structural location. Further, rather than this process limiting human imagination, I would suggest that it allows the most extensive bricollaging of narrative on a personal level and hybridisation on the level of culture and subculture. The important thing to stress here is that it increases *porosity* – it facilitates blurring, interpenetration and multiple reinterpretations.

The expansion of mediated interaction by use of cell phone and email is a phenomenon of exponential development and of exceptional significance. It introduces dialogic media after a time when most commentators were bemoaning the increasingly monologic and hierarchical nature of human communications. Indeed, as the late Douglas Adams (2001) argued in a programme on the future of broadcasting, human communication and scenarios have been, since the beginning of history, naturally interactive. It is only in the twentieth century that the monologue of non-interactive media imposed itself on the population progressively taking up more and more of their time. The twenty-first century promises a flourishing of interactive media which, in a way, is a return to what has been natural to humankind.

Such innovating technology immensely facilitates communication across borders and, particularly with the rapid development of blogs and personal websites, allows widescale decentralised sites of debate, a precursor of what we may see as the re-emergence of the public sphere. Thus the nineteenth century fora of public debate depicted by Habermas in *The Structural Transformation of the Public Sphere* (1989) which was subverted by the rise of the centralised mass media, becomes replaced by a virtual public sphere.

Hans Magnus Enzensberger, a major media theorist of the New Left writing in the 1970s, in a well-known article 'Constituents of a Theory of the Media', outlined the characteristics of the contemporary mass media and contrasted this with what an emancipated media would be like:

Repressive media use	Emancipatory media use
Centrally controlled program	Decentralized programmes
One transmitter, many receivers	Every receiver a potential transmitter
Immobilization of isolated individuals	Mobilization of the masses
Passive consumer behaviour	Interaction of participants, feedback
Depoliticization process	Political learning process
Production by specialists	Collective production
Control by owners or bureaucrats	Social control through self-organization

(Enzensberger, 1970, p. 173)

As many commentators have noted, there is a remarkable concurrence between the new media and Enzensberger's picture of emancipation. Does this mean that a public sphere of rational emancipatory politics is in the making? I do not think so: for every site of radical politics and debate, whether it is *Move On* or *Greenpeace*, there are many sites of a negative or backward looking nature. The flaw in the easy triumphalism of progress in the new media lies in the assumptions of both media theorists in the Frankfurt traditions from Adorno, to Enzensberger and of their critics.

For the Frankfurt theorists the actor is seen as easily manipulable, in thrall to the messages of the omnipresent mass media, passive actors in the flux of consumer capitalism. From this perspective, then, the new media would represent an escape from this tyranny – a site of emancipation in Enzensberger's terms. On the other side, critics such as John Thompson forcefully reject this image of the human order, rather, in the tradition of symbolic interaction they stress the creative, voluntaristic nature of human action. Quite rightly they stress that the gross manipulation postulated by the Frankfurt School fundamentally downgrades the human ability to interpret, discard, reinterpret and hybridise such messages and, moreover, as this is true of the conventional media it is even more true of the new media. Indeed for Thompson, even the conventional media become a source of greater public awareness, of a common human predicament and interconnectedness on a global scale. Witness the worldwide response and sympathy to tragedies from 9/11 to the tsunami; witness the interventions from Live Aid to Life 8. Virtual reality, then, in an era of globalisation becomes the site of a worldwide notion of a generalised elsewhere, a common humanity which powerfully and instantaneously cuts across borders and human divisions.

I will go quite a way down this optimistic line of reasoning, but not too far. For Thompson seems to ignore the fact that the material and ideological situation which people find themselves in make them prone to essentialisation, stigmatisation, and moral panics; their 'free' choice is already shrouded by insecurities, vertigo and instability. Thus the rise of a new public sphere of bloggers, and internet of choice and reflexivity, is full of much of the same essentialising garbage as the popular press (and some of it worse). Reason does not spring up automatically in these free zones, outside of the intervention of the centralised news media. The recent British moral panic about binge drinking is a case in point: precious few of the independent sources questioned dominant opinions. And the same is true for many of the other foci of public anxiety, witness paedophilia, drug use, teenage mothers, etc.

I have argued that the vertigo of late modernity, the insecurities of job, work, family, community, the idealisation of individualism, of personal narrative and fulfilment, spring from the vast changes we experience in industry and in the world of consumerism. Such a situation of forced reflexivity is underscored by the dramatic experience of pluralism whether in the flow of immigrant workers, the new consumer tourism or cultural globalisation. One response to this is an act of denial, of a process of othering which denies relativism and proclaims the absolute value of one's own culture, nation, religion, race, class or gender. It should be obvious that the new media, the creation of a virtual reality involving both vertical reference points through the proliferation of the conventional media or horizontal reference points through the internet and mobile phone, can easily be brought into the service of such essentialisations. Fundamentalist Islam, to take an example, can find global support on the airwaves; the internet and phone system can create an instant and intense community among a widely dispersed minority. Fundamentalist Christianity can and does do likewise: mobilising, for example, powerful political coalitions in the US elections. But, despite all of this, we should not act as if dystopia were determined and progress had very little help from the forces of change. For although I would eschew an easy optimism, in the last analysis the balance of forces tend to undermine rather than to shore up such essentialisation. The reasons for this are several, but they hinge around the level of cultural porousness which both the new configuration of media and the changing composition of the cities engenders. Let me first stress the brittleness of essentialism.

The porous community

Identity politics confronts a world in flux and commands it to stop. Because the flux is not going to stop, neither will identity politics. Many varieties will rise, flourish, fall, give way to others, some more strident, others (one can hope) more temperate. Today, some cultural fundamentalists defend the formulas of 'multiculturalism' as solutions to the riddles of national identity in a world where the powers of any nation or state are steadily being eroded. Other fundamentalists, probably more numerous, claim that multiculturalism, racial preferences, and the like are instruments of an elite of usurpers from Harvard and Hollywood who are uncivilizing a formerly robust nation. The apparent opposites are twins. What frightens both is the flimsiness of a culture where everything is in motion and authority has perpetually to prove itself, where marginality is no longer always so marginal and the fragments of identity are on sale everywhere from the university to the mall. In the minds of all fundamentalists, porousness makes for corrosiveness. A porous society is an impure society. The impulse is to purge impurities, to wall off the stranger.

(Todd Gitlin, *The Twilight of Common Dreams*, 1995, p. 223)

Throughout this book I have examined the paradox of identity in late modernity. Namely, that in no other time has there been such an emphasis on individualism and self-development, yet the building blocks for such a personal narrative are increasingly insubstantial: they are no longer embedded in a taken-for-granted world of continuity and certainty. One response to this ontological insecurity is to create a world of rigidity and essence, blind faith in existentialist terms, where nationality, or race, or gender or religion become seen as natural, reified things, places of security, shelters from the storm of uncertainty. And there can be no doubt that such a resort is widespread and virulent: whether it is the depiction of human nature as 'deep wiring', or to religious beliefs 'written in tablets of stone'. But such a place is by the same analysis scarcely secure or certain. In a pluralistic world of cultural hybridism and personal bricollaging, such essentialist cultures have borders which are perpetually precarious and porous. They are *brittle*

CONCLUSION: ROADS TO ELSEWHERE

creations which seem tough and rigid but which can break all too easily. It is this brittleness which is the source of the hyperbole surrounding their defence, the nervous energy of the attempts to maintain distance and difference, the vehement and visceral denunciations of those 'liberals' who refuse to countenance clear demarcation lines whether it be in the arena of 'correct' sexuality or the 'good' war.

These hard narratives of right and wrong, of righteousness and betrayal, come on strong but they can collapse easily. Take the narrative of war, for example, in the First World War 20,000 British troops died in one day at the Battle of the Somme, yet the battle raged on for three and a half months: martyrdom glorified, patriotism unabated. Just look at the war memorials, look at the list of names and the length of the columns. The number of American casualties in the Second World War was over 292,000, in Vietnam over 47,000, in the present Iraq War, to date, is around 3,000. The latter figure would be reached in just six months at the rate of deaths in Vietnam. Chris Hedges may be quite right about the attractiveness of war as a guiding narrative but one suspects that there is no longer such a stomach for it in the West. The anti-war demonstrations were out on the streets before the present Iraq War began and public opinion both in the US and the UK has swung against the intervention: the hubris has been quickly shattered.

The two processes which underscore such brittleness are hyperculturalism and interconnectedness. Both, as we have seen, are the result of changes in virtual reality (the expansion and configuration of the media) and experienced reality (the changing composition of the late modern city).

Hyperpluralism and the elusive other

Let me close this chapter by underlining that much of this analysis carries within it benign as well as deleterious possibilities: the situation is genuinely contradictory. In *The Exclusive Society* I was at pains to criticise the one-sided dystopian vision of many who write about the late modern predicament. The disembeddedness of the social world, the need for constant reinvention of narrative holds the possibility of existential liberation as well as the temptations of essentialism and reification. The accent on pluralism, both pre-given and newly created, of hybridisation, bricollaging and invention, create possibilities of tolerance as well as conflict and the generation of sharp and solid differences. The new technologies of internet, cell phone and multi-mediation allow for the democratisation of human communication and the generation of an interconnecting on a global scale at the same time as the media corporations coalesce into more and more gigantic conglomerates. As far as othering is concerned – as I indicated – the widespread precariousness of material position, the ever-present possibility of loss of job, of breakdown of marriage, of instability of community, of drug use out of control, of our children or the children of one's friends engaging in behaviour which one finds aberrant, alarming, or just distasteful, makes it more and more difficult to fixate on a deviant and distant other. There but for fortune is as likely a response as there *they* go again. Interconnectedness fosters shared suffering as well as shared values. The other becomes, as I put it in *The Exclusive Society*, *elusive*, and the ability to fix public antagonism on outgroups through the agitations of the sections of the popular media or the activities of populist politicians is far from a foregone conclusion. That is, widespread public frustrations, repressions and uncertainties need not of necessity lead to intolerance. The solution is in part political, the existence of progressive parties that do not perpetuate hiatus politics, that is, politics where the poor are not seen as a separate category, the other side of a late modern binary, but as having a great deal in common in terms of existential predicament and material interest with the vast majority of society.

The organisation of such politics reflects such contradictions and presents both perceptual barriers and windows. Thus, while the politics of class is occluded, and that of identity with its narrative basis in status exists in a pluralism of values which permits numerous platforms of opportunities and alternatives. Not the least consideration here is the transformation of the late modern city. If we look at New York, Toronto, London, Amsterdam, we see the development of the most extraordinary social formations. The key change is massive immigration so that a very large proportion of the population are first generation immigrants (Kasinitz et al., 2004). Further, that this level of immigration, although sometimes paralleled in the past, comes from a much greater number of countries and cultures. New York City, for example, had a high proportion of foreign immigrants in 1900 but mainly from one rather than four continents. Indeed it might be conjectured that the optimum conditions for othering are where one has a massive mono-culture with a tiny 'deviant' culture (e.g. gypsies) or, even more so, where we have a binary: a majority culture and a very large minority culture (e.g. Belfast, Protestant/Catholic; Bradford, English/Pakistani). Indeed binary cultures are probably more liable to stigmatisation and conflict than are monocultures. Multiculturalism has been with us for a long time, hypercul-turalism, where there is very many cultures and there is no longer a major-ity population – that is, the minorities are the majority – is a new thing. Underscore this with mass tourism – New York City is host to just under 40 million tourists a year, that is five times its population – and, of course, add to this the vast number of virtual reference points available out there in the mass media, and one has a situation of unprecedented pluralism. My suggestion is that in these circumstances the optimum situation for 'successful' othering has past. That this is where there is a large majority culture and a few easily definable 'multicultural' minorities. Rather, in hyperculturalism, levels of ontological insecurity are somewhat lowered because, although the upheaval and turmoil of life involves a constant rewriting of biography and personal narrative, this is true for nearly everyone. Further, that status denigration is more difficult because it becomes experientially obvious that there are many ways of life and that none are *ipso facto* normal.

Towards a politics of diversity

I have argued for the politics of diversity which stresses change rather than tradition, which values hybridisation and crossover rather than 'authenticity' and stasis, which involves a creativity of innovation rather than a resort to the essential and the given.

The organic community of the past is in terminal decline although not into a black hole of atomistic individuals devoid of trust as the more dystopian of commentators would have it. Rather it has reformed into the late modern community: virtual and mediated in part and global in its reach which touches down at the local sometimes substantially but always intermittently in the biography of each individual. It is in this new community, the Generalised Elsewhere, where old identities are discarded and new identities reconstructed. It is here both in the more general public sphere and the host of subaltern publics where concepts of appropriate and inappropriate behaviour, and the criteria of social worth and opprobrium are regularly debated. Never have so many people looked at so many people: never in human history has there been such a degree of reflexivity about human behaviour. Yet the paradox of identity, once again, is that it is precisely at the point in history where it becomes most apparent as a social construction that there is a widespread desire for essence and fixity.

But such a carapace of fixity and security is a chimera, a fading illusion. For the direction where we are going has also dramatically altered. Social inclusion as a goal has changed meaning from the Golden Age of the postwar period. Whereas inclusion once meant lifetime stabilities of work, family and locality embedded in a culture of homogeneity, inclusion must now entail re-assessment and change in all these spheres and the creation of narratives which can cope with instabilities and uncertainties of biography and the problems of identity in a diverse society. The fundamental flaw in the present discourse about social exclusion is that its terms of reference are inclusion into a world that is fast disappearing.

And it is here that I would differ from Zygmunt Bauman in this description of the dialectic of inclusion and exclusion, of othering and counterothering, in his emphasis on the *necessity* of such a process, that is, the baldness of the statement that an 'inclusive community is a contradiction'. Indeed, I venture a modicum of optimism that under conditions of hyperpluralism where many of the great cities of our time no longer have a majority of any identity or ethnicity, where we have a majority of minorities, the conditions of successful othering begin to falter. Couple this with a media which is less centralised and much more profligate, then a widespread sense is engendered that diversity is *natural* and that material deprivations of poverty, unemployment, uncertainty and insecurity are a *shared experience*. One might even argue that for certain cosmopolitan populations of the late modern world it is the homogeneity of culture that is seen as alien, as an other. That it is the uniformity, for example, of the suburbs and its perceived prejudices which provides a convenient other and defining reference for their own culture of tolerance and diversity,

Finally, let us look to the future. The transition to late modernity is one which involves the most dramatic changes in the fabric of society. Anthony Giddens describes it like a juggernaut sweeping all solid institutions aside, Francis Wheen (1999) in his biography of Marx wryly notes how the images of globalisation and the metaphor of the 'melting' of all that seemed solid in the Communist Manifesto is prescient more of the present time than in the nineteenth century. Indeed there is more than a slight resonance of today when we read of a world where there is 'uninterrupted disturbance of all social conditions, everlasting uncertainty and agitation ... fixed, fast-frozen relations, with their train of ancient and venerable prejudices and opinions are swept away'; such changes with heavy irony swept away the fossilised state socialist regimes of Eastern Europe just as they transform our lives in the West. Community, work, the family – all the major institutions of social order, face a transformation. Whether this is in the direction of greater equality and a sense of self-worth or towards inequality and essentialism is the central hub of the politics of the future.

BIBLIOGRAPHY

Adams, D. (2001) 'Broadcasting in the Digital Age', 28 April. London: BBC Radio 4.

Andersen, J. (1999) 'Social and System Integration and the Underclass', in I. Gough and G. Olofsson (eds), *Capitalism and Social Cohesion*. New York: Palgrave Macmillan.

Anderson, B. (2000) *Doing the Dirty Work*. London: Zed.

Anderson, E. (1999) *Code of the Street*. New York: W. W. Norton.

Back, L. (1996) *New Ethnicities and Urban Culture*. London: UCL Press.

Banfield, E. (1968) *The Unheavenly City*. Boston: Little Brown.

Barrett, M. (1988) *Women's Oppression Today*, 2nd ed. London: Verso.

Bauman, Z. (1995) *Life in Fragments*. Oxford: Blackwell.

Bauman, Z. (1998a) *Globalization*. Cambridge: Polity.

Bauman, Z. (1998b) *Work, Consumerism and the New Poor*. Buckingham: Open University Press.

Bauman, Z. (2000) *Liquid Modernity*. Cambridge: Polity.

Bauman, Z. (2004) *Wasted Lives*. Cambridge: Polity.

Bauman, Z. and Tester, K. (2001) *Conversations with Zygmunt Bauman*. Cambridge: Polity.

Beck, U. (1992) *Risk Society*. London: Sage.

Beck, U. (2000) *The Brave New World of Work*. Cambridge: Polity.

Bell, D. (1973) *The Coming of Post-Industrial Society*. New York: BasicBooks.

Berger, P. and Luckmann, T. (1966) *The Social Construction of Reality*. New York: Doubleday.

Berman, M. (1983) *All That's Solid Melts Into Air*. London: Verso.

Berman, P. (2004) *Terrorism and Liberalism*. New York: W. W. Norton.

Bhabha, H. (1993) *The Location of Culture*. London: Routledge.

Blair, T. (1993) 'Why Crime is a Socialist Issue', *New Statesman* (29 January), pp. 27–8.

Blair, T. (2001) Foreword to *Preventing Social Exclusion*. London: The Stationery Office.

Blok, A. (1998) 'The Narcissism of Minor Differences', *European Journal of Social Theory*, 1, pp. 33–56.

Bonnemaison, G. (1983) *Face á delinquance: prevention, représsion, solidarité*. Paris: La Documentation Française.

Bottoms, A. and Wiles, P. (1997) 'Environmental Criminology' in M. Maguire, R. Morgan and R. Reiner (eds), *The Oxford Handbook of Criminology*, 2nd ed. pp. 305–60. Oxford: Clarendon Press.

Bourdieu, P. et al. (1999) *The Weight of the World*. Cambridge: Polity.

Bourgois, P. (1995) *In Search of Respect*. Cambridge: Cambridge University Press.

Bourgois, P. (1998) 'Just Another Night in a Shooting Gallery', *Theory, Culture and Society* 15(2), pp. 37–66.

Brake, M. (1980) *The Sociology of Youth Culture*. London: Routledge & Kegan Paul.

Broks, P. (2003) *Into the Silent Land*. New York: Grove Press.

Brotherton, D. and Barrios, L. (2004) *The Almighty Latin King and Queen Nation*. New York: Columbia University Press.

Burchardt, T., LeGrand, J. and Pichaud, D. (2002) 'Degrees of Exclusion', in J. Hills, J. LeGrand and D. Pichaud (eds), *Understanding Social Exclusion*. Oxford: Oxford University Press.

Burchell, B. (1999) *Job Insecurity and Work Intensification*. York: Joseph Rowntree Foundation.

Burke, J. (2005) '600,000 and rising: How the British are Colonizing Spain', The *Observer*, 9 October, p. 19.

Buruma, I. and Margalit, A. (2004) *Occidentalism: The West in the Eyes of its Enemies*. New York: The Penguin Press.

Byrne, D. (1999) *Social Exclusion*. Buckingham: Open University Press.

Cabinet Office (2002) *United Kingdom National Action Plan on Social Inclusion: 2001–2003*.

Campbell, C. (1987) *The Romantic Ethic and the Spirit of Modern Consumerism*. Oxford: Blackwells.

Cartner-Morley, J. (2005) 'Beauty and the Bust', *The Guardian*, 23 September.

Castells, M. (1991) *The Informational City*. Oxford: Blackwell.

Castells, M. (1994) 'European Cities, the Informational Society, and the Global Economy', *New Left Review*, 204, (March–April), pp. 19–35.

Chakrabarti, S. (2005) 'Freedom Fighter', Saturday Interview, The *Guardian*, 10 December.

Christopherson, S. (1994) 'The Fortress City: Privatized Spaces, Consumer Citizenship', in A. Amin (ed.), *Post-Fordism*. Oxford: Blackwell.

Clarke, J., Gerwitz, S. and McLaughlin, E. (eds) (2000) *New Managerialism, New Welfare*. London: Sage.

Clarke, R. (1980) 'Situational Crime Prevention', *British Journal of Criminology*, 20(2), pp. 136–47.

Cohen, A. K. (1955) *Delinquent Boys: The Culture of the Gang*. New York: The Free Press.

Cohen, A. K. (1965) 'The Sociology of the Deviant Act: Anomie Theory and Beyond', *American Sociological Review*, 30, pp. 5–14.

Cohen, N. (2003) 'A kind, really nice boy', The *Observer*, 4 May, *Guardian Unlimited*, pp. 1–4.

Cohen, S. (2002) *States of Denial*. Cambridge: Polity.

Coleman, J. (1990) *The Foundations of Social Theory*. Cambridge, MA: Harvard University Press.

Colley, H. and Hodkinson, P. (2001) 'Problems with "Bridging the Gap": the Reversal of Structure and Agency in Addressing Social Exclusion', *Critical Social Policy*, 21(3), pp. 335–59.

Collinson, M. (1996) 'In Search of the High Life', *British Journal of Criminology*, 36, pp. 428–44.

Corrigan, P., Jones, T., Lloyd, J. and Young, J. (1988) *Socialism, Merit and Efficiency*. London: Fabian Society.

Crawford, A., Jones, T., Woodhouse, T. and Young, J. (1990) *The Second Islington Crime Survey*. Middlesex University: Centre for Criminology.

215

Currie, E. (1997) 'Market Society and Social Disorder' in B. Maclean and D. Milanovic (eds), *Thinking Critically About Crime*. Vancouver: Collective Press.

Currie, E. (1998) *Crime and Punishment in America*. New York: Metropolitan Books.

Dahrendorf, R. (1985) *Law and Order*. London: Stevens.

Dakers, S. (2006) 'The Hunger Within', The *Guardian*, Society, 4 January.

David, M. (2004) 'Clash of Civilisations', *The New York Times*, 13 May, A.25.

Davis, M. (1990) *City of Quartz*. London: Verso.

deBeauvoir, S. (1953) *The Second Sex*. London: Jonathan Cape.

DeKeseredy, W. and Schwartz, M. (1996) *Contemporary Criminology*. Belmont, CA: Wadsworth.

Department of Social Security (1999) *Opportunity for All: Tackling Poverty and Social Exclusion*. Cm 4445. London: The Stationery Office.

Dilulio, J. (1995) 'Crime in America: It's Going to Get Worse', *Readers Digest* (August), p. 57.

Dixon, W. (2001) 'Exclusive Societies: Towards a Critical Criminology of Post-Apartheid South Africa'. Institute of Criminology, University of Cape Town.

Douglas, M. (1966) *Purity and Danger*. London: Routledge and Kegan Paul.

Durkheim, E. (1951 [1893]) *The Division of Labour in Society*. New York: Free Press.

Durkheim, E. (1964 [1895]) *The Rules of Sociological Method*. New York: Free Press.

Durkheim, E. (1970 [1887]) *Suicide*. London: Routledge and Kegan Paul.

Dylan, B. (2004) *Chronicles: Volume One*. New York: Simon and Schuster.

Ehrenreich, B. (2001) *Nickel and Dimed*. New York: Henry Holt.

Ehrenreich, B. (2002) 'Maid of Order' in B. Ehrenreich and A. Hochschild (eds), *Global Woman: Nannies, Maids and Sex Workers in the New Economy*. New York: Metropolitan.

Ehrenreich, B. and Hochschild, A. (eds) (2002) *Global Woman: Nannies, Maids and Sex Workers in the New Economy*. New York: Metropolitan Books.

Engels, F. (1969 [1844]) *Conditions of the Working Class in England in 1844*. London: Panther.

Enzensberger, H. M. (1970) 'Constituents of a Theory of the Media', *New Left Review*, 64, pp. 13–36.

Ermisch, J. and Pevalin, D. (2003) *Does 'Teen-birth' have Longer-term impacts on the Mother?* University of Essex: ISER Working Papers 2003–28.

Etzioni, A. (1997) *The New Golden Rule*. London: Profile Books.

Faludi, S. (1999) *Stiffed: The Betrayal of the American Man*. New York: Putnam.

FBI (1998) *Terrorism in the United States 1997*. Washington DC: US Department of Justice.

Featherstone, M. (1985) 'Lifestyle and Consumer Culture', *Theory, Culture and Society*, 4, pp. 57–70.

Felson, M. (2002) *Crime and Everyday Life*, 3rd ed. Thousand Oaks, CA: Sage.

Ferguson, H. (2006) 'Second Thoughts', The *Guardian*, Society, 11 January, p. 4.

Ferrell, J. (1997) 'Criminological Verstehen: Inside the Immediacy of Crime', *Justice Quarterly*, 14, pp. 3–23.

Ferrell, J. (2004) 'Boredom, Crime and Criminology', *Theoretical Criminology*, 8(3), pp. 287–302.

Ferrell, J. (2006) 'The Aesthetics of Cultural Criminology', in Bruce Arrigo and Christopher Williams (eds), *Philosophy, Crime and Criminology*. Chicago: University of Illinois Press.

Frank, T. (2004) *What's the Matter with Kansas?: How Conservatives Won the Heart of America*. New York: Metropolitan Books.

Fraser, N. (1997) *Justice Interruptus: Critical Reflections on the Post-Socialist Condition*. New York: Routledge.

Fraser, N. (2000) 'Rethinking Recognition', *New Left Review*, 2/3, pp. 107–20.

Fraser, N. (2003) 'Social Justice in the Age of Identity Politics', in N. Fraser and A. Honneth (eds), *Redistribution or Recognition?* London: Verso.

Fraser, N. and Honneth, A. (2003) *Redistribution or Recognition?* London: Verso.

Freedland, J. (2005a) 'After the Aftershock', *The Guardian*, 13 July.

Freedland, J. (2005b) 'France is Clinging to an Ideal that is Pickled in Dogma', The *Guardian*, 9 November.

Freedland, J. (2005c) 'It May Well be Beyond Passé – but we'll have to do something about the rich', The *Guardian*, 23 November.

Freud, S. (1929) *Civilisation and its Discontents*. Harmondsworth: Penguin.

Friedman, L. (1999) *The Horizontal Society*. New Haven: Yale University Press.

Friedman, T. (2005) *The World is Flat*. New York: Farrar, Straus and Giroux.

Frith, S. (1983) *Sound Effects: Youth, Leisure and the Politics of Rock 'n' Roll*. London: Constable.

Gabriel, Y. and Lang, T. (1995) *The Unmanageable Consumer*. London: Sage.

Gaines, D. (1998) *Teenage Wasteland: Suburbia's Dead End Kids*. Chicago: University of Chicago Press.

Galbraith, J. K. (1992) *The Culture of Contentment*. London: Sinclair-Stevenson.

Gans, H. (1995) *The War Against the Poor*. New York: Basic Books.

Garland, D. (1996) 'The Limits of the Sovereign State', *British Journal of Criminology*, 36(4), pp. 445–71.

Garland, D. (2001) *The Culture of Control*. Oxford: Oxford University Press.

Giddens, A. (1984) *The Constitution of Society*. Cambridge: Polity.

Giddens, A. (1990) *The Consequences of Modernity*. Cambridge: Polity.

Giddens, A. (1991) *Modernity and Self-Identity*. Cambridge: Polity.

Gilroy, P. (1993) *The Black Atlantic*. Cambridge MA: Harvard University Press.

Gitlin, T. (1995) *Twilight of Common Dreams*. New York: Henry Holt.

Goldhagen, D. (1997) *Hitler's Willing Executioners*. New York: Vintage Books.

Gorz, A. (1999) *Reclaiming Work: Beyond the Wage-Based Society*. Cambridge: Polity Press.

Gregson, N. and Lowe, M. (1994) *Servicing the Middle Classes*. London: Routledge.

Gupta, A. and Ferguson, J. (1997) 'Beyond "Culture": Space, Identity and the Politics of Difference' in A. Gupta and J. Ferguson (eds), *Culture, Power, Place*. Durham, NC: Duke University Press.

Habermas, J. (1989) *The Structural Transformation of the Public Sphere*. Cambridge: Polity.

Hagedorn, J. (1991) 'Gangs, Neighborhoods and Public Policy', *Social Problems*, 38(4), pp. 429–42.

Hall, S. (1969) 'The Hippies, an American Moment' in J. Nagel (ed.), *Student Power*. London: Merlin.

Hall, S. (Steve) (1997) 'Visceral Culture and Criminal Practices', *Theoretical Criminology*, 1(4), pp. 453–78.

Hall, S. and Jefferson, T. (eds) (1975) *Resistance Through Ritual*. London: Hutchinson.

Hallsworth, S. (2000) 'Rethinking the Punitive Term', *Punishment and Society*, 2(2), pp. 145–60.

Hamm, M. (2004) 'Apocalyptic Violence: The Seductions of Terrorist Subcultures', *Theoretical Criminology*, 8(3) pp. 323–339.

Handler, J. (2000) 'Winding Down Welfare', *New Left Review*, 4, pp. 114–36.

217

Harrington, M. (1963) *The Other America*. New York: Macmillan.

Harrision, P. (1983) *Inside the Inner City*. Harmondsworth: Penguin.

Hayward, K. (2002) 'Crime, Consumerism and the Urban Experience', PhD Thesis, School of Law, University of East London.

Hayward, K. (2004) *City Limits: Crime, Consumerism and the Urban Experience*. London: Glasshouse Press.

Hayward, K. (2006) 'Beyond the Bing in Booze Britain: Market-led Criminality and the Spectacle of Binge Drinking', 34th Conference European Group for the Study of deviance and Social Control, University of the Peloponnese, Corinth, Greece, August 2006.

Hebdige, D. (1990) 'Fax to the Future', *Marxism Today* (January), pp. 18–23.

Hebdige, D. (1992) 'Redeeming Witness: In the Tracks of the Homeless Vehicle Project', *Cultural Studies*, 7(3), pp. 173–223.

Hedges, C. (2003) *War is a Force That Gives Us Meaning*. New York: Anchor.

Herrnstein, R. and Murray, C. (1994) *The Bell Curve*. New York: Free Press.

Hills, J., LeGrand, J. and Pichaud, D. (eds) (2002) *Understanding Social Exclusion*. Oxford: Oxford University Press.

Hirst, P. (1994) *Associative Democracy*. Cambridge: Polity.

Hirst, P. and Thompson, G. (1999) *Globalisation in Question,* 2nd ed. Cambridge: Polity.

Hobbs, D. (2002) 'Obituary of John Gotti', The *Independent*, 12 June, p. 18.

Hobsbawm, E. (1994) *The Age of Extremes*. London: Michael Joseph.

Hobsbawm, E. (1996) 'The Cult of Identity Politics', *New Left Review,* 217, pp. 38–47.

Hobsbawm, E. and Ranger, T. (eds) (1983) *The Invention of Tradition*. Cambridge: Cambridge University Press.

Hochschild, A. (2002) 'Love and Gold' in B. Ehrenreich and A. Hochschild (eds), *Global Woman*. New York: Metropolitan Books.

Holmes, R. and Holmes, S. (1994) *Murder in America*. Thousand Oaks, CA: Sage.

Home Office (2002a) *Secure Borders, Safe Haven: Integration with Diversity in Modern Britain* cm5387. London: The Stationery Office.

Home Office (2002b) *Community Cohesion*. London: The Stationery Office.

Home Office (2002c) *Building Cohesive Communities*. London: The Stationery Office.

Honneth, A. (2003) 'Redistribution as Recognition: A Response to Nancy Fraser' in N. Fraser and A. Honneth, *Redistribution or Recognition?* London: Verso.

Hood, R. and Jones, K. (1999) 'Three Generations: Oral Testimonies on Crime and Social Change in London's East End', *British Journal of Criminology*, 31(1), pp. 136–60.

Hough, M. and Tilley, N. (1998) *Auditing Crime and Disorder: Guidance for Local Partnerships*. Police Research Group, Paper 91. London: The Stationery Office.

Huggins, M. Haritos-Fatouros, M. and Zimbardo, P. (2002) *Violence Workers*. San Francisco, CA: University of California Press.

Hunt, J. and Hunt, L. (1977) 'Dilemmas and Contradictions of Status: The Case of the Dual-Career Family', *Social Problems*, 24, pp. 407–16.

Huntingdon, S. (1993) 'The Clash of Civilisations', *Foreign Affairs*, 71(3), pp. 22–49.

Hutton, W. (1995) *The State We're In*. London: Cape.

Ignatieff, M. (1999) *The Warriors Honor*. London: Vintage.

Jamieson, R. (1998) 'Towards a Criminology of War in Europe', in V. Ruggiero, N. South and I. Taylor (eds), *The New European Criminology*. London: Routledge.

Jamieson, R. (1999) 'Genocide and the Social Production of Immorality', *Theoretical Criminology,* 3(2), pp. 131–46.

Jones, M. (1999) 'Monica: The Real Woman Behind the Headlines', *Marie Claire*, 128 (April), pp. 30–36.

Jones, T., MacLean, B. and Young, J. (1986) *The Islington Crime Survey*. Aldershot: Gower.

Kaldor, M. (2003) 'Terrorism as Regressive Globalisation', 27 March, Open Democracy: www.opendemocracy.com

Kaldor, M. and Vashee, B. (1997) *Restructuring the Global Military Sector, Vol. 1: New Wars*. London: Pinter.

Karydis, V. (1996), 'Criminality of Migrants in Greece', *Chronicles* 9, pp. 169–76.

Kasinitz, P., Mollenkopf, J. and Waters, M. (eds) (2004), *Becoming New Yorkers*. New York: Russell Sage.

Katz, J. (1988) *Seductions of Crime: The Moral and Sensual Attractions of Doing Evil*. New York: BasicBooks.

Kelso, W. (1994) *Poverty and the Underclass*. New York: New York University Press.

Kennedy, M. (2005) *Without a Net*. New York: Viking.

Kiernan, K. (1995) *Transition to Parenthood*. Welfare Study Programme Discussion Paper, WSP/113. London: LSE.

Knox, P. (1995) *Urban Social Geography,* 3rd ed. Harlow: Longman.

Kontos, L., Brotherton, D. and Barrios, L. (eds) (2003) *Gangs and Society: Alternative perspectives*. New York: Columbia University Press.

Kristeva, J. (1991), *Strangers to Ourselves*. New York: Harvester Wheatsheaf.

Kyambi, S. (2005) *Beyond Black and White: Mapping New Immigrant Communities*. London: Institute of Public Policy Research.

Lea, J. and Young, J. (1982) 'The Riots in Britain 1981, in D. Cowell, T. Jones and J. Young (eds), *Policing the Riots*. London: Junction Books.

Lea, J. and Young, J. (1993) *What is to be Done about Law and Order?* 2nd ed. London: Pluto.

Lee, C. P. (1998) *Like the Night*. Manchester: Helter Skelter Publishing.

Lee, J. A. (1981) 'Some Structural Aspects of Police Deviance in Relations with Minority Groups' in C. Shearing (ed.), *Organisational Police Deviance*. Toronto: Butterworth.

Levitas, R. (1996) 'The Concept of Social Exclusion and the New Durkheimian Hegemony', *Critical Social Policy*, 16(1), 5–20.

Levitas, R. (1997) 'Discourses of Social Inclusion and Integration: From the European Union to New Labour', paper presented at the European Sociological Association Conference, University of Essex, August.

Liebow, E. (2003[1997]) *Tally's Corner*, new edn. Lanham, MA: Rowman and Littlefield.

Lister, R. (1998) 'From Equality to Social Inclusion: New Labour and the Welfare State', *Critical Social Policy*, 18(2), pp. 215–25.

Luker, K. (1996) *Dubious Conceptions: The Politics of Teenage Pregnancy*. Cambridge, MA: Harvard University Press.

Luttwak, E. (1995) 'Turbo-Charged Capitalism and its Consequences', *London Review of Books,* 17(21), 2 November, pp. 6–7.

Luttwak, E. (1999) *Turbo-Capitalism: Winners and Losers in the Global Economy*. New York: HarperCollins.

Lyng, S. (1990) Edgework: A Social Psychological Analysis of Voluntary Risk-Taking', *American Journal of Sociology*, 95(4), pp. 876–921.

Magnet, M. (1993) *The Dream and the Nightmare*. New York: William Morrow.

Mandelson, P. (1997) *Labour's Next Steps: Tackling Social Exclusion*, Pamphlet 581. London: The Fabian Society.

Mann, C. (1993) *Unequal Justice*. Bloomington, IN: Indiana University Press.

Marquand, D. (1998) *The Unprincipled Society: New Demands and Old Politics.* London: Fontana.

Marshall, I. (ed.) (1997) *Minorities, Migrants and Crime.* Thousand Oaks, CA: Sage.

Marshall, T. H. (1996 [1950]) *Citizenship and Social Class.* London: Pluto.

Marx, K. (1967 [1844]) *Economic and Philosophic Manuscripts* in L. Easton and K. Guddat (eds), *Writings of the Young Marx on Philosophy and Society.* New York: Anchor Books.

Massing, M. (1999) 'The End of Welfare?', *The New York Review of Books,* 46 (7 October), pp. 22–6.

Matthews, R. (2002) *Armed Robbery.* Cullompton, Devon: Willan.

Matza, D. (1964) *Delinquency and Drift.* New York: John Wiley.

Matza, D. (1969) *Becoming Deviant.* Englewood Cliffs, NJ: Prentice Hall.

Matza, D. and Sykes, G. (1961) 'Juvenile Delinquency and Subterranean Values', *American Sociological Review,* 26, pp. 712–19.

McEwan, I. (2001) 'Only love and then oblivion: Love was all they had to set against their murderers', The *Guardian,* 15 September, at *Guardian Unlimited,* pp. 1–4.

McLaughlin, E., Muncie, J. and Hughes, G., (1991) 'The Permanent Revolution: New Labour, New Public Management and the Modernization of Criminal Justice', *Criminal Justice,* 1(3), pp. 301–18.

Mcleod, J. (1995) *Ain't No Makin' It.* Boulder, CO: Westview.

McRobbie, A. and Thornton, S. (1995) 'Rethinking Moral Panic for Multimediated Social Worlds', *British Journal of Sociology,* 46(4), pp. 559–74.

McVicar, J. (1979) *McVicar: By Himself.* London: Arrow.

Mead, L. (1986) *Beyond Entitlement The Social Obligations of Citizenship.* New York: The Free Press.

Mead, L. (1992) *The New Politics of Poverty.* New York: BasicBooks.

Mead, L. (1997) *From Welfare to Work.* London: Institute for Economic Affairs.

Mednick, B., Baber, R. and Sultan-Smith, B. (1979) 'Teenage Pregnancy and Perinatal Mortality', *Journal of Youth and Adolescence,* 8(3), pp. 343–57.

Merton, R. K. (1938) 'Social Structure and Anomie', *American Sociological Review,* 3, pp. 672–82.

Merton, R. K. (1957) *Social Theory and Social Structure* (rev.ed). Glencoe, IL: Free Press.

Meyrowitz, J. (1985) *No Sense of Place: The Impact of Electronic Media on Social Behaviour.* New York: Oxford University Press.

Meyrowitz, J. (1989) 'The Generalized Elsewhere', *Critical Studies in Mass Communication,* 6(3), pp. 326–34.

Miller, W. (1958) 'Lower Class Culture as a Generating Milieu of Gang Delinquency', *Journal of Social Issues,* 14(3), pp. 17–23.

Miller, W. (1964) Foreword to Sydney E. Bernard, *Fatherless Families: Their Economic and Social Adjustment.* Waltham, MA: Brandeis University Research Center, Papers in Social Welfare No.7.

Mishel, L., Bernstein, J. and Schmitt, J. (2001) *The State of Working America 2000–1.* Ithaca, NY: Cornell University Press.

Mooney, G. and Danson, M. (1997) 'Beyond Culture City: Glasgow as a Dual City' in N. Jewson and S. MacGregor (eds), *Transforming Cities.* London: Routledge.

Mooney, J. (2003) 'It's the Family Stupid: New Labour and Crime', in R. Matthews (ed.), *The New Politics of Crime and Punishment.* Cullompton, Devon: Willan.

Mooney, J. and Young, J. (2000) 'Policing Ethnic Minorities' in B. Loveday and A. Marlow (eds), *Policing After the Stephen Lawrence Inquiry.* Lyme Regis: Russell House.

Mooney, J. and Young, J. (2003) 'Video Games: Overview Research', *Video Games and Aggression*. Middlesex University: Centre for Criminology.

Morley, D. (1986) *Family Television*. London: Comedia/Routledge.

Morley, D. (2000) *Home Territories: Media, Mobility and Identity*. London: Routledge.

Morley, D. and Robins, K. (1995) *Spaces of Identity*. London: Routledge.

Morrison, W. (1995) *Theoretical Criminology*. London: Cavendish.

Morrison, W. (2003) 'Criminology, Genocide and Modernity: Remarks on the Companion Criminology Ignored', in C Sumner (ed.), *Blackwell Companion to Criminology*. Oxford: Blackwell.

Murray, C. (1984) *Losing Ground*. New York: Basic Books.

Murray, C. (1990) *The Emerging British Underclass*. London: Institute of Economic Affairs.

Murray, C. (1994) *Underclass: The Crisis Deepens*. London: Institute for Economic Affairs.

Murray, C. (1996) 'Rejoinder', in D. Green (ed.), *Charles Murray and the Underclass*. London: Institute for Economic Affairs.

Murray, C. (1999) 'All Locked Up in the American Dream', *The Sunday Times* (7 February) p. 5–7.

Nelson, J. (1995) *Post-Industrial Capitalism*. Newbury Park, CA: Sage.

Newman, K. (1999) *Falling from Grace*. Berkeley, CA: University of California Press.

Newman, K. (2000) *No Shame in My Game*. New York: Vintage Books.

Nietzsche, F. (2005) *The Genealogy of Morals* (trans. Richard Hooker), www.wsu.edu:8080/~dee/MODERN/GENEAL.HTM

Nightingale, C. (1993) *On the Edge*. New York: Basic Books.

Offe, C. (1985) 'Work: The Key Sociological Category?' in C. Offe *Disorganized Capitalism*. Cambridge: Polity.

Olalquiaga, C. (1992) *Megalopolis*. Minneapolis: University of Minnesota Press.

O'Malley, P. and Mugford, S. (1994) 'Crime, Excitement and Modernity', in G. Barak (ed.), *Varieties of Criminology*. Westport, CT: Praegar.

Oualhaci, A. (2006) 'The "Riots" in the French Banlieue', unpublished paper.

Painter, K., Lea, J., Woodhouse, T. and Young, J. (1989) *The Hammersmith Crime and Policing Survey*. Middlesex University: Centre for Criminology.

Pakulski, J. and Waters, M. (1996) *The Death of Class*. London: Sage.

Parenti, C. (2000) *Lockdown America*. London: Verso.

Parkin, F. (1971) *Class Inequality and the Political Order*. New York: Praeger.

Peck, J. (1999) 'New Labourers? Making a New Deal for the "Workless Class"', *Environment and Planning C Governmental Policy*, 17, pp. 345–72.

Pelecanos, G. P. (1998) *King Suckerman*. London: Serpent's Tail.

Pelecanos, G. (2000) 'Interview', The *Guardian*, 16 July, p. 13.

Percy-Smith, J. (2000a) 'The Contours of Social Exclusion' in J. Percy-Smith (ed.), *Policy Responses to Social Exclusion*. Buckingham: Open University Press.

Percy-Smith, J. (2000b) 'Political Exclusion' in J. Percy-Smith (ed.), *Policy Responses to Social Exclusion*. Buckingham: Open University Press.

Perry, A. (2002) 'Teenage Pregnancy and the Midwife: Examining the Social Exclusion Report', *Midwifery Matters*, No.93 (Summer).

Pitts, J. (2001) *The New Politics of Youth Crime*. London: Palgrave.

Pitts, J. (2006) 'New Labour and the Racialisation of Youth Crime', in J Hagedorn (ed.), *Gangs in the Global City: The Limitations of Criminology*. Champaign, IL University of Illinois Press.

Plummer, K. (1995) *Telling Sexual Stories*. London: Routledge.

Power, A. and Tunstall, R. (1997) *Dangerous Disorder: Riots and Violent Disturbances in Thirteen Areas of Britain 1991–1992.* York: York Publishing Services.

Pratt, J. (2000) 'Emotive and Ostentatious Punishment: Its Decline and Resurgence in Modern Society', *Punishment and Society*, 2(4), pp. 417–40.

Prescott, J. (2002) 'Social Exclusion in the Twenty-First Century', speech to Fabian Society, London.

Presdee, M. (2000) *Cultural Criminology and the Carnival of Crime.* London: Routledge.

Raban, J. (2004) 'Emasculating Arabia', The *Guardian*, 13 May, pp. 1–5 (*Guardian Unlimited* http://www.guardian.co.uk).

Radford, J. and Stanko, B. (1991) 'Violence Against Women and Children' in K. Stenson and D. Cowell (eds), *The Politics of Crime Control.* London: Sage.

Ranulf, S. (1964 [1938]) *Moral Indignation and Middle Class Psychology.* New York: Schocken.

Rees, T. (1982) 'Immigration Policies in the United Kingdom', in C. Husband (ed.), *'Race' in Britain.* London: Hutchinson University Library.

Reiner, R. (1997) 'Media Made Criminality' in M. Maguire, R. Morgan and R. Reiner (eds), *The Oxford Handbook of Criminology*, 2nd ed. Oxford: Clarendon Press.

Rieff, D. (1993) *Los Angeles: Capital of the Third World.* London: Phoenix/Orion.

Rifkin, J. (1996) *The End of Work.* New York: Putnam.

Ritzer, G. (1993) *The McDonaldization of Society.* Newbury Park, CA: Sage.

Rollins, J. (1985) *Between Women: Domestic Workers and their Employers.* Philadelphia: Temple University Press.

Rosaldo, R. (1993) *Culture and Truth.* Boston: Beacon Press.

Rose, N. (1999) *Powers of Freedom: Reframing Political Thought.* Cambridge: Cambridge University Press.

Ross, A. (1999) *The Celebration Chronicles.* New York: Balantine.

Ruggiero, V. (2000) *Crime and Markets.* Oxford: Clarendon.

Runciman, W. (1966) *Relative Deprivation and Social Justice.* London: Routledge and Kegan Paul.

Sahlin, M. (1976) *Culture and Practical Reason.* Chicago: University of Chicago Press.

Said, E. (2003) *Orientalism*, 25th Anniversary Edition. New York: Vintage Books.

Sales, R. (2002) 'The Deserving and the Undeserving? Refugees, Asylum Seekers and Welfare in Britain', *Critical Social Policy*, 27(3), pp. 456–78.

Sassen, S. (2002) 'Global Cities and Survival Circuits' in B. Ehrenreich and A. Hochschild (eds), *Global Woman: Nannies, Maids and Sex Workers in the New Economy.* New York: Metropolitan.

Sayer, A. (1992) *Method in Social Science*, 2nd ed. London: Routledge.

Scarman, L. (1982) *The Scarman Report.* Harmondsworth: Penguin.

Scheler, M. (1923) 'Das Ressentiment im Aufbau der Moralem' in *Van Umsturz der Werte* I, Leipzig.

Schelsky, H. (1957) 'Ise die Dauerreflektion Institutionalisierbar?' *Zeitschrift fòr Evangelische Ethik* 1, pp. 153–74.

Schor, J. B. (1993) *The Overworked American.* New York: Basic Books.

Schwartz, D., Grisso, A., Miles, G., Holmes, J., Wishner, R. and Sutton R. (1994) 'A Longitudinal Study of Injury Morbidity in an African–American Population', *Journal of American Medical Association*, 271(10), pp. 755–60.

Scottish Council Foundation (1998) *Three Nations: Social Exclusion in Scotland.* Edinburgh: SCF.

Seabrook, J. (1984) *The Idea of Neighbourhood.* London: Pluto.

Sennett, R. (1991) *The Conscience of the Eye*. London: Faber.

Sennett, R. and Cabb, J. (1993) *The Hidden Injuries of Class*. London: Faber and Faber.

Sennett, R. (1998) *The Corrosion of Character*. New York: W. Norton & Co.

Shaw, M. (2003) *War and Genocide*. Cambridge: Polity.

Shipler, D. (2004) *The Working Poor: The Invisible America*. New York: Knopf.

Shulman, B. (2003) *The Betrayal of Work*. New York: The New Press.

Sibley, D. (1995) *The Geographies of Exclusion*. London: Routledge.

Sillitoe, A. (1958) *Saturday Night and Sunday Morning*. London: W. H. Allen.

Simmel, G. (1950) 'The Metropolis and Mental Life', in *The Sociology of Georg Simmel*, trans. K. H. Wolff. New York: The Free Press.

Simon, J. (2001) 'Entitlement to Cruelty: The End of Welfare and the Punitive Mentality in the United States', in K. Stenson and R. Sullivan (eds), *Crime, Risk and Justice*. Cullompton, Devon: Willan.

Smith, M. (2001) *Transnational Urbanism*. Oxford: Blackwell.

Social Exclusion Unit (1999a) *Bringing Britain Together*. London: The Stationery Office.

Social Exclusion Unit (1999b) *Teenage Pregnancy*. London: The Stationery Office.

Social Exclusion Unit (1999c) *Bridging the Gap: New Opportunities for 16–18 Year Olds*. London: The Stationery Office.

Social Exclusion Unit (2001) *Preventing Social Exclusion*. London: The Stationery Office.

Social Trends (2005) *2005 Edition*. London: The Stationery Office.

Sothcott, K. (2003) 'The Seductions of War and the Existential Origins of Military Atrocity', Middlesex University: Centre for Criminology.

Sykes, G. (1958) *The Society of Captives*. Princeton NJ: Princeton University Press.

Sykes, G. and Matza, D. (1957) 'Techniques of Neutralization', *American Sociological Review*, 22, pp. 664–70.

Taylor, I. (1999) *Crime in Context*. Oxford: Polity.

Taylor, L. and Mullan, B. (1986) *Uninvited Guests*. London: Chatto and Windus.

Therborn, G. (1986) *Why Some Peoples are More Unemployed than Others*. London: Verso.

Thompson, G. (2000) 'Economic Globalisation?' in D. Held (ed.), *A Globalizing World? Culture, Economics and Politics*. London: Routledge.

Thompson, J. (1995) *The Media and Modernity*. Cambridge: Polity.

Tomlinson, J. (1999) *Globalization and Culture*. Cambridge: Polity.

Touraine, A. (1971) *The Post Industrial Society*. New York: Random House.

Townsend, P. (1979) *Poverty in the United Kingdom*. London: Penguin.

UN (1999) *World Investment Report 1999: Foreign Investment and the Challenge of Development*. UN: UNCTAD.

Unger, C. (2004) *House of Bush, House of Saud*. New York: Scribner.

Valentine, C. (1968) *Culture and Poverty*. Chicago: University of Chicago Press.

Veit-Wilson, J. (1998) *Setting Adequacy Standards*. Bristol: Policy Press.

Wacquant, L. (1996) 'The Comparative Structure and Experience of Urban Exclusion in Chicago and Paris' in K. McFate, R. Lawson and W. J. Wilson (eds), *Poverty, Inequality and the Future of Social Policy*. New York: Russell Sage Foundation.

Wacquant, L. (1997) 'Three Pernicious Premises on the Study of the American Ghetto', *International Journal of Urban and Regional Research*, 20(2), pp. 341–53.

Wacquant, L. (1998) 'Inside the Zone: The Social Art of the Hustler', *Theory, Culture and Society* 15(2), pp. 1–36.

Wacquant, L. (2000) 'The New "Peculiar Institution": On the Prisoners Surrogate Ghetto', *Theoretical Criminology*, 4 (3), pp. 377–89.

Wacquant, L. (2001) 'Deadly Symbiosis: When Ghetto and Prison Meet and Merge', *Punishment and Society* 3 (1), pp. 95–134.

Wacquant, L. (2002) 'From Slavery to Mass Incarceration', *New Left Review*, 13 (January/February).

Wacquant, L. (2002) 'Scrutinizing the Street: Poverty, Morality, and the Pitfalls of Urban Ethnography', *American Journal of Sociology*, 107(6), pp. 1468–532.

Waldfogel, J. (1997) 'Ending Welfare As We Know It: The Personal Responsibility and Work Opportunity Act of 1996', *Benefits*, September/October, pp. 11–15.

Walklate, S. and Evans, K. (1999) *Zero Tolerance and Community Tolerance*. Aldershot: Ashgate.

Weber, M. (1958) 'Class, Status, Party' in H. Gerth and C. Wright Mills (eds), *From Max Weber*. London: Routledge and Kegan Paul.

Webster, C. (2003) 'Race, Space and Fear: Imagined Geographies of Racism, Crime, Violence and Disorder in Northern England', *Capital and Class*, No. 80, pp. 95–123.

Webster, F. (1995) *Theories of the Information Society*. London: Routledge.

Welch, M. (2000) *Flag Burning: Moral Panic and the Criminalization of Protest*. New York: deGruyter.

Wellman, B. (1982) *Studying Personal Communities in East York* (Research Paper No. 128) University of Toronto: Centre for Urban and Community Studies.

Wheen, F. (1999) *Karl Marx*. London: Fourth Estate.

Willis, P. (1977) *Learning to Labour*. Aldershot: Gower.

Willis, P. (1990) *Common Culture*. Milton Keynes: Open University Press.

Willis, P. (2000) *The Ethnographic Imagination*. Cambridge: Polity.

Wilson, W. J. (1987) *The Truly Disadvantaged*. Chicago: Chicago University Press.

Wilson, W. J. (1996) *When Work Disappears: The World of the New Urban Poor*. New York: Knopf.

Wolfe, T. (1988) *The Bonfire of the Vanities*. New York: Bantam Books.

Wright, E. (2004) *Generation Kill*. New York: Bantam.

Wright Mills, C. (1940) 'Situated Actions and Vocabularies of Motive', *American Sociological Review*, 5(6), December.

Young, I. M. (1990) *Justice and the Politics of Difference*. Princeton, NJ: Princeton University Press.

Young, J. (1971) *The Drugtakers*. London: Paladin.

Young, J. (1973) 'The Hippie Solution: An Essay in the Politics of Leisure', in I. Taylor and L. Taylor (eds), *The Politics of Deviancy*. London: Penguin.

Young, J. (1981) 'Beyond the Consensual Paradigm' in S. Cohen and J. Young (eds), *The Manufacture of News*, revised ed. London: Constable.

Young, J. (1994) 'Incessant Chatter' in M. Maguire, R. Morgan and R. Reiner (eds), *The Oxford Handbook of Criminology*, 1st ed. Oxford: Oxford University Press.

Young, J. (1999) *The Exclusive Society*. London: Sage.

Young, J. (forthcoming), *The Criminological Imagination*. Cambridge: Polity.

Young, M. (1999) '1999 Hugh Weldon Memorial Lecture' London: BBC.

INDEX

Moss, K 13, 186, 206
Move On 207
Moynihan, D 16
Mugford, S 20, 57
Mullan, B 189
multiculturalism 135, 145–6, 165, 171
Murder in America 160
Murray, C 19, 24, 45, 80, 82, 101,
    103, 106, 119
Muse, A 132

narcissism of minor differences 39–40
narrative
    community as 178
    guiding 5, 184–7, 198
    war as 168–9
National Deviancy Conference 19
nationalism 141, 178–9
Nelson, J 100
Nemesis Effect 185
New Labour 12, 79, 102, 104–111, 134
New Politics of Youth Crime, The 128
New York 9, 31, 173–4, 211
Newman, K 48, 87–90, 98, 101
Nickled and Dimed 95
Nietzsche, F 10–11, 152
Nightingale, C 25, 38–39, 51–52, 57, 143
9/11 154, 161–2
No Shame in My Game 87

Occidentalism 162–7, 160, 165–6
*Occidentalism: The West in the Eyes
    of its Enemies* 152
Offe, C 78–81, 101
Ohlin, L 55
Olalquiaga, C 27
O'Malley, P 20, 57
On the Edge 25
Only a Pawn in their Game 187
ontological insecurity 6–7, 9, 13, 35,
    62, 178, 198
*Opportunity for All: Tackling Poverty and
    Social Exclusion* 126
Orientalism 149–150, 154–7, 160–1, 165
Other America, The 89
othering 11, 23, 141–3, 198, 211–13
    and dehumanisation 35
    conservative 5–6, 203
    liberal 5–6, 24, 73–5, 202–3
    of immigrants 140–1
Oualhaci, A   148

Painter, K 126
Pakulski, J 64–65, 71
Parenti, C 19, 103
Park Slope 31

Parkin, F 62
Pearse, P 170
Peck, J 138
Pelecanos, G 44, 53
Percy-Smith, J 102, 126, 128
Perry, A 116
Phillips, M 146
Pichaud, D 120
Pitts, J 110–111, 119, 128
Plummer, K 182
politics
    distributive 199–201
    of hiatus 11, 202, 211
    of identity 60, 66, 68–71
    transformative 11, 129, 198–9
Pope Benedict XVI 11
porosity 206
positivism 9
Post-Industrial Capitalism 100
postmodernism 71
Poverty in the United Kingdom 120–121
Power, A 128
Pratt, J 41
Prescott, J 108
Presdee, M 19–20
Presley, E 186, 206
Prevalin, D 115
Preventing Social Exclusion 126
prison
    American gulag 12, 14, 155
Pruett, T 170
public sphere 192–3, 207–8
Purity and Danger 92

Raban, J
racism 141
Radford, J 106
Ranger, T 141
Ranulf, S 42–43
rational choice theory 20, 56–7,
    118–9, 203–6
Rees, T 138
Reiner, R 168
relative deprivation
    and narrowing of differences 37–8
    downwards 36–7, 41–5
    economic and status 62
    fraternal and egoistic 48–9
    global 36, 155, 192
ressentiment 10–11, 42, 45, 154
Rieff, D 29, 91, 92
riots 128
    in France 147–8
    in Northern towns 133–6, 144–7, 164–5
    of 1980s 139–40
Rifkin, J 78

Ritzer, G 78
Rollins, J 96
Rosaldo, R 8
Rose, N 103
Ruggiero, V 25
Rules of the Sociological Method, The 12
Runciman, W 37, 48, 62

Sahlin, M 20
Said, E 149–150, 161
Sales, R 137
Sarkovsky, N 147
Sassen, S 93–94
Saturday Night and Sunday Morning 74
Sayer, A 63
Scarman Report, The 128
Scarman, L 128
Scheler, M 42
Schor, J B 43, 60
Schwartz, D 47–48
Schwartz, M 47
Scottish Council Foundation 110
Seabrook, J 47, 183
Secure Borders, Safe Haven: Integration and Diversity in Britain 134
Seductions of Crime 54
segregation 145
Self-Portrait 187
Sennett, R 79, 176–178
servants
  as Feudal 96–8
  invisibility 91–8
  to middle class 29–30
service class 93–4, 100–1, 121–3
Servicing the Middle Class 30
Sharif, O 153
Shaw, M 151, 158–159
Sheehan, C 170
Shipler, D 95
Shulman, B 90
Sibley, D 19, 141
Sillitoe, A 74
Simmel, G 181
Simpson, O J 50, 206
situational crime prevention 106
Slayer 191
Smith, M
social exclusion 18–35, 102–4
  and criminal justice system 125–6
  and humiliation 55
  and political exclusion 126–9
  and South Africa 33
  and Thatcherism 106
  Anglo-Saxon model 101
  causes 109

social exclusion *cont.*
  crime 110–112
  the 'weak' thesis 102, 124–5
  three theories 103
Social Exclusion Unit 18–19, 85, 101, 104, 107–113, 118, 124, 127
Social Exclusion 124
social isolation 19, 24, 55, 103
social reproduction theory 52–4, 57–8, 67
Social Trends 114
solipsis 99, 202
Sothcott, K 161, 166
Stanko, B 106
States of Denial 166
status 62, 70–1
Stiffed 63
stop and search 32
Structural Transformation of the Public Sphere, The 207
subterranean values 166–8
Suicide 186
suicide bomber 158
Sultan-Smith, B 115–116
Sutton, R 48
Sykes, G 51, 166–167

Tally's Corner 122, 204
Tanweer, S 162
Taylor, I 43
Taylor, L 189
techniques of neutralisation 166–7
teenage pregnancy 112–119
Teenage Pregnancy 112
Teenage Wasteland 191
terrorism
  definition 150–1
  symmetry of violence 157
terrorists
  home grown 162–5, 170–1
Tester, K 47, 49, 51, 76
Thatcher, M 105, 109
Therborn, G 100
Thomas, C 192
Thompson, E P 68
Thompson, G 38
Thompson, J 2, 4, 187, 190–191, 206, 208
Thornton, S 188
Three Nations: Social Exclusion in Scotland 110
Tilley, N 105
Tomlinson, J 27
Tomlinson, M 187
Toronto 9
Touraine, A 72
Townsend, P 120